Praise for *Clear Leadership*

"Practically focused, clearly written, and deeply thoughtful, *Clear Leadership* provides the keys to authenticity and productivity in organizations."

Robert E. Quinn, author of *Change the World;* ME Tracy Collegiate Professor of Organizational Behavior and Human Resource Management, University of Michigan

"Applying the principles outlined in *Clear Leadership* has made a difference in the way we communicate in our small business. I usually start out saying, 'This will never work,' only to see, after a few minutes of dialogue, layers of misunderstanding beginning to fall away. We are working and talking together better. Happier, too."

Colin L. Genge, President, Retrotec Inc.

"*Clear Leadership* revolutionizes the way we think about leaders and leadership. It breaks out of the quick-fix mold of reactionary leadership with a holistic description of the characteristics for organizing collective action successfully. Here is the bible for everyone whose life can be enhanced by the effective coordination of human resources, be it in the family, community, or workplace."

Hedley G. Dimock, author of *Groups: Leadership and Group Development* and *Intervention and Collaboration: Helping Organizations to Change*

"Here at last, in *Clear Leadership*, is a science of communications expressed so well that individuals at all levels in a company can both understand the destructiveness of office politics and personality conflict, and develop the skills they need to steer clear. This is a book with the potential to redefine your corporate culture and to improve almost all aspects of your working life."

Sebastian Moffatt, President, Sheltair Group Inc.

"I have had the pleasure of working with Gervase Bushe to implement his methods, and I can testify to their powerful and positive effects. At last, an effective and human way of improving organizational working culture and team effort."

Alf Bogusky, director/curator of the Southern Alberta Art Gallery; executive director of the Art Gallery of Windsor, the Edmonton Art Gallery, and the Vancouver Art Gallery

"Rich with practical wisdom and real-life examples, *Clear Leadership* provides a commonsense approach for cutting through the mush and creating organizations where learning and high performance are more than just another slogan. This is a must read for anyone who wants to learn practical ways to start making a difference in his or her organization *now*!"

Martin L. Kaplan, organizational consultant

CLEAR
LEADERSHIP

CLEAR
LEADERSHIP

HOW OUTSTANDING LEADERS MAKE
THEMSELVES UNDERSTOOD, CUT THROUGH
THE MUSH, AND HELP EVERYONE GET
REAL AT WORK

GERVASE R. BUSHE

Davies-Black Publishing
Mountain View, California

Published by Davies-Black Publishing, a division of CPP, Inc.,
1055 Joaquin Road, Suite 200, Mountain View, CA 94043;
800-624-1765.

Special discounts on bulk quantities of Davies-Black books are available to corporations, professional associations, and other organizations. For details, contact the Director of Book Marketing and Sales at Davies-Black Publishing, 650-691-9123; fax 650-623-9271.

07 06 05   10 9 8 7 6 5 4 3 2
Printed in the United States of America

Library of Congress Cataloging-in-Publication Data

Bushe, Gervase R.
        Clear leadership : how outstanding leaders make themselves understood, cut through the mush, and help everyone get real at work /
Gervase R. Bushe—1st ed.
            p. cm.
        Includes bibliographical references and index.
        ISBN 0-89106-152-5
        1. Leadership. 2. Communication in management. 3. Labor
productivity. 4. Industrial management. I. Title.
        HD57.7.B874 2001
        658.4'092—dc21

                                                    00-064533

FIRST EDITION
First printing 2001

Contents

Preface

This book describes the kind of leadership required to get great results from empowered organizations. It is written for managers, professionals, consultants, team leaders, and team members— anyone who wants to increase their effectiveness in 21st-century organizations. In an empowered organization leadership can come, and must come, from everyone. Leadership is anything that helps the organization achieve its purpose or improve its ability to achieve its purpose. In particular this book focuses on the skills needed for teams and organizations to be able to learn from their experience, recognize and change problem patterns, and create synergy. Any group of people who can do that will have a sustainable competitive advantage over those who can't.

This book describes in detail the skills and processes needed to have organizational learning conversations. A learning conversation is a kind of inquiry into problem patterns that leads to a change in those patterns. The book describes barriers to those conversations typically found in organizations and shows how to overcome them.

The main impediment to organizational learning is a condition I call *interpersonal mush*. Interpersonal mush exists where people are trying to make sense of each other without clear, descriptive interactions. Instead, we make up stories to explain what we see, and these stories get acted on as if they were reality. Over time organizations become composed of pockets of competing fantasies about what is going on and why. I will describe a number of negative consequences of interpersonal mush and show the importance of clear leadership, a kind of leadership that creates the interpersonal clarity required in the new, team-based, empowered organizations.

Clear leadership is based on four deep skills: those of the Aware Self, the Descriptive Self, the Curious Self, and the Appreciative Self.

I call them "deep" skills as they are the foundation for effective use of all other leadership and human relations techniques. While many books offer platitudes about things like self-awareness, this book offers detailed, practical definitions and many anecdotes and examples to explain what it is, why it's important, and how to become more skilled at it. For example, the book argues that the most important aspect of self-awareness for organizational learning is the ability to know one's experience in the moment, as it is happening. A model of four elements of experience provides a practical tool that weaves together the four skills. As another example, the difference between the Descriptive Self and "being open" is explained in some detail, showing why "being open" is usually not an effective way to increase clarity and build good working relationships. Applications of these skills to issues of organizational learning, decision-making, and change are described in detail, and skill-building techniques and exercises are included at the end of each skill chapter.

The primary audience for this book is managers, team leaders, team members, and staff professionals in companies that are trying to be non-bureaucratic and that are seeking help in how to be more effective in positively influencing others. Another primary audience is people who consult to those managers and professionals: organization development and other types of management consultants and trainers. Instructors of university courses in interpersonal relations, teamwork, managing people, and organization development might also find this book of value. I hope you do.

Acknowledgments

A ny book of this kind has been influenced by numerous colleagues, teachers, clients, students, and friends. This book is filled with their stories, and I am grateful to them. I have expressed that gratitude in part by changing the names, sometimes the gender, and the nonessential details of their stories to protect their identities.

Eight people have had the most influence on the ideas in this book and I want to acknowledge them. Hedley Dimock and Irene Devine mentored me into the field of group dynamics and organization development. I got my early training as a T-group facilitator from them, as well as my introduction to the work on organizational change in the 1960s coming out of places like NTL, MIT, Boston University, UCLA, Case Western Reserve, and the University of Michigan. Those familiar with that body of work will see its echoes here, though, I think, changed and recast in ways that make the ideas of those pioneers more practical and, ultimately, more effective for practicing managers.

My next mentor, Ian Macnaughton, mentored me into my soul. He revealed the secrets of the unconscious mind and taught me just about everything I know about the deep and dark places of the human psyche and the wisdom of the body. As coach, counselor, colleague, and friend, he has taught me a great deal about my own fusion, disconnection, and differentiation (important ideas I'll discuss in this book), and, by extension, how to help others learn about theirs.

I have had a number of consulting partners over the years, but the one who has had the greatest impact on the ideas in this book is, without a doubt, Tom Pitman. Tom embodies many attributes of the "clear leader," and through him I have developed a more grounded and, at the same time, more visionary sense of what is possible and practical in creating empowered organizations.

Each year I try to give myself a significant learning experience by attending a personal or professional development course of at least a week's duration. I want to acknowledge two such courses that had an impact on the ideas in this book. The first was a "Self-Differentiation" course run by John and Joyce Weir. The experiences I had there profoundly deepened my understanding of how fusion and differentiation operate in an interpersonal context. The second was a "Differentiated Leadership" course with Ron Short and John Runyon. There I was first introduced to family systems theory as a way of looking at team dynamics and to Ron's "learning from experience" model. In that course I found the organizing principle that helped me reformulate my previous 15 years of work: what I call in this book the Descriptive Self. It was there that I also experienced the group methodology that I now use in teaching managers the skills of clear leadership. The way I think about experience and organizational learning has been strongly influenced by Ron and John.

A major impetus for the research for this book was a year's sabbatical in 1992–93 when I joined the start-up team of Stentor, the Canadian telephone industry's joint venture in the face of a newly deregulated long-distance market. We had less than a year to integrate hundreds of employees from three different companies and take on international competition. Up until then I had been focusing on how to design empowered organizations. At Stentor the design issues were clear to me, yet it became even more clear that design was not enough and I was launched on the path of inquiry that led to here. Thanks to Don Calder and the managers and employees of "PMG 2"—that was quite a ride.

Some people read earlier drafts of this book and need to be thanked for making an effort to give me useful feedback. Thanks to Bev Behrman, Hedley Dimock, Marty Kaplan, Steve Lawler, Bob Quinn, Sally Ann Roth, Allison Smillie, Pat Supene, John Toma, Al Weisman, and Chuck Wilmink. They offered many wise thoughts and I probably didn't use enough of them, so these people can't be held responsible for the final version. My editor at Davies-Black, Alan Shrader, made numerous suggestions that have, I hope, increased the clarity and ease of reading the book.

Finally, I want to acknowledge the Faculty of Business Administration at Simon Fraser University. They have provided the time, patience, and resources to allow me to be a "clinical researcher," one who studies others by trying to help them. In the academic world, where success usually comes to those who do a lot of quick empirical research, crunch numbers, and rarely talk to the people they study, it is a rare and precious thing to be given both the low teaching loads and the long time lines that clinical research requires. My colleagues seem to think that it is a good thing that I spend considerable time in the "business world," that my students and research benefit from this. That is not as common a presumption as nonacademics might suppose, and I am grateful for it.

Introduction

On Becoming a Clear Leader

Do you want to work in an organization where you can tell the truth of your experience? Do you want people to tell you the truth? Do you want to work in an organization where you are clear where you stand, clear where other people stand, and able to learn from your experiences together? No matter where you are currently positioned in your organization, you can provide the leadership necessary to create those kinds of interactions in your work environment. The skills of clear leadership are the same whether you are the leader of a maintenance crew, a member of a new product development team, or the executive of a major corporation. They come from an understanding about human nature and how we humans organize ourselves and an integration of the four deep skills that I will explain in detail in this book.

In the past 25 years we have witnessed a dramatic change in the way we organize large companies and grow smaller ones. The nature and causes of these changes are now widely understood. The microprocessor revolution is changing everything. It looks like the new organizations will be based more on the principles of alliance and partnership—where employees are empowered to take initiative and make decisions—than on authority and control. Everywhere we look in business we see the breakdown of tall hierarchies, the use of teams, the reorganization of functional departments into cross-functional groups, and the reduction of centralized control, allowing more local autonomy. Companies are getting rid of one-size-fits-all rules and making people interact, negotiate, and come to agreement, focusing more on results and less on procedures. The changes have been less dramatic in the public sector, but attempts are being made to do similar things there too. This has happened out of necessity: The new structures cope with a greater pace of change and uncertainty at less

1

cost than bureaucracy can. I don't think we've seen the end of this revolution in organizing and I don't know what label we'll end up giving it. In this book I refer to these 21st-century businesses as "empowered" organizations to recognize that the wider dispersion of power is a core difference between them and bureaucratic organizations.

At the same time I have witnessed a much less dramatic change in how people lead and manage those companies. The need has, perhaps, been less dramatic up to now. Those responsible for planning and implementing organizational change often still operate out of old leadership styles and values. Here and there, however, I have come across a person whose behavior gets the kind of results that deserves the name "leadership." This book is about what these people do that is different from what most managers and employees do. I call this clear leadership because what these people do is create a climate where people are willing to express their own truth and listen to other people's truth, where working together is based on accurate understanding, not assumptions. This isn't about being "nice" or making things "safe." It is about changing the way we think about "truth" and "being diplomatic" and "people skills" so that a very different kind of conversation can take place.

We are leaving behind the legacy of the industrial revolution and are in the midst of the microprocessor revolution. The way companies structure and organize is being transformed. I believe that these new organizational structures create a need for new interpersonal and leadership skills and we can see hints of this new leadership style here and there at various levels in various organizations. I think the change has not yet been as dramatic as that in organizational designs and organizing processes, because the competitive advantage of this new leadership style has not become so visible. To the extent that it appears randomly in random organizations, people only recognize that "Bill does things differently" or that "the culture of that organization is really unique." Wherever the competitive advantage of clear leadership is recognized, however, companies demand at least some of these abilities in their managers, a trend I believe can only grow.

People have been talking about managing and leading in ways that empower for well over a decade now, but our companies haven't really made a great deal of progress—in spite of a plethora of training programs, books on empowerment, leadership assessment instruments, and the like. Many describe what is needed but few explain how to do it. What is needed is a deeper set of skills.

This book will show you a way of understanding organizing processes and the basic interpersonal skills that can make you effective in our 21st-century organizations. As it turns out these skills are simple, but tough. By that I mean that they are easy to explain and demonstrate but tough to actually live day to day and master. Western society has trained us so thoroughly that these skills require a way of being that is alien for many of us. Yet they are the skills that I see exceptional leaders, the clear leaders, using every day. Most of us don't act this way. Not because we lack the courage, caring, or basic personal integrity, but because we don't know how! No one ever taught us. Few people have had the role models to show them how to take these basic attitudes and intentions and turn them into effective ways of working with and managing other people.

To act in these simple but profoundly different ways requires not only some new techniques, but some new ways of thinking about people, human interaction, and the nature of leadership. In this book I'll begin by explaining what is going on, under the surface, between people in the workplace. I want you to understand the cause of the poor interpersonal dynamics that seem to plague all organizations. It isn't just "problem people." Rather, it is a system of interaction that most of us take as normal and natural. The way most of us have learned is the "right way" to treat other people is what, in fact, creates organizations that don't treat people well at all.

The problem is captured in the following story.

In their weekly meeting Lynette, a new manager in the customer service group, describes her unit's poor performance results and what she intends to do to improve them. As she talks other managers listen politely and a few (always the same ones) ask a few questions "for clarification." At the end of her presentation the boss thanks her and says he looks forward to reviewing the results of her plans in another month, and the meeting moves on. But many things have not been said. More than one manager at the meeting does not really agree with Lynette's analysis of the problems but says nothing about it. Some say nothing to avoid embarrassing Lynette, others to avoid being seen as quarrelsome. Doug wonders if Lynette is competent and really understands the situation. Marlene believes Lynette knows perfectly well what is going on but has chosen not to talk about the whole story in order to protect people in her department. Bruce thinks Lynette is trying to protect herself by covering up the real problems in her unit. Sondra thinks Lynette is well intentioned but taken advantage of by her employees. Others have other thoughts and opinions which they keep to themselves.

After the meeting, some of them get together in smaller gatherings, over coffee or lunch, and the conversation turns to what they think is really going on in Lynette's department, what Lynette is really going to do about it, and her reasons for what she is and isn't saying about it. Differing opinions are examined and discussed, and in future interactions with Lynette people look for tips and clues to support or refute their different opinions about her real thoughts and feelings. In time, these managers come to develop firm opinions about Lynette's real motivations and competence. Of course, none of this is ever discussed or checked out with Lynette. Over the next few months various images of Lynette, her strengths and weaknesses, her motivations, and her agenda develop among the smaller groups, and these guide future interactions with Lynette.

Lynette is fully aware of what is going on in her department and has some excellent ideas about what to do about it but, due to the perceptions she had developed of her current boss before becoming his subordinate, believes it is not a good idea to be completely truthful, especially since some of his behaviors are part of the problem. She is a little surprised by the lack of cooperation she is receiving from her peers. They don't say anything in meetings but she notices the lack of follow-through on things she thought they had agreed to. She attributes this to competition and "politics," unaware that her co-workers are actually concerned about the accuracy of her analysis of the problems and the motivations behind her plans. "Why waste energy and resources on a doomed effort?" is the thinking behind much of the noncooperation.

In particular, she distrusts Bruce, whose cooperation she really needs. She sees him as unwilling to deal honestly, always covering his ass. She had heard that Bruce didn't like women in management and had found her initial interactions with him awkward. He seemed uptight and never looked at her directly. She never talked about this directly with Bruce, of course. Instead, when his behavior got to be too much she talked to Marlene, who helped her ventilate and strategize how to work around Bruce.

Bruce, in turn, distrusts Lynette, who never seems to deal with him directly and always seems to be trying to go around him in ways that discredit him. The only explanation he has for her behavior is that she is trying to discredit him, either so he'll take the blame for her problems or to take his job. He thinks Marlene, whom he finds a pain in the butt, is just that way because of her personality.

> *All these factors, of course, make it that much more difficult for Lynette to implement her plans and get results, and this situation further reinforces those who suspect she isn't really competent. In desperation, at another meeting she brings up her need for more support from other departments to improve performance. A certain nervous tension fills the room, and her boss, a "team player," moves quickly to smooth things over. Lynette's complaint is not examined in much detail and everyone professes their willingness to be more supportive. While Lynette's co-workers are well intentioned, their behaviors, and the beliefs behind them, don't really change. An endless cycle of lunchtime conversations, unexamined assumptions, and avoidance of issues results in continued mediocre results and increasing stress from all the gossip and politics at work.*

If this appears at all familiar to you, then you have some inkling of the territory this book is about. I believe that in this story lies the basis of group and organizational dysfunction and a lot of unnecessary misery at work. I describe this group as living in *interpersonal mush*. Interpersonal mush occurs when people's understanding of each other is based on fantasies and stories they have made up about each other. It is impossible for a group or organization to be anything more than mediocre if it is full of interpersonal mush. Changing this to *interpersonal clarity* is the basis for creating highly effective and satisfying working relationships and organizations, where people can stop endless repetition of the same destructive patterns and, instead, learn together to create more effective ways of operating. In this story, anyone could have provided leadership by taking the first steps to create interpersonal clarity. Clear leadership can be practiced by anyone, regardless of their level in an organization. It's also true, however, that those with authority set the tone for the rest of the organization. The effects of clear leadership are amplified the more authority one has.

Traditional command-and-control organizations are built to be able to operate in spite of the interpersonal mush. An organization that relies on people to take personal initiative and collaborate cannot. In this book I will show you that the key skill of managing people in empowered organizations is that of creating an environment where they are willing to tell the truth about their experience and learn from it. This is what creates interpersonal clarity. The reason it is so essential will become clear as the book unfolds. Let me just note here that if people you work with are not telling you what they really observe, think, feel, and want, then you cannot really lead them—in fact, you can't really even know the consequences of your own attempts to lead, manage, or influence them.

One company president who interviewed me as a potential consultant asked me what I could do for him. I said that mainly what I do is get people to tell each other the truth. He said, "No way—you can't do that! No one can do that! Can you really do that? If you can do that, you're worth your weight in gold." His 40 years as a very successful leader in various companies had taught him how difficult, and how precious, the truth is to a leader.

In this book I will show you why achieving simple, honest interaction among people is so difficult. It's not just because people are liars—no one starts out that way. It's not just because people are scared, lack self-esteem, or are afraid of "hurting others" or causing embarrassment or anger, though all that is some of it. Nor is it really "human nature." I will discuss some basic truths of the human mind that lead to under-performance and poor working relationships, and I will describe the skills of working with people that can create a totally different scenario—one in which people learn together and base their interactions on facts and the truth.

The basis for understanding how to work well with people consists of two core realities of the human mind. One is that we are perception-generating beings. The other is that we are sense-making beings. When you fully grasp what this means and the implications of these ideas separately and together, you are on the road to understanding why people do what they do and therefore to being able to influence their actions and perceptions meaningfully, which is the basis of great leadership.

Perception Generation

I believe the most basic truth about humans is that we are constantly generating a stream of percepts, the building blocks of perception. We do this when we are awake or when we are asleep. We do this with or without sensory stimulation. From a position of the most extreme scientific doubt, we can never be sure if what we perceive is real—but we can be sure that we perceive. There is strong evidence that our perceptions are shaped by what is going on both outside of us and inside of us. But even without anything going on outside of us, we will continue to generate perceptions. Sensory deprivation tanks, where a person floats on buoyant water in a completely dark and soundless chamber, proved that. If you stay in a sensory deprivation tank long enough, you will start to create perceptions that you can't distinguish from what we normally call "reality." We call these perceptions "hallucinations."

Percept generation is a constant, ceaseless process unless you have spent many years and a great deal of discipline to quiet the mind. Few people have. As a result it is almost always valid to assume that you and others are constantly creating a stream of percepts. In this book I will call this stream of percepts, and your internal reaction to those percepts, your *experience*. Even as you are reading this sentence you are having an experience. Your experience is made up of the percepts you are generating and your reactions to those percepts.

The sensory part of your experience consists of the words you are reading, the atmosphere in which you are reading this, the quality of light, the comfort of your body, and so on. While sensory input influences your percepts, experience is not just the literal apprehension in the mind of what is going on outside the mind. Not everyone will read these words exactly as I have written them. It is quite normal for people to read the same sentence yet experience different things. You have probably heard that if ten people observe a crime there are ten different reports of what happened. It is a common teaching trick in introductory psychology classes to have someone burst into the class, do something out of the ordinary, and then suddenly leave. Different people in the class will report seeing different things—even the color of the person's hair, the clothes they were wearing, and any other "objective fact"! The ideal of "objective observation" is seldom, if ever, achieved. To be interpersonally skillful you must give up the idea that what you believe you saw or heard is always the truth. Until you do so you will not be able to create conditions where people learn together from their collective experience, and you will not be able to really work with other people well. You need to learn—if you haven't already—to treat your perceptions as hypotheses that always need further investigation and continuous updating.

The perceptions you are generating are part of your experience and so are the reactions you are having to those perceptions. These are the thoughts, ideas, judgments, feelings, bodily sensations, wants, and desires you are having as you read this. For example, somebody might be thinking, "This is obvious, I already know this." Another might be thinking, "This is an interesting way of putting these ideas." Someone might be feeling frustrated at the "psychobabble" and wondering if the book is worth reading any further. Someone else might be excited to find me putting words to things they've had a sense of before. The possible reactions to the varying perceptions of readers like you are extensive, maybe even infinite. That's how it is with human experience.

Note that my way of talking about human experience is different from another common way of using the word: as a description of what happened to you in the past. From the point of view of this book experience is not what happened to you last week or the things you put on your resume. Experience is not what happens to you but the reactions you create out of what happens to you moment by moment. And so a fundamental truth is that you, I, and everyone else all create our own experience.[1]

If you can believe that everyone reading this book will be having a personally unique experience at this point, then I pose a question to you. Who is having the right experience? This turns out to be a crucial question for developing the attitudes that will make you effective as a leader, follower, or colleague in empowered teams and organizations. I will take this up in greater detail in Chapter 3.

Sense-Making

The second key human process is sense-making. As human beings we appear to have a deep need to make sense of ourselves and others. When we make sense we explain our perceptions within a framework that provides consistency and meaning to what we are perceiving. There are many aspects to this that I will take up in the next chapter, on sense-making, but let me point out here the key thing for working with people. When we try to make sense of other people's behavior we almost always make up a story about *their experience*. That's what Lynette's peers were doing with her. They were making up stories about what Lynette's "real" thoughts, feelings, and intentions were. How much a story is pure fantasy or is based on some reality depends on two things: the quality of a person's observation and the willingness of those being observed to describe what their experience is. Neither of these behaviors is well developed in traditional organizations. Skills of human observation depend first and foremost on self-observation and self-awareness, and these are not taught in schools or in many families. Describing our experience to others is also not taught in schools or many families and, more often, is frowned upon. As a consequence, most interpersonal encounters, especially those in work organizations, are best described as two or more people having different experiences while making up stories about what is going on in each other's minds: stories that are never checked out.

These stories then become the input for further episodes of sense-making, shaping future perceptions and experiences that build on and reinforce each other, further making us certain that what we believe we see is the truth, and we never check that out with the people we are making up the "truth" about. Executives make up a story about workers and workers make up a story about executives. Managers in one department make up stories about managers in another department. People who work together every day make up stories about each other. On and on it goes, so organizations are composed of multiple, competing fantasies of what is going on and why, stories that are rarely discussed openly and almost never examined in a way that could prove or disprove them. Where this is taken to an extreme organizations become crazy-making places—places that generate stress and mixed messages and can literally drive people crazy.

Clear leadership is a set of skills that work with, rather than against, these two realities of the human mind. I will show you how the skills are related to our new forms of organizing and how they are the basis for "organizational learning"—a type of learning that leads to improvements in how people work together.

Clear Leadership for Interpersonal Competence

New forms of organizing create, implicitly, new definitions of interpersonal competence. Henry Mintzberg pointed out many years ago that bureaucracy is a type of organization that builds conflict right into its structure.[2] By giving most of the power to just a few people who decide the best way to do things, and then ensuring that everyone else does what they are told, lots of pressure points get created. You usually find different departments in conflict with each other, different levels of hierarchy in conflict with each other (especially labor and management), even customers and suppliers in conflict with the company. In bureaucracy, the trick is to get the work done in spite of all the conflict. People who are able to maintain momentum in the face of repressed conflict, smooth things over, be articulate and persuasive, avoid creating awkwardness or embarrassment, maintain the veneer of harmony, and get people with different interests to compromise are seen as having good people skills—and in bureaucracy they do.

But, as most people realize, empowered organizations are based on a different logic, one where principles of partnership, alliance, and the utilization of everyone's intelligence mean that conflicts cannot simply be ignored and repressed by the force of authority. Instead, an ability to get things in the open and clear the air, to build real commitment to decisions, to develop synergistic teams, to be able to openly discuss failures and successes and learn from everyone's experience is what's required. In this book I will show you what I believe are the four foundational skills that make all that possible: the skills of partnership and leadership in synergistic groups. Clear leadership is a foundation; all other techniques for managing people and groups don't really work very well if you aren't using clear leadership as a platform to operate from.

The skills of clear leadership reflect a set of post-modern assumptions, a different way of thinking about people and society than most of us grew up with. Throughout this book I use the phrase, "telling the truth of your experience." It's an awkward phrase but the best I've been able to come up with for talking about a kind of truth that is different from "the" truth. Believing that there is more than one kind of truth is one assumption of what academics call post-modernism. I bring this up because one of the reasons for the lack of clarity in organizations is the tendency to try to assess everything against the standards of objective truth. When it comes to managing and working with people, most of the "truths" we are dealing with are not objective. That is probably why people who are well trained in matters of objective truth, like engineers and accountants, are often viewed as having poor people skills. Again, I don't think it is an innate deficiency—just a lack of understanding and training in what "the truth of experience" is and how to go about thinking about it, talking about it, and learning from it.

Even as children, we learn the difference between objective and subjective truth. *Objective truths* are truths that can be measured and validated independent of your percepts or mine. This is the truth of science and technology. Subjective truth is based totally on what is going on in each individual. For example, there is an objective truth to how much you get paid at work. What you think, feel, and want regarding how much you get paid is a subjective truth. Objective truth is based on our ability to objectively measure whatever we are talking about. When someone says what they think, feel, or want, how do you know if it is "true"? Subjective truth has to do with the quality of a person's awareness and the authenticity with which they express it. Subjective truth is what I mean when I talk about the truth of your experience. While modern society has made great strides in developing ways of assessing and validating objective truths, we are still novices at assessing and validating subjective truths. Yet subjective truth is an essential part of working with people, and its importance is amplified in empowered organizations. One of the challenges of clear leadership is to get clear about your subjective truth and the subjective truth of others you work with. It is a challenge because we often try to treat subjective truth the same way we treat objective truths.

There is a third kind of truth, *inter-subjective truth*. This consists of things that are true because you and I agree they are. So much of what is "true" in organizations is inter-subjective truth. What is success? What is quality? How much customer service is enough? The answers to questions like these in an organization are inter-subjective truths. Inter-subjective truths are the essence of social reality and they are always co-created. Everyone involved contributes to the creation, maintenance, and change of the reality or truths they face at work. Again, we don't have very developed methods of assessing and validating this kind of truth or even thinking about it. Building teams and organizations, however, is a lot about inter-subjective truth, and the skills in this book are very concerned with understanding, creating, and changing inter-subjective truth.

Even though I use the term *clear leader* throughout the book I want to make it clear that these skills are useful to anyone, regardless of their position, who works in an organization based on principles of teamwork, personal initiative, and partnership. A person provides *leadership* when they do something that helps a group or organization achieve its goals or increase its effectiveness. Anytime anyone helps a group of people increase their clarity or come to agreement, they are providing leadership. You can provide leadership whatever your position in an organization. I will show you how managers and professionals use these skills to gain clarity and agreement among people working together.

The skills of clear leadership are self-awareness, descriptiveness, curiosity, and appreciation. We all have some skill level in all four areas. In this book I want to describe what the mastery of those skills looks like. When you master something, you embody it. When a great guitarist plays music, or a great fencer fences, they don't think about what they are doing: something else in them takes over. The skill itself takes over. Similarly, to master the skills in this book a person must be able to embody them—to allow them, in a sense, to take over. In four chapters I will describe the nature of the Aware Self, the Descriptive Self, the Curious Self, and the Appreciative Self.

The Aware Self knows, moment to moment, what she is thinking, feeling, observing, and wanting. She understands the processes she uses to create her experience. She is clear how much of her experience is based on facts and how much is her sense-making. The Descriptive Self is able to help other people empathize with him. He can describe all the facets of his experience clearly. He is able to describe difficult, confrontational aspects of his experience in a way that doesn't make others defensive but elicits a willingness to listen and understand. The Curious Self is a master at getting other people to be descriptive. She is able to observe, question, and probe until she fully understands, as much as humanly possible, another person's experience. Others feel comfortable telling her the truth of their experience. The Appreciative Self works through imagination and conversation to find the best in people and processes. He is able to see what he wants more of as already existing, even if just in small ways, which he then works to amplify and strengthen.

I will show you how to integrate these skills to gain clarity and agreement. Clarity comes from clearing out the interpersonal mush and sometimes requires an *organizational learning conversation*. This is a conversation where people level with each other about their experience so that they can learn about and change the troublesome patterns of organizing they find themselves in. Agreement comes from the ability of a group to think together and make decisions. I will describe how clear leadership can create a foundation for effective decision-making and continuous learning in organizations.

The personal attribute that underlies a person's ability to use clear leadership and create an atmosphere that supports others using these skills is her level of *differentiation*. A person acts in a differentiated way when she is able to be separate from and simultaneously connected to other people. What that means is that her experience is not simply in reaction to other people. Her thoughts and feelings cannot be emotionally hijacked by other people. She doesn't attain this state of certainty and clarity by isolating herself from others, however. A differentiated leader wants to know what other people think and feel without taking responsibility for their experience or demanding that they have different thoughts and feelings. Most of us can learn to be more differentiated in our interactions with others. Most managers are too separate from their

employees and disconnected from their experience, or they are overly connected, so their own experience becomes wrapped up in that of
their employees. In the chapter on fusion, disconnection, and differentiation I will describe these issues in much greater detail.

The issue of authority is an important thread that is woven
throughout this book. Contrary to popular images of the new organization, empowered organizations do not decrease or eliminate
authority even if they do flatten hierarchies—quite the contrary.
Authority and hierarchy are two separate things. Authority is the
power to make and enforce decisions. Empowered organizations create much more authority than bureaucracies do because in empowered organizations authority is dispersed widely. More people are
authorized to make decisions and take actions that obligate others in
the organization to make complementary decisions and take complementary actions. That is one of the reasons why clear leadership from
many people is necessary for these organizations to work well. But
empowered organizations still require some hierarchy for focus and
control. Hierarchy, because of the uneven power it creates, can get in
the way of people telling their truth to one another. The many ways
in which managerial authority is a two-edged sword, both supporting
clear leadership and being a barrier to clear leadership, are discussed
in various parts of this book.

Here is a true, summarized vignette (the actual episode lasted
over 30 minutes) of an example of organizational learning by a group
of managers. They are led by a clear leader, Pierre, with a subordinate, Stan, who is also using the skills of clear leadership. It is an
example of a group working in interpersonal clarity.

---

*It has been four months since the president, Pierre, declared his and the
Board's intent to change the sole emphasis the organization has had for
the past ten years on Product A and introduce a new product, B. As he
sits in a meeting of his executive committee, Pierre is worried that the
vice-president of the unit responsible for Product A (Stan) is resisting
this change. He was very unhappy with Stan's performance at yesterday's
Board meeting, where he seemed confused and not in line with the new
strategy. Pierre was also concerned by the very negative reaction some
Board members voiced about Stan once he left the room. He values
Stan, who has been an outstanding performer for many years, but real-
izes that he really doesn't know what Stan thinks about the change in
strategy. As the discussion turns to the new strategy, the president takes
leadership in telling the truth of his experience:*

"Stan, the Board meeting yesterday raised confusion for me and I want to get clear with you about where each of us stands on the Product B strategy. I raise this here because it affects all of us and we all need to be clear on what each of us thinks about this. So let me begin. I was concerned by your apparent confusion yesterday, as I thought we had discussed the new product strategy fully and were all in complete agreement. It raises in my mind some doubts about whether you really support the Product B strategy, and, frankly, I'm starting to be concerned that you might resist it because you're afraid it will take resources away from Product A. I want you to be clear about where you stand on this and I want us to find a way for you to feel fully behind both products A and B."

Stan, who is visibly disturbed by Pierre's remarks, asks questions to get more clarity about Pierre's perceptions.

Stan: *"Could you tell me what, exactly, I did that caused you concern at the meeting?"*

Pierre: *"There were a number of times when you were fielding questions that you made statements that are contrary to the strategy the Board has endorsed. For example, when Brian asked about the marketing strategy you talked about a tie-in building on the brand recognition of Product A when we've decided it's better to keep the two products distinct in our clients' eyes."*

Stan: *"Any other things?"*

Pierre: *"Well, yes. Your response to Marilyn about product launch, and what you said to Herschel about expected cost of capital were not what we had agreed to."*

Stan: *"Just so I'm clear, Pierre, can you tell me what you think I said and what we've agreed to?"*

Pierre goes on to describe what he heard Stan say at the meeting and what he thinks was wrong with what Stan said.

Stan: *"OK, I think I'm clear on what you're unhappy about, but before I respond to what you've just said, Pierre, I just want to check if there are any other reasons why you think I might not be fully behind the change."*

Pierre: *"Well, since you asked, I was taken aback a week or so ago with a conversation I had with Barbara [one of Stan's direct reports], who seemed to have some pretty confused fears about what effects this change is going to have on your department. Then I noticed a similar set of thoughts coming from Kevin [another of Stan's managers]. It got me wondering just how much of that is coming from you."*

Stan: *"Were they talking about having to shift people to the new business unit? [Pierre nods] Yeah, I know what you're talking about. Anything else causing you to wonder where I'm at?"*

Pierre: *"No, that's about it."*

Stan: *"OK, well let me start by saying I'm somewhat taken aback by all this—I had no idea that things went sideways at the Board meeting, so I guess I'm glad you are telling me about it and I do want you to know that I'm fully behind Product B. Let me deal with the meeting issues first. With Herschel I think I must have just not gotten my thoughts out clearly because I agree with what you are saying about our financing and how much debt we're willing to take on. But I have to tell you that I am confused about our marketing strategy and launch plans because I thought we had decided to build on the brand recognition and tie-in with Product A."*

Pierre: *"No, no—that got decided at least a month ago."*

Robert: *"I have to tell you, Pierre, I'm with Stan on that one. I thought the opposite as well."*

Susan: *"I didn't know a decision had been made."*

Pierre: *"I don't understand this; we talked about this issue for weeks and then at the last meeting of the Board's Strategy Committee a decision was made to keep the two products separate and distinct in our sales campaign."*

Robert: *"Well I remember the discussions but I thought we were all leaning toward product tie-in. I don't remember hearing that the Strat Committee had made a decision."*

Errol: *"I knew about it from the meeting you had with the marketing group, Pierre, but I don't know if it ever came up here."*

Pierre: *"Oh hell, I thought I had announced that at our last meeting."*

At this point Pierre tells the group about the decision the Board's Strategy Committee had made and their rationale. A discussion ensues and it becomes clear that this is the first time the group has heard about and discussed this decision.

Stan: *"To finish off with the issues you were bringing up, Pierre, it's true that people in my unit are afraid that they are going to lose resources to Product B. I don't think it's going to be nearly as drastic as some of the concerns some people have, but obviously some resources are going to have to be redirected and we haven't really decided on what this is going to be yet. Frankly, I think the sooner we decide that the better, because the uncertainty is starting to fuel a lot of speculation, and since I don't really know what is going to happen there's not a lot I can tell folks to calm them down. But you need to understand that as far as I'm concerned, bringing on Product B is absolutely essential to the future health of our company and I am 100 percent behind it."*

Pierre: *"I'm glad to hear that, Stan, but why are your people not on the bus too?"*

Stan: *"Oh, I don't think anyone questions the wisdom of moving into the Product B space, Pierre; it's just that no one's sure what the ramifications for Product A will be and that is creating a lot of rumors and unfounded gossip. Last week someone asked me if we were closing down the Product A unit."*

Pierre: *"That's ridiculous! Product A is the core of this company. Isn't that obvious?"*

Stan: *"I think it is to us but there does seem to be some confusion in the ranks."*

Errol: *"I'm having a similar experience, Stan. A couple of days ago I overheard a conversation in the cafeteria where some people were guessing how Product Unit A was going to be reorganized."*

Stan: *"I think the buzz coming from below is causing some of the concerns you are hearing from my managers, Pierre."*

Pierre: *"Are any of the rest of you picking this up?"*

The group launches into a discussion about the effects that the organization's culture, with 10 years of sole focus on Product A, is having on implementing the new strategy. Some of this is news to Pierre, and together they develop a picture of a pattern of misperceptions and misguided fears that are surfacing in the organization. Everyone affirms that Product A is still the backbone of the company and that a new emphasis on Product B should not have to mean a decrease in support for Product A.

Pierre: *"We'd better do something to clear up the confusion we've created. I think Colette's team on resourcing Product B is just about finished. I'll ask her to speed up and we can use their report to make some clear announcements throughout the company that will end all the uncertainties about who is going to be working where. Susan, can you get the communications people geared up for this? I want to make it a priority. We don't need a lot of unfounded fears and rumors getting in the way of moving Product B to market quickly and effectively.*

"I'm sure glad we had this conversation, though I'm a little sorry that it started from my misgivings about you, Stan. I see that I have some responsibility for what happened at the Board yesterday so I guess I owe you an apology."

Stan: *"Thanks, Pierre, but I have to take some responsibility for not having checked out my facts before the presentation. I wonder if we can huddle before Board meetings in the future just to make sure I have my ducks in line."*

Pierre: *"I think that would be a good idea."*

And the group moves on to deal with other items on the agenda.

Sound like fantasy land? If it does, you have spent too much of your working life in the interpersonal mush of organizations where leaders do not create a climate for organizational learning. You may not be able to see it yet, but by the end of this book you will recognize in this story a set of critical skills that these people were using to create this interaction. In this vignette you see an organizational learning conversation in action. It is the basis for any sustained high performance in organizations that want their employees and managers to feel committed, take initiatives, negotiate agreements together, and coordinate their actions with one another. A lot of this book is about the perceptions, attitudes, and skills required to have learning conversations in organizations.

Some months before the event I've described took place, this was a typical organization where people didn't talk about their perceptions and concerns openly, where face-saving and backroom conversations were the order of the day, and where people often didn't know what others thought of them and didn't treat each other as trustworthy. As it turned out, virtually all the people in this organization were decent, trustworthy, and yearning to work in an organization that didn't give them ulcers. It was not their lack of integrity or intention that made their system the way it was. It was simply a lack of the basic skills that I will show you in this book. Once they had those, and authorities willing to create a new culture where telling the truth of one's experience was accepted and valued, the result was a place where people could talk easily and honestly about what was really on their minds and so make sane and sensible decisions that got followed through on.

Clear leadership is about creating clarity in every interaction and every group you are a member of. It requires understanding the nature of experience and the reasons it seems so difficult to get people to tell the truth of their experience to each other. So let's turn first to one of the bedrock understandings about people that clear leaders share—that we are sense-making beings—and let's examine the critical implications of that understanding for the kinds of organizations we create.

PART ONE

Clarity and Mush in Organizational Life

Where Interpersonal Mush Comes From and What It Does to Organizations

The content may be different, but the process described below goes on in organizations every day, all over the world. It seems to be a process beyond culture, something that is true of all human beings. To boil it all down I call it sense-making. Read the following scenario and see if it is at all familiar to you.

Bill, the General Manager for the Eastern Division, entered the room where his direct reports had been waiting ten minutes for their weekly meeting to begin. They knew he had been on the phone to headquarters on the West Coast and paid close attention to how he appeared as he entered. Rumors had been circulating about impending budget cuts, and given the losses over the past three quarters, none in the room would be surprised if it happened. Bill briskly apologized for being late and launched into the first item on the agenda, a report on a project in one of the departments. The meeting went on following the agenda, and once all items were finished Bill immediately left the room and returned to his office.

After the meeting people met in pairs and trios, sometimes including others who had not been in the meeting, to compare perceptions. Shirley thought Bill seemed flushed and angry when he entered the room. Jason didn't notice the anger but agreed that Bill did seem a little more curt than usual and seemed eager to leave the meeting and get back to something. They discussed how unusual it was for Bill to leave so quickly and not stick around to chat a little. They agreed the phone call from the West Coast must have been bad news and wondered why Bill wasn't willing to share it with them. Shirley said, "It's just not like Bill to leave us all up in the air like that."

Meanwhile Roger and Fernando were gathered around Kimberly's cubicle, where she was telling them she had heard from a colleague on the West

Coast that another division had gotten a sizable cut in their operating budget. Fernando and Roger agreed that Bill wasn't "acting normal" in the meeting and figured that he had been told they would be facing cuts as well. They wondered why he didn't say anything about it in the meeting, and all three tossed around theories ranging from the idea that he had been told not to say anything until there was a companywide announcement to the thought that he was going to be firing someone in the room and wanted to wait until that person was told privately before announcing it. Roger mentioned that he was already prepared for taking 20 percent out of his department's budget and Fernando said he'd better start planning for that as well. They parted agreeing to let each other know if they heard anything new.

In another part of the building, Jennifer was telling Margaret about the last time she had seen Bill "so upset," in a previous job when Bill's boss had closed down a project that Bill felt was close to success and hadn't been given the opportunity to prove itself. "But you know," Jennifer went on, "Bill is a company man and he closed it down without ever publicly grumbling about it; at least I never heard him say anything about it." Margaret agreed that Bill never lost his cool; it was something they admired about him.

We are all sense-making beings; that is, we will work at trying to make sense of something that is important to us until we are satisfied. We are all detectives in the interpersonal mush, building hypotheses and theories, looking for clues, fitting the pieces together until we have a satisfactory answer to the mystery of why someone did or said what they did. Then we stop until the next mystery comes along that needs to be solved. It appears that we don't just do it in trying to make sense of others. We even do it to ourselves. There is evidence to show that we make up stories about ourselves to make sense of what we see ourselves doing,[1] but in this book I'll only focus on how we do that with each other.

In the preceding vignette Bill's direct reports are trying to make sense of his behavior at the meeting. Notice a few common characteristics of sense-making processes. One is that Bill's actions are being placed in a larger context: the knowledge that the division has been losing money and the rumor of impending budget cuts. In order for us to make sense of something, it has to fit with what we already believe to be true, the bigger picture. Another characteristic is that what Bill doesn't say or do is given just as much scrutiny as what he does say and do. Nonverbal actions are given meaning. Notice that people are making up fantasies about his experience, about what is going on in his head. One thinks he's angry, another thinks he was eager to leave the room. Also, people are trying to understand him within the general picture they have of him ("he's a company man"). For us to be satisfied with our sense-making, current stories have to fit with past sense-making. A third characteristic is that people are talking to others to try and make sense of Bill. Where there is interpersonal mush, we rarely go to the person we are trying to make sense of to check our stories out—we seek out third parties. When the event we are trying to understand is new or different it's as though some part of us knows that we are on thin ice in trying to make sense of others, so we seek out someone else to help us. Sometimes this isn't even others in the organization—a spouse or close friend will do.

The sense-making process is over when we have a story that we now treat as "the truth." We no longer treat the story as a possible scenario but as what happened, and we align our future perceptions and actions based on these "facts" unless new information surfaces that forces us to revise our story. If the new information is vague and ambiguous, however, it can easily be ignored or distorted to fit.

Are you curious about what was going on with Bill in the story above?

As it turns out, Bill had received an important phone call from his boss that he was preoccupied with. The Senior VP had just told him that he agreed with the argument Bill had been making for months that divisional losses were due to his division being under-resourced, especially in sales and marketing. Because of cuts going on in other parts of the company Bill's boss could not see how their budget could be increased at this time, but he was prepared to fight to ensure that the division did not get a cut in budget if Bill could put together a convincing business plan and find a way to transfer budget he already had into sales. If there was improvement in profit figures, he would work to increase the budget in the future. He also advised Bill not to say anything about it because it was far from a sure thing and, with cuts going on elsewhere in the company, others might try to work against them if rumors started circulating.

In this case people were way off in the stories they were making up, but for our purposes here it really doesn't matter. Whether our stories are near or far from accurate doesn't matter—what matters is recognizing that this process is endemic to human relations. It cannot be stopped. So in work relationships we have two choices: let people make up stories about what is going on in us or tell them what is going on in us. If we don't tell them, they make it up. It's as simple as that.

What could Bill do, having been told not to mention the substance of the phone call? Well, what did Bill do? Like most people he thought if he said nothing then people wouldn't think there was anything going on. WRONG. People who work closely together day in and day out are picking up all kinds of cues all the time (and making them up). Those with authority are the most closely watched for clues about "what is really going on." Bill had no idea of the impact he was having on the people in the meeting. Clear leaders know that people will notice any incongruity and use it as fodder for new rounds of in-depth sense-making. Bill had a number of choices for how to influence the sense-making that was bound to follow after such an important phone call, but these were pretty much out of his awareness. In this book I will argue that the best strategy is almost always to be a *Descriptive Self*; that is, to tell the truth of your in-the-moment experience. Let me just give you an example of what he could have said:

I just had an important call from my boss. I am not at liberty to tell you what it was about and that troubles me, because I'd like us all to be honest and up front with each other, but I also understand his concern and agreed to stay silent. There may or may not be some good news for us in the near future. I want you to know the call was not bad news. I'm excited and a little distracted but I think that is all I can say and it's important right now that we don't start any rumors, so, please, just hang on and let's continue with our meeting as planned.

If Bill had said something like this, he would be letting the people he works with see what was going on in him at that moment without violating any agreement with his boss. He would be describing his here-and-now experience, so people would not be forced to make it up. Any stories they now made up would likely be more accurate, making the interpersonal climate less mushy and more clear.

Would saying this stop people from sense-making? Probably not. They might still meet in small groups after the meeting to fantasize what the good news was about. But it would stop a rush of negative, fearful fantasies that had managers spending their time thinking about how to chop 20 percent of their budget, and all the fallout that would come from that passed on down through the division. More important, however, is the effect of being a Descriptive Self day in and day out. It's not about the one-time hit of telling the truth of your experience, but the long-term impact on an organization where people tell the truth of their experience. If Bill used clear leadership, his subordinates would feel comfortable asking him directly what was going on and talking about their fears so that they would have Bill's direct input into the stories they settled on as "the truth." Any one of them would have felt comfortable saying something like, "Bill, I know you were on a call to headquarters and you seem a little distracted. Naturally I'm wondering if that was bad news about our budget." But such an inquiry doesn't often happen in an organization characterized by interpersonal mush. People don't ask each other directly what is going on, so a lot of energy goes into sense-making. In a climate of interpersonal clarity instead of mush, people are more willing to suspend their sense-making, believing that they will get a satisfactory explanation from Bill as soon as possible, because they have in the past.

Telling the truth of our experience is really quite simple, but so rare in organizations that some business people at first react to my message as if I were coming from Mars. To them, interpersonal mush is a normal way of life and anything else is a utopian dream. So let's pause for a moment and consider why most of our organizations exist in interpersonal mush.

Why We Live in Interpersonal Mush

Most people do not describe what is going on in themselves. It doesn't seem like a natural thing to do. This tendency does not necessarily come from malicious intentions, fear, distrust, or any other negative reason. It is just that we have never been taught to do so. Some people are even taught *not* to do so; they've been told that describing their experience makes them seem too self-centered. Most of us have never even thought that it might be useful or important to describe our experience to others. We have few role models of Descriptive Selves, and even when we are around those who do use clear leadership skills successfully, it's not immediately obvious what they are doing. I remember one very bright woman engineer in my Executive MBA class who, at first, said I was nuts to tell her to be a Descriptive Self at work. Then one week she came to class flushed with the realization that during a regular meeting at work she had finally noticed that the three most influential engineers in her organization were also the most Descriptive Selves at work.

Growing Up

We learn most about how to act around other people in the first group we belong to, our family of origin. In our families we were children and our parents were adults. As such there was a huge imbalance in experience, knowledge, and power. There are lots of things that might go on in adults' lives that they would not want to describe to the children (e.g., spousal problems, work fears). The problem with saying nothing is that the children will make up a story about what is going on, and why they are excluded.

As the children turn into teenagers they develop their own reasons not to tell their parents everything that is going on in their lives, so the parents make up stories about their children's lives. In most families parents and children come, to some extent, to make up what is going on in each other's minds. Even in the least dysfunctional family, there still develops a level of interpersonal mush that children learn is the normal way to interact with others.

Then we hit adolescence, where normal developmental processes make us desperately want to fit in and belong. Most of us learn that it is not OK to have a different experience from our peers—that we are expected to have similar thoughts, feelings, and wants in order to fit in. Then there is the double whammy of sexual relations, where there is so much vulnerability. We learn to look for clues, get information from third parties, but never ever approach the object of our interest head-on—too scary. High school is a perfect breeding ground for living in interpersonal mush, where we learn how to keep up appearances and repress renegade thoughts, feelings, and wants. We learn how to operate in a world where it really isn't safe to be fully open and different, and we don't expect others to be open and different with us either. The successful ones have learned how to operate effectively in interpersonal mush, even how to use it to their advantage in their normal, well-intentioned attempts to do well, be liked, and achieve in the world.

Hierarchy and Authority

In organizations a third force makes interpersonal mush so prevalent: hierarchy. Having a hierarchy means that some people have authority over others. There is a difference between good authority and bad authority (which I describe in Chapter 7), and a difference between too much authority and just the right amount. In order to organize a group of people effectively, we need to create the right amount of authority, that is, clarity about who is responsible for what and who has final decision-making power over what. One problem with a lot of large organizations is that the structure of hierarchy is haphazard, poorly designed, and more of a barrier to effective organizing than a support. It would take us too far afield to go into this topic, which is covered well elsewhere.[2] But even where hierarchy in a system is well designed it creates interpersonal mush because of the *reactions to authority* most of us develop in the family, school, and religious institutions. Basically, most of us learn to duck and cover around authority. We learn to try and figure out what the authority wants us to say or do and then say or do that when they are around. We learn to keep to ourselves the thoughts and feelings that we believe might make authority angry, upset, or less than pleased with us. The effect is that interpersonal mush is greatest in situations of unequal power, especially where one person or group feels dominated or oppressed by another.

A basic rule of thumb—and any manager who doesn't realize this is wandering around in the dark—is that information distorts on the way up in hierarchies. Less and less of the real story makes its way up the hierarchy as people put positive spins on things, censure unpopular views, hide less-than-favorable results, and so on. A funny description of this process, using coarse but common language, has been passed on to me by different students over the years. It's called "The Plan" (see the box on page 28). I don't know who originally wrote it. It may have been passed on to you. To me it is not only a description of how hierarchy creates interpersonal mush, but a template of the kind of story people lower down in hierarchies tend to create about people higher up in hierarchies. No one knows if a process like this

THE PLAN

*In the beginning was the plan
and then came the assumptions
and the assumptions were without form
and the plan was completely without substance
and darkness fell upon the faces of the workers.*

*And they spake unto their Supervisors, saying:
"The plan is a crock of shit and it stinketh."*

*And the Supervisors went unto their Department Heads, and said:
"It is a pail of dung, and none may abide the odor thereof."*

*And the Department Heads went unto their Group Managers, and
said unto them: "It is a container of excrement, and it is very strong,
such that none may abide it."*

*And the Group Managers went unto their General Manager, and said
unto him: "It is a vessel of fertilizer, and none may abide its strength."*

*And the General Manager went before the Vice-Presidents, and said:
"It promoteth growth and it is very powerful."*

*And the Vice-Presidents went to the CEO and said unto him:
"This powerful new plan will actively promote the growth of this
company and all its business units."*

*And the CEO looked upon the plan, and saw that it was good,
and the plan became policy.*

really takes place, but for many workers and middle managers, it is a story they are too likely to believe.

People who have authority have power over us. The more power we perceive them to have, the more our survival and prosperity appear to depend on them. What they do, think, feel, and want affects us. So they are the most likely targets of our sense-making. We don't bother trying to make sense of people and actions that we don't attach any significance to. But our boss, our boss's boss, the president—these people can do things that do matter to us. So we try to make sense of what we know and see. A lot of the stories that are made up in organizations are attempts to make sense of what authorities are up to. Authorities are the object of a full and rich fantasy life amongst organizational participants. That cannot be stopped. If there weren't a lot of fantasies going on about them it would mean they were insignificant.

What I am trying to make clear is that even in a world of good intentions it's easy to create interpersonal mush. In fact, it is often good intentions that create the mush in the first place. Abe doesn't want to hurt June's feelings so he doesn't tell her some of his truth. Sheryl doesn't want to cause unnecessary concern so she doesn't tell her truth. Rhana doesn't want to disrupt the meeting so she doesn't ask a question to get clear about Jack. Of course, when we seek to protect others we are also often protecting ourselves, but that doesn't diminish the irony that one of the most debilitating realities of human association does not come from dysfunctional people or bad intentions—just from normal folks muddling through life doing what they learned to do in their family of origin and schools. It is also true that there are some unsafe social situations, work environments, and business relations where it is not a good idea to be a Descriptive Self, but these are not prevalent and do not account for the pervasiveness of interpersonal mush.

Why Is Interpersonal Mush "One of the Most Debilitating Realities of Human Association"?

Interpersonal mush is the cause of most of the "people" messes we find ourselves in. If you watch situation or romantic comedies on TV or in the movies, you will notice that they usually involve people getting into some kind of interpersonal mix-up based on misperceptions. If you follow the story line these are always based on some critical moment when someone did not tell the truth of their experience. If they had, there would have been no mess or mix-up to try and resolve. TV and movie sit-coms are not that serious, but our work lives and our family lives are. They are our lives, and when the interactions in these lives are based on misperceptions, inaccuracies, and mix-ups the results can be a lot less than funny. Our sense-making has long-term consequences and when our stories are inaccurate we end up living in a make-believe world. And as I'll explain below, our make-believe worlds are usually *not* rose-colored: they are often less pretty than the real one.

We See What We Believe

Part of what makes a new story satisfactory is that it fits with what we already believe to be the truth, that is, our past acts of sense-making. This has two effects. One is that we tend to make up explanations and rationales for others' actions that fit with ones we've made up in the past. You can see that happening with Bill's subordinates in the story at the beginning of this chapter.

The second effect is that we tend to see and hear things that fit with our previous stories and miss things that don't fit. Our beliefs distort our perceptions. Most people recognize that this happens but don't notice when they themselves are doing it. As a consequence we live in a world of our own construction, fairly unaware of what is accurate and what's inaccurate. Both effects make it hard to see what is not already in our sense-making repertoire.

Sense-making in an environment of interpersonal mush might be neutral if we were as likely to err toward the positive as the negative side of things. I mean, isn't it possible that the story I make up about you has you being more courageous, more concerned, more honest, more trustworthy than you really are? Couldn't my story be inaccurate that way? Well, it could and it can. Sometimes we do make up stories that put people on a pedestal that doesn't really fit. But that isn't normally what happens, especially in organizations.

Our Stories Tend to Be More Negative Than Positive

It is an unfortunate truth that the stories we make up, and the stories that get made up about us, tend to be more unfavorable than the reality. In a vacuum of information, people tend to assume the worst, and this is particularly true in work organizations. The result of interpersonal mush is that what we believe about the organizations we work in, and the people we work with, is often worse than the reality. Executives are seen as more heartless and cruel than they really are. Organizations are seen as more political and unbending than they are. Co-workers are seen as more insensitive and uncaring than they are. Subordinates are seen as lazier and more careless than they are.

I would go as far as saying that the greater the interpersonal mush, the more negative the stories that go around. A vicious cycle is created where I become less willing to tell the truth of my experience because it is too dangerous, thus increasing the interpersonal mush, which is what makes it seem dangerous in the first place. Interpersonal mush drives out our ability to see the basic humanity in each other—the loving, caring people who are just trying their best to do what they feel is rightfully expected of them by others.

One reason we fantasize the worst is as a defense. It's a way of preparing ourselves for the worst-case scenario. This defensive stance is amplified when a person is feeling insecure. Interpersonal mush teaches us that being negative is more "realistic," so we take that belief with us into ambiguous situations. Environments of interpersonal mush feed off our fears and increase our sense of threat. But these are not what start the mush in the first place. There are a couple of reasons for this normal, human way of sense-making, which psychologists have uncovered over the 20th century. Let me describe them to you.

The Fundamental Attribution Error

One of the things psychologists have found is that when we make up a story about another person's behavior the first thing most of us do is look for external causes or "sufficient justification" for the behavior. For example, if I see you standing by a car at the side of the road with the hood up I will probably assume that you are having car problems. You may be standing there for a totally different reason; it may not even be your car. But seeing you beside a car with its hood up gives me sufficient justification to believe that your behavior (standing by the road) was caused by car problems. I have created a story that satisfies me and my sense-making ends. Now, if I can't find an external reason for your behavior, then I will assume that the cause is internal (e.g., your character, values, motivation, personality). The fundamental attribution error is the common tendency to assume that the cause of someone's behavior is internal when it is really external.

A typical way in which this plays out at work is as follows. When I mess up (such as missing a deadline), I can almost always show you how it was caused by the situation I am in. When I see you mess up, however, I assume it is because you have some kind of defect (you have no sense of time, you're over-emotional, you're incompetent, unmotivated, and on and on). Just about everything we do is shaped to some extent by the situation we perceive ourselves to be in. Research has shown that situational factors are far better predictors of behavior than any personality or other internal factors. But when we make up stories, we only work with the facts that we have. If we don't understand the situation the other person is in, then it can't get included in our stories. To create a satisfactory story with sufficient justification, we make up internal justification.

It is even more complex than that, because what really counts is not the objective situation the person is in, but the situation *they perceive* themselves to be in. Remember, ten people in the same "objective" situation will be having 10 different experiences and therefore their experiences will actually be of 10 different situations.

Projection

Another reason why the stories we make up are often more unfavorable than the reality has to do with where the raw material for our stories comes from. *Projection* is a psychological theory used to explain some things that have been observed about perception. Basically, it means that we see outside of ourselves what is inside of ourselves. To some extent, we are projecting ourselves onto the world around us all the time. For example, when I'm happy, the world seems like a happier place. When I'm depressed, the world seems like a more miserable place.

One of the reasons we are projecting all the time is that it is almost impossible to perceive things that we don't have inside ourselves. Most of us know what it is like to learn a new word that we had never seen before, and then see it all over the place. What has happened is that until we learn that something exists, it is almost impossible for us to see it (I'll see it when I believe it). In Chapter 4 I describe what I call *mental maps*, products of past learning that shape what we experience in the future. When it comes to interacting with people, we tend to see what is on our maps and miss what isn't. This is why being able to work well with people requires a deep knowledge of ourselves; the more we can understand all the different parts of ourselves, the more complicated our maps become, and the more we can see in other people while at the same time recognizing the difference between what is us and what is them.

Projection can be used to defend ourselves from becoming aware of parts of ourselves we don't want to be aware of. All cultures socialize people by telling them that certain qualities are good, positive, and acceptable, and other traits are bad, negative, and unacceptable. We learn and are encouraged to deny and repress these "bad" qualities, but they exist within us nonetheless. Numerous studies show that people who are most "psychologically healthy" in the sense of feeling happy, being optimistic, having a desire to achieve and accomplish in the world, and so on, have an inflated, overly positive and illusory view of themselves and the world. People who are successful and confident tend to forget their failures and exaggerate, in their memories, their successes; to ignore their negative actions and focus on their positive social values.[3] It appears that people who have the most "accurate and realistic" view of themselves can also be depressed and fatalistic. So it is not at all unusual for people to be repressing and denying parts of themselves they see as small, bad, inferior, or weak. The people who succeed in business and organizations are the most likely to do this. So what happens to these repressed parts? They become the raw material that gets used in stories to explain other people's failures and less-than-perfect actions.

The theory is that part of me wants me to see all of me, the bad as well as the good, but another part defends me from seeing it. When I am pushing myself to see something about myself I can avoid it through a kind of mental jujitsu where I let the image slip past myself and land on you. By using split-off material in my sense-making I get to kill two birds with one stone: create a satisfying story about you and defend myself from dealing with parts of me I don't like. In organizations people make up stories about the reasons other people are doing what they do by taking their own negative motivations and projecting them onto others. I deny the part of me that is competitive so I see you as competitive. I don't want to see my own pettiness and jealousy so I see you as petty and jealous. To avoid confronting my own vindictiveness I use it to make up a story about you where you act the way you do because you are a vindictive person.

I have found that there has to be *something* about the other person that hooks the projection in the first place. We don't project a quality randomly. The other person has to have some characteristic that makes the projection seem to fit. Before I will project my competitiveness onto you, I have to see you doing something that looks competitive. My projection of jealousy onto you is probably hooked by some jealousy you have. But I am not really seeing your jealousy anymore, just my own projection. And here is the kicker. Because you are doing a good job of helping me not see it in myself, I will want to keep that projection in place. I will look for evidence to continue to see you acting jealously because that relieves me of having to confront my own jealousy. So on top of the normal sense-making process of seeing what I believe, projection also gives me a motivation to not see anything that might change my story.

The clear leader understands these normal tendencies of human sense-making. He understands that he is a sense-making being just like everyone else, and so he is likely to be projecting and making attribution errors. Therefore people using clear leadership skills are constantly open to the possibility that their stories are inaccurate. Clear leaders know they can't stop themselves from sense-making; they have to do it, so they ask people to tell them the truth of their experience. This gives these leaders more accurate input into the stories they are making up, so they can project less and make fewer attribution errors. Clear leaders try to understand how the world looks from the perspective of other people, getting clear about the other person's experience and not making up what is going on in their head. They work at helping other people get clear about each other. Most importantly, clear leaders tell others what is going on in themselves so that there are fewer attribution errors and less projection being placed on them. By doing this, they reduce interpersonal mush and create the conditions for interpersonal clarity.

It is true that there are personal characteristics that also contribute to the amount of interpersonal mush going on. It's not just a product of socialization at home and in the family. Clear leadership requires clear psychological boundaries, and a lack of these boundaries, in managers, makes it almost impossible to get rid of interpersonal mush and create interpersonal clarity in organizations. But that is an issue that takes us away from focusing on sense-making, interpersonal mush, and interpersonal clarity in organizations, so we'll save that for the next chapter.

What Is the Effect of Interpersonal Mush on Organizations?

Interpersonal mush is sustained by an organizational culture that does not expect or support people in being Descriptive Selves and by managers who do not work at creating interpersonal clarity in the workplace. Interpersonal mush is endemic to most organizations, large and small. As a result, many organizations are much less than they could be. We assume teams and committees will be time-wasting and laborious, that bureaucracy will put up barriers to innovations, that people are unmotivated and will resist change. That's just the way it is, isn't it?

I know it doesn't have to be that way, because I've seen many instances where things are different—work groups, departments, divisions, and whole companies where the mediocrity we call "normal organization" is far surpassed by an environment of high motivation, real synergy, rapid innovation, and mastery of change. I have come to the conclusion that the one common factor in every instance I have seen is the presence of clear leaders—people who use a basic set of skills that create interpersonal clarity. It's not the structure, technology, market, product, or service that makes the difference. It's interpersonal clarity. Before I talk about how people create interpersonal clarity, I want to make sure you are convinced that interpersonal mush is at the core of so much organizational dysfunction, and I'd like you to imagine what an environment might be like if instead of hiding our experience from each other, we told each other the truth of it. Let's start with the more obvious consequences and then move on to the more subtle issues.

Fragmentation Increases and Subcultures Form

In an environment of interpersonal mush people seek out others they can sense-make with. They tend to form into fairly stable cliques that develop a common set of perceptions about others. The team, division, or organization becomes fragmented into these subcultures. It is difficult to get real communication, cooperation, or agreement about anything because people in the different subcultures are operating out of different sets of assumptions. The people in each subculture reinforce each other's perceptions, so it becomes difficult to get any of them to see a different point of view. This pattern can escalate to a situation where the members of each subgroup think they have truth and goodness on their side and other groups are wrong-headed or evil. Inter-group conflict increases the fragmentation, the isolation, and, therefore, the amount of inaccurate fantasy in each group's stories about the other groups. There are real, reasonable reasons for people and groups to have conflicts in organizations—I would even say that is healthy. What is unhealthy is when conflicts are based on misperceptions and inaccurate stories that groups are making up about each other.

An Environment of Distrust and Cynicism Develops

In an environment of interpersonal mush, we aren't clear on what others are experiencing, why they are doing or saying what they do. This ambiguity and uncertainty creates a certain amount of anxiety. It's not safe, though we can't be exactly sure why (yet when pushed we can make up some good stories for why it's not safe). In a lot of organizations, especially smaller and younger ones, there is a kind of benign interpersonal mush where I don't *distrust* people, I just don't trust them. For many, this is as good as it gets in business. I don't expect my co-workers or leaders to do anything malicious, but I would feel vulnerable if I told them how I really think about things. I keep parts of my experience to myself and don't expect anyone else to tell me the truth of their experience.

Then there is the less benign form of interpersonal mush, where I feel like I have to watch my back. Unfortunately, the normal human tendencies described earlier inevitably lead environments of benign interpersonal mush, over time, to become less benign. The stories that get made up are more and more negative. People get more and more cynical as they attribute worse and worse motives to the actions of leaders and co-workers. Organizations become places of distrust. They come to be seen as a "jungle" where it makes sense to look after yourself and not worry too much about others who might, unfortunately, be damaged by your actions. After all, they wouldn't shed a tear for you, would they? Hey—it's kill or be killed in the jungle. Interpersonal mush can create a spiral of distrust and actions based on that distrust that further fuel the distrust, creating the reality that, initially, was just a story someone made up to explain someone else's behavior.

People, Especially Leaders, Can't See the Consequences of Their Own Actions

Here's another tendency of human thinking that psychologists have unearthed. When I judge myself, I do so based on the intentions I have. I decide whether my motivations are good or bad before I decide whether what I did was good or bad. But when I judge you, I do it on the basis of the effect you have on me. Unless I ask, I don't know what your intentions were. In a relationship of interpersonal mush, I don't ask. So I make it up, and I do so based on how your actions landed on me.

In an environment of interpersonal mush, I'm not likely to even tell you the effect you are having on me. In the world of interpersonal mush, victory goes to those who keep a cool and calm appearance, who never seem ruffled or anxious. You could be making me irritated, confused, or hurt, but I'm unlikely to want to let you see that, especially if you have authority over me. As a consequence you may not have a clue what effect you are having on me. And, of course, the story I will make up about you will not be a pleasant one.

Let me tell you a story from one of my undergraduate classes.

In this course, student teams had a series of tasks that earned them points which eventually made up part of each member's grade for the course. One of the early tasks was for each team to make a class presentation on a topic, with points for the quality of the presentation itself. One group selected a young man from China who had been in North America less than a year and whose English was almost unintelligible. I gave this group very low marks, trying to make the point that teams need to utilize their resources effectively. Making this person do the presentation was poor resource utilization. Many students in the class were embarrassed for the poor guy and angry at me for this decision. Outside of class, students began to discuss my "racist" decision. Someone had heard that I was involved in a men's support group, and in the interpersonal mush this was quickly turned into a "white supremacist men's group." Soon, there were concerns that I was sexually harassing women in the class. For weeks the atmosphere in the class degraded while an active fantasy life amongst the students was built on and embellished. As the authority I heard about none of this until one student cautiously approached me to ask if I really was a member of a white supremacist group. Fortunately, I could and did bring this out into the open and it provided a great learning experience for the students in what happens in interpersonal mush (though I'm sure some students weren't totally convinced of my innocence).

In this case, the structure and content of the class made working the issues very appropriate. Few leaders, especially in work organizations, have this luxury. Instead, negative reactions and perceptions can spiral into a poisonous work environment that has no basis in reality. From the point of organizational effectiveness, perhaps the most damaging result is that those with authority and responsibility for making good decisions get the least accurate feedback. If there is a negative culture toward authority in the organization, they become isolated and cannot get good information about the effect they are having on the people they lead. As a result, they become unable to lead in any meaningful way.

An Active "Organizational Unconscious" Is Created

In organizations characterized by interpersonal mush, two separate worlds develop. Imagine organizations for a moment using the metaphor of the human mind. In our minds we talk to ourselves and there can be many different voices—or perspectives—saying things, making judgments, urging different courses of action, offering opinions. Some of this we are very aware of. We call that the *conscious* mind. It tends to be the rational, logical part of the mind, the part we focus our awareness on. Just below that are parts of the mind we are less aware of. It is the level of daydreams, where we talk to ourselves and make up stories that we can't quite remember 10 minutes later. At this level of mind other less rational parts urge us to do one thing over another, interpret things one way instead of another, suggest certain courses of action and ignore others. Psychologists talk about this *subconscious* mind as a very powerful determinant of what we do. Contained here are what psychologists call *scripts* and *schemas*, and some therapies, like neuro-linguistic programming and rational-emotive therapy, operate mainly on this subconscious level of the mind. The idea is that we are talking to ourselves all the time; we have an inner dialogue but we don't pay attention to all of it. Some is outside our awareness, but that doesn't mean it doesn't affect us. In fact, the effects can be very powerful because we're not aware of them. Without awareness, we can't be choiceful in how we respond to those voices.

In organizations full of interpersonal mush a similar thing happens—there is a conscious, rational part of the organization and there is an unconscious inner dialogue that has powerful effects on the organization. The conscious, rational part is the things that are said between people in official forums of organizational business—events like committee meetings, departmental meetings, workshops and offsite retreats, and strategic planning sessions. What is said here is discussable by all employees who are in attendance, and in that sense the organization as an entity is consciously aware of it.

Before and after these events, however, are things people talk about in smaller groups or in confidential conversations. These conversations are full of interpretations, judgments, feelings, and preferences about the discussions and decisions made in official forums, which these people would not verbalize in a larger group. The organization as an entity is only partially aware of these conversations, and to the extent that these perceptions, interpretations, and judgments are not discussable in any official forum of organizational business, they are out of awareness. They are like the inner dialogue of the human mind that operates at a subconscious level, and they have a powerful effect on organizational actions.

By definition, the inner dialogue is about things that are *not discussable*—thoughts, feelings, and wants that people don't feel comfortable saying out loud except to a small circle of intimates. The very fact that an inner dialogue exists usually indicates that people don't fully agree or support what is going on in the conscious part of the organization. Yet it is here that people are making sense of what is going on. The stories they create, the "truth" that they then operate on, is not being created in the conscious, rational part of the organization but in the subconscious, inner-dialogue part! Because it is not discussable in official forums of organizational business, it can't really be dealt with in the normal operation of the business. In effect, interpersonal mush creates an unconscious part of the organizational mind that powerfully affects how people experience the organization and therefore act at work. And this unconscious part tends to be at odds with the conscious part—that's why it exists in the first place.

Poor Implementation and Follow-Through Result

The presence of this inner dialogue explains why some apparently good, well-supported plans and actions are not followed through on or are poorly implemented. I am still amazed at how willing people are to appear to be supporting managerial decisions or actions that they really have grave misgivings about. In interpersonal mush there are rules or norms that people have to follow if they want to belong. Generally these involve certain thoughts that are OK and those that aren't, certain feelings that are OK and those that aren't, and certain intentions or wants that are OK and others that aren't. Successful managers learn that they have to couch their plans and actions according to the thoughts, feelings, and wants that are OK. One result can be that groups agree to things that no one individual actually wants. The effect on follow-through is obvious. I'm aware of one managerial group that planned layoffs for seven months without actually following through on them. The discrepancy between their words and actions was becoming so great that they were starting to really fall apart. With the help of a consultant they finally told the truth of their experience to each other and discovered that everyone hated the decision they had made. All of them felt unhappy about what they were proposing to do, particularly the way in which they had planned to go about making the layoffs. They did not like how they would feel about themselves—but that had not been OK to talk about. In this organization, decisions were supposed to be impersonal, based on the organization's needs and not personal needs. It is not that uncommon for organizations to make the personal needs of managers and employees undiscussable or only discussable in the service of the organization. Of course all that does is increase the interpersonal mush and ensure spotty implementation of poorly supported decisions. In this case, once the managers told each other their real experience, they were able to make plans and decisions they were willing and able to act on decisively.

People Are Unable to Learn from Experience Together

Under conditions of interpersonal mush people can't learn from their experience together because they are not describing their experience. People are not getting accurate information about the effect they are having on others. Different subgroups have no idea what stories are being made up about them by other subgroups. Important thoughts, feelings, and intentions are not talked about openly so people make up fantasies about each other. Without real information, learning cannot take place.

Organizational learning is a term I use throughout this book, so let me be clear what I mean by it. Organizational learning is a term that has come into popular usage and, as typically happens with every new management fad, the meaning of it becomes watered down and it comes to mean just about anything. Since organizational learning is a concept, you cannot prove that one definition is more correct than another. Rather, you can ask which definition is more useful, provides a new and more powerful lens, and leads to insight and action. I believe that the approach to organizational learning in this book is a practical and doable method for increasing organizational effectiveness and renewal.

From my point of view, organizations are a network of relationships among people. These relationships take place in the context of particular goal and task demands, though the relationships have a meaning and life beyond the formal tasks and goals of the organization. An organization is found in the patterns of relationships that get formed and are repeated over time. An organization is not its tasks or goals; an organization has tasks and goals. An organization is not its people; an organization has people that come and go. An organization is not its products, markets, or technologies. Rather, an organization is found in its processes of organizing—in the repetitious patterns of how people relate to each other, gather and interpret information, solve problems, make decisions, manage conflict, and implement change while accomplishing the organization's purpose.

I define *learning* as the outcome of an inquiry that produces knowledge and leads to change. All three components (inquiry, knowledge, and change) have to be present for an episode of organizational learning to take place. Knowledge that doesn't come from inquiry is revelation, not learning. Knowledge that does not lead to change might be called conceptual learning, but without practical results it's not organizational learning.

Organizational learning takes place within the relationships that make up the organization. From this point of view, learning is a social, not an individual, phenomenon. Organizational learning happens when two or more members inquire together and produce knowledge that leads to a change in their patterns of organizing. It is the change in patterned relations that makes learning organizational and not simply individual.

You can have technological learning, where the organization implements new technologies. You can have skill development, where people learn new techniques. But organizational learning means that a change in the organization, that is, in the patterns of organizing, has taken place. The patterns of organizing are "how things really get done around here." It's the way your department typically interacts with other departments. It's the way you typically deal with that fellow in purchasing. It's how you and your boss deal with new tasks. All the typical ways in which you and others in the organization interact while doing the business of the organization are what I mean by "patterns of organizing" or "patterns of interaction." Unless these change, the organization doesn't really change. Perhaps you have gone through a major restructuring where, after the dust settled, people said "nothing really changed." Nothing really changed because the patterns of interaction didn't change.

Under conditions of interpersonal mush, organizational learning simply isn't possible. There isn't any inquiry into our various experiences, and, at best, learning is about things—like technology or markets or products. It is useful learning, but it's not organizational learning.

The Same Problem Patterns Never Go Away

With interpersonal mush the patterns of organizing don't change unless something happens in the group's or organization's environment that forces a change. The problem patterns, the typical interactions that make us less effective, de-motivate us, and reduce our capacity to understand the real issues, never go away. The same boring meetings go on and on. The same petty conflicts never get resolved. The same round of mindless budget cuts happens each fall. The same lackluster performance becomes not only tolerated but expected.

Attempts to change these problem patterns through such methods as team building workshops, survey feedback, managerial training, strategic planning, and process reengineering have little or no
effect on the problem patterns if they do not create more interpersonal clarity. Rational discussions where people make lists of good
intentions, create organizational visions, and write values statements
soon disappear, chewed up in the interpersonal mush.

People need to make sense of problem patterns as much as anything else. Because interpersonal mush seems normal, it doesn't get
blamed for these problems. Sometimes people make up stories about
how it's "the system" that needs to change. More often we make sense
of problem patterns by blaming individuals—the fundamental attribution error. In most problem patterns it is clear to me how it's the
other person who is the problem. It's because they have bad intentions, are incompetent, don't listen, are on a power trip, whatever. So
we figure nothing can be done about it except get rid of the person,
or work around them. The last thing we'd think of doing is to talk
about our here-and-now experience with that person. But as it turns
out, that is the only real solution, because the problem pattern is as
much a function of the interpersonal mush as of anything else.

This is one of the reasons that the ideas in this book are simple and
powerful. They're simple because it doesn't matter what the problem
appears to be, there is one solution that almost always makes it better:
increase the interpersonal clarity. That won't solve technical, product,
or market problems but it will lead to solutions to organizational problems. They're powerful because every time two or more people inquire
into their in-the-moment experience of a problem pattern they develop
new knowledge about the pattern that leads to a change in the pattern.
The only way this result will not happen is if they stop short of following the inquiry before everyone is totally clear.

Our Inability to Manage Change Makes Us Victims, Not Masters, of Change

An organization in interpersonal mush has fragmented subgroups
who have different stories about each other, leaders who can't see
the consequences of their actions on those they are leading, an inner
dialogue that is in opposition to the plans and decisions that are
announced and apparently agreed to, poor implementation and follow-
through, and an inability to learn together from experience. No wonder change seems so hard to plan and implement. No wonder resistance

to change seems endemic to organizational life. And no wonder real changes in problem patterns seem to occur only in a crisis—only when the environment of the group or organization has changed so much that its current patterns of organizing can no longer sustain it.

Many of the transformational changes seen in organizations in the past two decades were forced on the organization by the environment. People don't feel they are in control of what is happening, and that includes the people at the very top. So many of the changes they make seem forced on them by the market and competitors. And so few of the change programs that companies spend millions of dollars on seem to return much change at all. I know of one large progressive company where no one is willing to champion any change program because every one of the change programs of the past two decades, from quality circles to process reengineering, is remembered as a failure. Yet, at the same time, this company has totally transformed from a sleepy, bureaucratic, inward-focused firm to an innovative, dynamic, market-focused global competitor. But the people in this company feel like victims, not masters, of change, and fear of the future is greater than at any time in the past 20 years.

Even the new "empowered" organizing processes that have made clear leadership indispensable (e.g., breaking down tall hierarchies, using teams, breaking down functional departments, reducing centralized control and allowing more local autonomy, de-bureaucratizing, getting rid of rules and making people interact and negotiate, focusing on results and not procedures) have been forced on organizations. Little of this was actually planned by any company.[4] Piecemeal adaptations to threats from competitors, new technology, new products, and new processes have accumulated over time, willynilly, in most of today's organizations. Only in retrospect, when talking to journalists, can companies point to triumphs of planned change. Unless a company has a healthy dose of interpersonal clarity, the problems of interpersonal mush doom any large-scale planned change efforts from the start.

People Get Stress Disorders

Most of the focus to this point has been on the negative impact of interpersonal mush on organizational effectiveness, but I would be remiss if I didn't point out the negative impact it has on people in the workplace.

One of the dirty secrets of current corporate life in North America and Europe is that increasing numbers of employees are on sick leave for various kinds of stress and emotional disorders, ranging from depression to chronic fatigue syndrome. It is almost an epidemic. I think a contributing cause is the negative interpersonal mush people live day in and day out at work. Sure, there are other causes, such as too much work with too few resources, reduced job security, and incessant competition, but interpersonal mush makes it all that much worse. When my daily experience is of secrecy and gossip, where it isn't safe to tell the truth of my experience, when I am constantly having to hunt for clues to fuel my sense-making, after a while I burn out. If I'm lucky, I get out and do something else. But if I feel trapped by mortgage payments and the children's education and a myriad of other obligations and responsibilities, that is a hard place to be.

Why is this situation having such an impact now? Because the destructuring and reengineering that has been going on in Western organizations for the past decade has created environments where interpersonal mush is more toxic. One of the great advantages to bureaucratic organization is that there is a rule for everything, and a center of responsibility for everything. If you and I have a conflict, there is someone else who can resolve it for us. If you want something from me, we only have to look in the rule book to see if you should get it. It may not be effective, it may create great barriers to innovation, but it does create a work environment where things move more slowly and with less uncertainty. When you take the rules away, and tell employees to figure out the best way to do things locally, there is now a great deal more uncertainty. I no longer have the rule book to put between me and you. I have to deal with you not just as a role, but as a real human being. In the world of interpersonal mush, this is a very stressful development.

Let me give a concrete example. In the good old bureaucracy, if an employee asked to leave work early to deal with a problem child at school, his supervisor simply had to find out what the policy was and enforce it. There was nothing personal about it. The supervisor and the employee's interaction was completely bound by their respective roles. The supervisor didn't really have to think about it—just enforce company policy. If the supervisor said "no," the employee might not have liked it, might even have made up a story about the supervisor, but in the bigger picture everyone understood that this interaction was embedded in a larger, impersonal system.

Now take the same request in a destructured, "empowered" organization. It is a whole different experience. The supervisor has to make the decision, and the employee is bound to experience it as personal. The supervisor has to trade off a whole host of issues—this employee's morale, the needs of the organization, what is happening on that particular day, the precedent this will set for other employees, and on and on. It is much more stressful for the supervisor. In an environment of interpersonal mush, these stresses are not talked about. The supervisor is unlikely to ask for more information to gauge how important this request is. The employee might not think his personal life is any of the supervisor's business anyway. The supervisor is likely to give her decision without describing to the employee what her experience in making that decision is or finding out what the impact on the employee is. Feeling awkward about saying no, she might just send a curt email. The employee gets to fantasize all sorts of things from this email. Maybe he makes up a story about the supervisor being cold and uncaring. Maybe he makes up a story that he is out of favor and on the way out. Who knows? What I do know is that the daily grind of interpersonal mush in an "empowered" organization, where people need to, but are not willing to, describe and discuss their patterns of organizing, drives just about everyone crazy.

Summary

We are sense-making beings. Nothing you or I can do will change that. As sense-making beings we are compelled to make sense of people and events that are important in our lives. We do this by looking for sufficient external justification for their actions. If we don't find it, then we make up a story about what is going on inside of them, what their experience is. When people who work together are mainly making up stories about each other's experience without checking them out you have interpersonal mush, where it is impossible to achieve anything great as a team or organization. The old adage "a camel is a horse created by a committee" describes the outcome of interpersonal mush, and the fact that in most of our committees, teams, and organizations, interpersonal mush prevails.

Sense-making doesn't just occur around big decisions or events, or when people are acting mysteriously or not saying much. Most of us are sense-making in every interaction and conversation we have.

As Jennifer listens to her co-worker discuss the new product plan, she makes up a story about how much he really knows about what he is saying, what his purpose in talking is, how he feels about the plan, and what he wants from her. She does this without even noticing that she is doing it—it is as natural as breathing. We can't really stop ourselves from doing this; the best we can do is understand that our stories are usually wrong in some way and learn how to go about checking them out before we act as if they were real.

Because of normal human tendencies of sense-making, the stories we make up about each other and the organizations we work in tend to be more negative than positive. And because future acts of sense-making are based on past acts of sense-making, negative spirals are created that lead to organizations full of cynicism and distrust. People are afraid to tell their managers what they really think, so managers get less and less accurate feedback and ultimately can't see the effects of their actions on others. An organizational unconscious is created where people's real thoughts, feelings, and wants become undiscussable and therefore unmanageable. As a result, decisions that people appear to agree to are poorly implemented, and resistance to change seems endemic. With the increasing breakdown of impersonal, bureaucratic rules and regulations, within which people didn't really have to deal with each other as people but as roles, the necessity of negotiating agreements and managing conflict between peers makes interpersonal mush a highly stressful environment to work in.

What makes clear leaders effective is that they create environments of interpersonal clarity. They do this by recognizing that everyone is having a different experience, asking people to tell the truth of their experience, and leading by being a Descriptive Self. This sounds simple and, in a way, it is. But it is also tough. It is tough because of the clarity and strength of personal boundaries that is required. Part of the reason for interpersonal mush is our early socialization in the family and at school. Part of it also, however, depends on the personal character and actions of the people with authority. Clear leaders are able to create interpersonal clarity because they have clear boundaries, a state called differentiation. So let's turn now to understanding why people perpetuate interpersonal mush and what is required to effectively use the skills of clear leadership.

Understanding the Foundations
of Clear Leadership

There is a dilemma that we face as human beings. We want two things that seem to be opposite or mutually exclusive. On the one hand we value our individuality, our ability to be self-defined, to find and walk our own path. On the other hand we value belonging, having others who care about us, both for the intimacy and for the sense of community. Looked at from the flip side, we fear the isolation and loneliness that too much separation from others could bring but at the same time we fear the demands for conformity and the feeling of being stifled by others' expectations that can come from close relationships.

This set of contradictory pulls, what I'll call the paradox of individuality versus belonging, is at the heart of a lot of the unproductive behavior found in organizations. It is the source of two key anxieties that affect people's behavior. One is separation anxiety, the fear of being isolated and alone. The other is intimacy anxiety, the fear of being too close and engulfed. These are, for the most part, deeply unconscious and primitive anxieties. By unconscious, I mean that we can be anxious and act on that anxiety without being aware of what is motivating our actions. I'll talk more about that later.

Separation anxiety is that tug to give in when you see the disappointment in someone else's eyes. It's the part of you that is willing to let go of rationally determined goals and plans when it appears that others will disapprove or feel hurt. *Intimacy anxiety* is that desire to push away when you are feeling crowded and closed in. It's the part of you that stops listening to others, gets annoyed, and wants to take action without any more input from those whose cooperation is needed. The push and pull of these two basic, normal, human anxieties leads us to adopt strategies that help relieve the anxiety but get in the way of interpersonal clarity. I call these fusion and disconnection.[1]

Think of a continuum of interpersonal behavior. At one extreme is too much closeness—where I lose myself in others. I don't have any sense of my own boundaries; my emotions and desires are just reactions to what others say and do. This is a state of fusion, described in more detail below. At the other extreme is too much separation, where I have no awareness of others. I have no sense of what others think, feel, or want and no curiosity or caring about them. My actions take only my own needs into account, not those of others. This is a state of disconnection.

Neither end of this continuum is healthy for people, groups, or organizations. Let me give you some examples:

The manager who "hides out" is often motivated by his separation anxiety. If he lets people get too close to him he finds it hard to say no without feeling anxious. He fears that asking others what they want will make it too difficult to pursue his vision, so he avoids them. As a result he loses track of what is actually happening in his organization and undermines his ability to effectively manage toward his vision.

The manager who tries to be all things to all people is mainly acting out of her separation anxiety too. She also has a hard time saying no but has given up on self-definition and seeks mainly to belong. As a result she cannot provide a guiding vision for the people who work for her and therefore cannot create anything new.

The manager who demands a high level of formality and shuns any display of emotion by self or others is often gripped by intimacy anxiety. Contact with people is physically draining to her and she needs to maintain as much distance as possible to be able to interact with others. As a result she really does not understand the feelings and motivations of the people who work for her.

The manager who is constantly joking and "zinging" others, who seems friendly but never gets into a serious interpersonal discussion, is also motivated by his intimacy anxiety. Here as well, contact with others is avoided, but in a way that appears informal. This is usually even more confusing to people, especially after they find their attempts to get some real contact are rebuffed. As a result, this manager is unable to develop much loyalty or real team spirit and is unaware that people feel attacked by his jokes.

As you can see, the same underlying anxiety can result in totally different behaviors. In each case the result of unconscious anxiety creates problems for organizational success.

Effective managers balance these extremes in a place that's been called differentiation. When I am differentiated I am both separate from and connected to you. My experience is not simply a reaction to you. I have clear boundaries where I am clear about my own experience separate from yours. At the same time I am curious about you and care about what is going on in you. I am able to stay in connection with you while not losing myself. I am not pushed around by either intimacy anxiety or separation anxiety.

This, I believe, is the key personal difference of leaders and members in outstanding teams and outstanding organizations: they are able to stay differentiated in their work interactions. Clear leaders are able to be clear about performance expectations and stay true to their vision while listening to and seeking to understand the fears and objections of the people who will have to carry out that vision. They are willing to listen until they understand and can demonstrate that understanding, but not willing to have their agenda "emotionally hijacked" by others. Because of this they do not get anxious in the face of interpersonal clarity. They welcome it.

When managers don't welcome interpersonal clarity they act in fused or disconnected ways and so perpetuate the interpersonal mush going on. Let's get a fuller understanding of these two states before returning to a deeper appreciation of differentiation.

Fusion—Demanding That Others Manage My Anxiety

I am in a fused relationship with you when my thoughts and feelings are simply in reaction to you. How I feel depends on what you say or do. The more fused I am with you, the more my awareness and experience is determined by you. For example, in some ways I am fused with my wife and when she is angry I get anxious (separation anxiety). I notice I get more tentative in my actions, I look for ways to calm her down. At that moment, her needs take priority over my own. Seems normal, doesn't it? Well, fusion is normal in the sense that almost all of us learned to be fused in our family of origin. But it turns out to be a fairly unhealthy thing for relationships, groups, and organizations because fusion maintains the interpersonal mush.

When you are fused with me you give me messages, implicit or explicit, about how I should be for you to feel OK. In other words, you want me to have certain kinds of experiences, and not have other kinds of experiences. In the example above I didn't want my wife to feel angry because then I didn't feel OK. Notice that it doesn't matter what or who she is angry about. Her anger comes up and my separation anxiety quickly follows. So I try to stop her from having the experience of anger. If she is angry with me I try to mollify her. If she is angry with someone else I try to get her to see she needn't feel angry. Eventually she learns that if she is feeling angry and just wants to express it, talk to someone about it, she had better do it with someone other than me. She learns to hide this experience from me, and as a result I develop a less-than-accurate view of her real experience.

This is one way that fusion causes interpersonal mush. If I am having an experience that, in your fusion, causes you to be reactive to me, I get the message that having that experience is not OK or that I had best not tell you about it. You may get angry or you may cry, you may withdraw, or scold me, or try to fix my problem, give me a pep talk or tell me why I shouldn't be having that experience, whatever. I get the clear message that my experience is not acceptable to you. So I learn to keep it to myself, to hide it from you. And we are on the road to interpersonal mush.

If I weren't fused with my wife, when she got angry I would notice that she was angry but not react to it. My experience in that moment would not be determined by her. I would see she was having a particular experience and I might be curious about it. What I wouldn't do is take on responsibility for her feelings—as though I make her feel this or that, as though I have the power to create her experience. The truth is that it is very hard for me to not feel some fusion with my wife. As children it may be impossible for us not to feel fused with our parents, or them with us. But let's leave that aside and talk about fusion at the workplace.

While you and I may intellectually agree that I, not you, create my experience, when I am fused with you I hold you responsible for my experience. You are making me feel such and such. And in a sense that is correct, because when I am fused my personal boundaries are weak and porous. Fusion is about fuzzy personal boundaries. I am not clear where I end and you begin. When I have weak boundaries your actions do have a big impact on me. When I make it your problem by demanding that you have only certain kinds of experience, I am creating interpersonal mush. Managers who are fused with their subordinates will train their subordinates to express only certain kinds of thoughts and feelings. Subordinates learn that when they say things that are out of bounds, their supervisor gets anxious and life gets uncomfortable. Maybe the boss gets angry or emotional or critical or argumentative or concerned, or tries to fix their attitude. There are a lot of ways to shut people down. So the subordinates learn to hide the truth of their experience when it doesn't fall into what is acceptable to their boss.

Fusion, of course, is a continuum that ranges from extreme, pathological forms of fusion (where a person literally can't tell the difference between herself and the object of her fusion) to mild cases of boundaries getting a little blurred. The way I think of fusion is not as a characteristic of a person so much as a description of an interaction. I act fused in some interactions and not in others. Usually I'm not aware I am doing it when I'm doing it: fusion is a reactive process, not one we participate in consciously or by choice.

People who act in fused ways with their co-workers encourage and perpetuate interpersonal mush. The co-workers learn what is not OK to say or do and avoid those things. If someone is having an experience she believes would push her co-worker's fusion buttons, she keeps it to herself. Here are some examples:

Sheera learned that if she disclosed her sadness over some of the decisions they were making about layoffs, Brian would castigate her for being unprofessional. In this case, Brian's fusion caused him to unconsciously feel responsible for Sheera's sadness and then become annoyed at her for "making him" feel bad.

Paul learned that if he tried talking to Lars about his doubts over his ability to do the job, Lars would belittle his doubts and tell Paul why he had no reason to doubt his competence. In this case, Lars' fusion caused him to feel his own fears of inadequacy, which he quickly tried to squelch through "fixing" Paul.

Sue-yee learned that if she expressed her excitement about something at work Bernice would quickly respond with ridicule and cynicism. In this case, Bernice's fusion caused her to feel pain over her own lost excitement, which was kindled whenever Sue-yee got excited.

Odile discovered that Al would snap at her every time she talked about things she'd like to physically change in her work environment. In this case, Al's fusion led him to feel responsible for getting Odile what she wanted; and since he couldn't, he felt frustrated.

But fusion doesn't only happen with other people. It can happen with things and ideas as well. We are fused whenever we confuse ourselves with something that is not ourselves. For example:

Robert found that whenever he tried to plan moving the department to the new building with Juanita, she became withdrawn and unresponsive. In this case Juanita was fused with her office and felt physically ill at the thought of having to move.

Ali learned that whenever he brought up hard questions about Rick's marketing strategy Rick would attack him in some way. In this case, Rick was fused with his strategy and heard Ali's questions as personal attacks.

Stories like these are a dime a dozen. They permeate organizational life. In each case one person learned to keep a part of their experience hidden from another. Each instance on its own is probably a tolerable state of affairs. But when they are all added up, work becomes a place where we find ourselves continually censoring what we say and do so that we don't have to deal with the consequences of other people's fusion. And, as described in the previous chapter, the long-term consequences for team performance and organizational effectiveness are staggering.

Maybe the most debilitating thing about other people's fusion is that we don't want to check our stories out because we're afraid of the fused, anxiety-driven response we'll get from the other person. If I see you as less than perfect I may be afraid that if I raise issues I have with you, I might get your defensiveness instead of your interest, and that could make my working relationship with you even worse. Maybe you'll get angry or emotional. Maybe you'll look as if you are listening and interested but actually be quite angry and take it out on me when I'm not around.

Marvin and Holly were members of a quasi-police team of about eight people responsible for investigations and enforcement of certain laws. It was potentially dangerous work and required a healthy level of trust and mutual respect between team members. When I was called in there was an identified "men versus women" issue in the team. As we worked to get clear what that was about, it turned out there was not one issue at all—in fact, just about everyone had a different set of issues. But these had all gone under the label "men versus women," as this had been a useful way for the women in the team to talk to each other about some problems they had with some of the men without getting any real clarity. Once everyone told the truth of their experience of the "men versus women" issue, the real complexity of all the undealt-with issues became apparent. The one that looked like it would be the most difficult to resolve involved Holly and Marvin.

Team members did most of their work independently but it was required that members pair up when needed for safety reasons. Holly and Marv had been on the team for over five years but had not worked together for over two years. Holly thought that Marv was avoiding working with her but had been afraid to confront Marv over it. When she did try to broach the issue with Marv, she found he would get aggressive and angry, and she would quickly back off. For his part, Marv had avoided working with Holly, though for reasons she had no inkling of. He had come to the conclusion that Holly's personality was the problem and there was nothing he could do to change that.

When Marv owned up to the fact that he did not want to partner with Holly, he began by saying he found Holly "an embarrassment." Holly had a very difficult time listening to him after that. As his story came out she would interrupt with tangential issues and ramble until no one, including herself, knew what her point was. She would point out flaws in Marv's behavior that had nothing to do with what he was talking about. At that moment, Holly's experience was fused with what Marv was saying. What Marv was saying was making Holly very anxious. She lost all curiosity about Marv's experience and was reacting in a way that normally would have brought the conversation to a grinding halt.

With some coaching Holly was able to stop her reactions and listen to Marv until she understood him. She found out that in a case where she had been paired with Marv over two years ago, Marv had found her behavior inappropriate and dangerous. After tracking down and appre-hending someone considered highly dangerous, Holly had flirted with the suspect! She did this in front of members of another police agency, which made Marv even more angry as it seemed to reduce the appear-ance of professionalism of the whole team. Marv had decided that Holly was more interested in her romantic life than the work of the team and in general was not serious about the job.

Once he had been heard, it was time for Marv to listen. Holly told him that the reason she had "flirted" with the detainee was to find out where he had stashed his gun, which, she reminded Marv, she had been able to do. She pointed out that in dealing with detainees the women needed to use different strategies from the men, that they couldn't use intimidation and force to gain compliance. Marv was visibly affected by what was clearly a completely different way of understanding Holly's behavior, but he was not yet convinced. "How about how you are always taking really long coffee and lunch breaks?" he demanded—another sign that Holly didn't take the job seriously. Holly said, yes, she did sometimes take extra time at breaks but there were a few things he didn't know about. First, he wouldn't know that she was always in the office at least an hour before starting time. Second, she kept a record of her long breaks and subtracted those from her vacation days. Marv was stunned; subtracting breaks from vacation days seemed beyond the call of duty to him.

At that point, both Marv and Holly had gotten past their fusion with each other's stories enough to be able to pull apart all the stories they had made up about each other over the past two years, and they agreed to try starting over in their working relationship.

What usually happens with the Marvs and Hollys of the world is that each requires the other to act in a way that doesn't surface uncomfortable feelings. Marv didn't like how he felt when Holly would attempt to broach their not working together, so he would act aggressively enough to get her to back off. Holly didn't feel good when Marv called her an embarrassment, and she tried to get him to take it back. Her reactivity didn't allow her to listen and understand what Marv meant by that, so she would find some way to get Marv to shut up, perhaps apologize, and nothing between them would change.

One consequence of fusion is that a person might not really want to know the truth of another person's experiences if it falls outside their comfort zone. If I am fused with you there is a part of me that is going to avoid asking you about your real thoughts and feelings if I am afraid that I won't like what I'll hear. But I can't stop myself from sense-making about your experience, so I make it up. One of the great ironies of fusion is that people often don't ask others what their experience is because the story they've made up is pretty bad and they'd rather not hear it. In my experience as a consultant helping managers clear out interpersonal mush, I've found that the truth is almost never as bad as the fantasies that preceded it. By making up stories instead of just asking and getting clear, people perpetuate the fusion between them and add to the interpersonal mush in organizations.

Authority—Compounding the Problem

Authority amplifies the problems of fusion and anxiety because authority, just by itself, creates anxiety for many people. If someone has authority over me they can influence my life for good or ill. I, also, am more fused with authority: I am more concerned about their approval, and my boundaries are not as strong around them. The reaction authorities have toward me has a much bigger emotional impact on me simply because they have authority. That in itself is likely to make me cautious about being real. On top of this I, like most people, have had a number of bad experiences with fused authorities at home, school, and work. I've had teachers and bosses who didn't react well when I told them the truth of my experience, and I learned I had better be careful what I say.

As a manager some people working for me are going to feel more fused with me simply because I'm their boss. Because of the anxiety there will be even stronger filters between me and them, and their sense-making about me will be less determined by the facts and more by their internal state. If I do anything to tell them it is not OK to be real around me, my authority will amplify the impact of it. The smallest voice inflection, the most innocent remark can land hard on someone I have authority over, causing them to make up a story that supports increased caution and distorts further interactions.

On top of that, many people already come to interactions with a bias against authority—it is one of the central dilemmas of Western society at the beginning of the 21st century. Just think of the general contempt and distrust with which political, corporate, military, religious, educational, and judicial authorities are held these days. A lot of people expect to be treated poorly, unfairly, discriminatingly, and with callous disregard for their welfare by authority. Sense-making makes it likely that they will perceive such disregard in their manager's behavior. Interpersonal mush makes it almost a certainty. Once you begin, as a manager, to learn what people who work for you are really making up about your thoughts and feelings toward them, you will be astounded, I assure you. I still am even after knowing this stuff for decades.

Authority is really a two-edged sword. On the one hand, it makes authorities live in a fishbowl, where every action and utterance is scrutinized for meaning and they are suspect until proven trustworthy. On the other hand, it gives a manager greater visibility and greater prominence in the psyche of their subordinates. This initial influence, if it isn't squandered, can be very helpful in allowing managers to set the tone, the norms, and the climate of interaction. The further up in a corporate hierarchy, the stronger the authority dynamics that swirl around. The only people an authority can influence to be real with them are those they've made an effort to personally interact with so those people can learn that the authority is trustworthy. Those who do not get a chance to test the authority's trustworthiness will always be cautious around them. As discussed in the previous chapter, the managers who don't realize this live in a fantasy world where they cannot see the consequences of their actions. The amount of distortion can be so great that a senior manager can believe that everything in his organization is fine while the troops are looking for ways to bail out. It's not that uncommon.

Fusion Can Also Mean No Leadership

Up to now I've been concentrating on how fusion can cause one person to close down another person, creating interpersonal mush. There is another consequence of fusion that gets in the way of leader effectiveness as well. When I'm fused I can try to change myself so that you will have a different, nicer, or better experience. That creates weak and ineffective leadership.

This is often what's happening with managers who do not seem able to make hard decisions or stay focused on an objective. Anyone who tries to do anything significant where a lot of other people are concerned is almost sure to encounter some resistance. This is especially true of change. The psychological dynamics of transition ensure that most people will experience some loss and grief in any change. Managers who are fused with their subordinates can be emotionally hijacked by other people's hurt or sadness. They can also be affected by anger and outrage, but I've found that people are more likely to get hooked by tears than aggression. If I am fused with you and believe that what I am doing is hurting you (taking responsibility for your feelings), then I am going to stop doing it or feel incredibly miserable myself.

Managers who try to ensure that they are liked by everyone generally don't accomplish much. In general I've found that people initially love managers who create no anxiety for them, managers who make few demands and who search for consensus on all issues. Over time, however, they get impatient with the lack of clarity and action from such managers. Outstanding teams and organizations require leaders who have a vision of the team or organization at its best and are willing to push hard to accomplish that. This sometimes means stepping on toes, maybe even a knock-down-drag-out fight. The clear leaders I've seen do not constantly try to ensure that everyone agrees with them. Not at all. They just want to know exactly where people stand and why so that they understand the situation and aren't causing unnecessary problems. A clear leader needs to be able to hear the misery he is causing people as he forces them to adopt a new and better technology, and not lose his vision because of it. Clear leaders can't be fused with the people they lead or they will either cave in to other people's emotions or avoid hearing altogether. In order to be hardnosed leaders, some people therefore go to the opposite extreme: disconnection. Let's turn to look at that.

Disconnection: A Different Kind of Reactivity

At the other end of the continuum, disconnection comes from choosing extreme individuality without any connection to others. Again, there is a continuum from the pathological disconnection of the sociopath to the mild disconnection of someone just not paying much attention to others. Instead of fuzzy boundaries the person who acts disconnected has boundaries that are too rigid, not allowing anything to pass in or out. Like fusion, a disconnected response can come from either intimacy or separation anxiety. It is easier to see it as a response to fear of closeness, but it can also be motivated by not wanting to feel the pain of separation. Because I don't want to experience separation, I can stay disconnected and therefore feel nothing.

Disconnection is a state where I have little sense of you. When fused, I don't know where you end and I begin. When disconnected, I don't notice that I don't know much about you. I'm aware of you as an object, a role, or a means to an end but I have no curiosity about what goes on inside of you. I don't wonder what your experience is, or, if I do, my sense-making is totally driven by internal stimuli. I don't much care what effect I am having on you, but not because I've decided to not care. A disconnected response is as unconscious as a fused one is. When I'm disconnected it doesn't even occur to me to pay attention to what effect I am having on you. I might even be embarrassed by my lack of curiosity if someone points it out to me. This is a crucial distinction. When I'm fully aware that I am closing myself off from you and can choose a different response if I want, then that is not disconnection in the way I mean it. Similarly, if I choose to care about the impact I am having on you and change my behavior, fully aware of what I am doing, that is not fused behavior either. In these two examples I am making a conscious choice, aware of what I am doing. But a fused or disconnected response to another person is a reactive response. We don't think about it, we just do it. In a sense, we are out of control—the fusion or disconnection controls us.

A disconnected response is just as reactive as a fused response, but in the opposite direction. Because it's a reactive state it also creates interpersonal mush. A disconnected response, however, tends to be reactive to the whole person while a fused response is more often reactive to the specific behavior. This means that if I am disconnected from you, I tend to do things to avoid being emotionally affected by you. The person who is disconnected from her colleagues doesn't make demands on others to act in ways that make her feel OK. Instead, she enters and exits situations to control her anxiety. She avoids situations, interactions, and people that might cause her to not feel OK.

You could argue that disconnection is just a different manifestation of fusion. Underneath disconnection is often a fear of becoming fused if I allow myself to get too close. It is also a case of weak boundaries, but one where I am in a sort of all-or-nothing state. I can keep my boundaries up as long as I keep them up rigidly. If I relax them at all, the floodgates will open. But dealing with disconnection is quite different from dealing with fusion, and I have found it makes more intuitive sense to people if I portray differentiation as a midpoint between the problematic form of belonging (fusion) and the problematic form of individuality (disconnection).

Disconnection appears to be quite prevalent amongst senior managers in organizations and looks different from fusion in that the person is not likely to be emotionally hijacked and is not demanding that people express only certain kinds of experience. Rather, disconnected managers show little interest in their subordinates' experience. They give the appearance that other people's experience is irrelevant to the business at hand. They tend to show no curiosity about the impact of their ideas or actions. They don't inquire into other people's thoughts, feelings, and wants.

There is another kind of disconnected interaction that managers can have that looks different. This is where they solicit information about other people's experience but provide no information about their own experience. The new manager who talks to everyone, solicits their opinions and views, says little about his own, and then suddenly announces a set of changes can be operating in a very disconnected way. If he is managing his anxiety about what others might think, feel, and want concerning his plans by having no openness to being reasonably influenced, he's being disconnected. What he avoids is a discussion about his own experience—his thoughts, feelings, observations, and wants. It never occurs to him to ask others what they think, feel, and observe about his own experience.

The person who is disconnected is still sense-making just like everyone else. She is making up stories about other people that she considers important, but does it with even less primary information. If someone says something that creates a sense of closeness, the person using disconnection will find a way to distance herself from the remark—a glare, a joke, a change of subject; it's a knee-jerk reaction quite often outside the person's awareness. In a disconnected relationship, a person won't be affected by praise or by criticism; neither is really allowed to register.

A manager who often interacts disconnected from his subordinates can make explicit attempts to separate the business at hand from people's experience. The problem is that his subordinates' experience determines how they make meaning out of the business at hand. The two factors are inseparable. Managers who say things like "feelings are irrelevant to the decision" are just acting on the basis of their own fears or anxieties. Most people would acknowledge that feelings are strong determinants of how people work together. The disconnecting person is afraid of connecting, so he talks as if it were not legitimate.

In Western organizations disconnection tends to look more "professional" than fusion. In fact, I have found some people equate disconnection with professionalism, contending that professional managers keep a distance and don't allow themselves to care about employees. This might work, even be effective, in bureaucratic work systems, but it is deadly in empowered organizations. In the last few chapters I described how new, nonbureaucratic organizations create a very different interpersonal reality that requires managing interpersonal contact. I also described the problems of authority and hierarchy and how they create interpersonal mush. There is already a tendency by subordinates to keep authorities in the dark about the effect they are having and about the stories people are making up about them. When the authorities are operating out of a disconnected state, the combination ensures that they will have little chance to give the kind of leadership outstanding organizations require. Disconnection is a kind of "professionalism" organizations cannot afford.

Rob is typical of a disconnected leader trying to create change in his organization. Rob had been the CEO of this professional, knowledge-based organization for about 10 years and was strongly identified with it by people inside and outside the company. It had been successful in pursuing a particular strategy, but Rob had decided that the company needed to make a major adjustment to its strategy. This meant that some parts of the organization which had been central under the old strategy would now have a different role.

Rob made pronouncements about the changes and tried to explain the logic behind them but experienced the anxiety created in others by his new vision in ways that made him uncomfortable. I watched him have a lot of difficulty listening openly to the fears and concerns of people in the organization. As I got to know him I learned that when people described problems they were having he felt that he was responsible for taking away their fear. In addition, so many of these fears and concerns seemed unreasonable to him that he was able to create a story that allowed him to dismiss them: "It's just resistance to change," he said. "People will get over it once they see that the changes are good for everyone." So he became more and more distant and difficult to communicate with. He had less and less time for meetings. He was away more. He was difficult to reach. He even stopped returning phone calls to his vice-presidents.

Out of this vacuum of information those most concerned with the changes became increasingly anxious. The lead manager of the department most affected, Mario, reasoned that the lack of contact with Rob meant he was in imminent danger of losing his job, so he placed more and more pressure on himself to perform. He became less and less clear about what Rob really wanted, and the more anxious he became, the more he tried to please, the less competent he appeared. Mario's actions puzzled Rob, who believed that Mario had been a great asset to the company but began to resign himself to the possibility that Mario would have to go.

The people who worked for Mario felt even more unsure about the changes. They, of course, were aware of Mario's anxiety but had little information, so they made up stories about what was going on. Naturally, these were not pretty stories. They thought Mario and Rob were getting ready to downsize their department and lay people off. Actually, Rob thought that they were a highly skilled group and did not want to lose any of them, but none of that was communicated because to Rob it seemed so self-evident, especially because they were having problems with other companies raiding their top personnel. Their morale was sinking into the toilet and this was having an effect on the rest of the organization, who were increasingly unclear about the real nature of the now ambiguous changes. Rumors were rampant.

When people broached the topic of the meaning of the changes for the department, Rob would act annoyed and reply in a brisk way. This was a manifestation of his unconscious anxiety, as he feared that if he listened to them they would try to talk him out of the change and he would have a hard time standing firm. They, of course, only heard his annoyance and, already fearing for their jobs, would stop any questioning for fear of his anger. At the point where I was hired to do some executive development, the best people in the department, unbeknownst to Rob, were polishing their resumes and getting ready to leave. Rob knew there was some discomfort but he assumed that Mario was communicating the actual nature of the changes and that people would quickly get comfortable with them. Everyone had a fantasy about what was going on and everyone was, in some way, wrong.

For this to change, Rob had to recognize his disconnection and understand that he was avoiding people because interaction made him feel bad. That led him to face his fusion and see how his deep caring for the people who worked in the organization caused him anxiety in the face of their discomfort. As we worked to uncover all the stories and experiences swirling through the senior levels of the organization, Rob faced the irony that his disconnection was causing even more discomfort to the people he valued than the change in strategy he was pursuing, and this was a major revelation for him. As Rob came to understand the logic of being separate and connected at the same time (differentiation), he began a process of learning how to stay firm with his principles, values, and vision and not take on responsibility for the experiences that other people created from that. At the same time he wanted to hear what experience was being created so he could influence it, make it more realistic, stop wildly inaccurate speculations, and ensure that key people knew they were, in his perception, key people.

FUSION	← DIFFERENTIATION →	DISCONNECTION
Too connected	Separate and connected	Too separate
No boundaries	Choiceful boundaries	Rigid boundaries
Reactive to the interaction	Choiceful during the interaction	Reactive to the person
Own experience based on other people's experience	Wants to know what others are experiencing but stays true to self	Has little or no idea what others are experiencing

Figure 1 • Fusion, Disconnection, and Differentiation

Differentiation—Resolving the Paradox

Differentiation is finding a place where belonging and individuality are not mutually exclusive, where I am both separate from you and connected to you at the same time. Differentiation is about having clear boundaries, being clear what my experience is and the difference between that and your experience. Differentiation is about knowing the difference between the data I have and the stories I make up with it. Differentiation is about acknowledging that your experience will always be separate from mine and acting on your desire for belonging without demanding that my internal state be a certain way. Differentiation is about being true to myself and true to the relationship I have with you. It is about putting equal emphasis on my needs and our needs, whether "our" is two people, a group, or an organization. In order to do this, differentiation means being totally aware of what my truth really is—knowing what my experience is and what is really motivating my thoughts, feelings, and actions. Obviously this is a lot easier said than done. As one of my friends says, differentiation is a razor-wire balancing act that you never get completely right. It is a commitment to living a certain way, with as much failure as success.

There are at least five elements to what I call acts of differentiated leadership.

- When a person is acting in a differentiated way, she knows, first of all, what her experience is, that is, being an Aware Self. She is aware of the choices she has and the choices she is making. Awareness is the basis of differentiation, and without it differentiation may be impossible to achieve. I'll cover this in greater depth in the next chapter.

- Second, a person acts in a differentiated way when she openly seeks to understand the experience others are having, that is, being a Curious Self. She notices when she is making up stories to fill in the gaps of her knowledge and asks questions to get more accurate information. She wants to know the impact she is having on others, not necessarily to change her mind but so that she will know what is really going on. She acts in a differentiated way when she communicates to others that she really wants to know the truth of their experience and can listen to them dispassionately and openly.

- Third, a person is acting in a differentiated way when he is describing his experience to others, that is, being a Descriptive Self. This is not the same as "being open," where you tell people whatever is on your mind. It is where you describe the truth of your experience, fully aware that it is only one experience and no more valid or invalid than anyone else's experience.

- Fourth, a person is acting in a differentiated way when he is clear about his scope of authority, what decisions he has made and expects to be implemented, and what decisions he is making for which he is seeking others' input. He is clear in his own mind about where he does and doesn't want other people's input and how much authority he is willing to delegate to others. He acts in a differentiated way when he makes his position about this clear to others.

- Fifth, a person is acting in a differentiated way when she is clear about the basis of her actions and can describe these to others. Her actions are not motivated primarily by anxiety or other reactive emotions. She allows herself to be informed by emotion, to understand the message the feeling is sending her, but not to be overwhelmed or controlled by emotion or unconscious motivations.

Learning to be differentiated is a lifelong journey. It is a life path, a way of being. Some people decide that they want it all: they want to be self-defined, true to their own needs and wants, and yet also be in close, partnership relationships with others that support the growth and self-definition of both people. These people, whether they call it this or not, have chosen differentiation as the way they want to be.

Almost everyone is able to be differentiated in some interactions. The less emotional baggage we have toward someone the easier it is to be differentiated. And all of us have relationships where we have a great deal of trouble being differentiated. The most difficult are with our family of origin. As we develop ourselves we are able to be differentiated in more and more of our relationships, but this requires conscious work and the strong intention to be differentiated in our relations with others.

Differentiation Is About Healthy Boundaries

Psychological boundaries is the term increasingly used to describe and explain many of the psychological and relationship issues normal people face. Healthy boundaries are those where I know the difference between what is me and what is not me and can choose what I let in and what I don't. They are a necessary part of being differentiated. It's not always clear what is really inside of me and what is outside. In fact, most of us mix that up all the time. If I believe a story I've made up about you is really about you, then I'm confusing me with you. If I think I am responsible for how you feel, then I am confusing me and you. Healthy boundaries also require not confusing my thoughts and ideas with the things they are meant to represent. As I will describe in the next chapter, we all create internal representations or "mental maps" of external realities, and we are forever confusing them. And differentiation requires that I be able to separate out my past from my present. Again, that is not as easy as it sounds. We are constantly reacting to things in the present with feelings, attitudes, and perceptions fueled by past experiences.

One of the places where people often confuse the boundary between themselves and others is found in the phrase "you make me . . ." (angry, sad, happy, upset, mad, whatever). When I say this I am saying that you are creating my experience. I am confusing you with the person who really creates my experience, me. *Next to the principle that I create my own experience is the principle that I am responsible for the impact you have on me.* You are not "making me" feel or think or want anything. I make me do those things. Let me give you an example.

Laurie, a new clerk, was transferred to my department. She seemed a little ditzy. Her manner of speaking was weird, like someone with a mental deficiency. She was pleasant and smiled a lot but sometimes seemed a little spaced out and appeared not to follow the conversations around her. I decided she wasn't too bright and left it at that. I avoided giving her work that was in any way complicated. For months she was fine doing simple work with a smile on her face.

One week she filled in for one of our senior clerks and gave me a report writeup that was first-class. Not only that, she hesitantly pointed out changes she had made to increase the clarity of it. They were excellent changes. I was a little shocked. This was not what I had expected. I started paying closer attention to her but still saw the same slightly spaced-out behavior and heard the same lispy speech. Then one day I noticed she wore little hearing aids. I asked her about them and she blushed and then confided that she had been virtually deaf from birth but didn't like to tell anybody. From that point on none of her behavior changed but my experience of her changed completely. I have come to see her as extremely bright and courageous.

Notice that I created my own experience of Laurie. One minute she is a somewhat spaced-out, mentally deficient person. The next, she is brilliant and courageous. Her behavior didn't change at all, only my awareness. She didn't create the impact she had on me, I did.

A differentiated person takes the position "I am responsible for the impact you have on me *and* I am responsible for the impact I have on you." You'll notice that whether it's me impacting you or you impacting me, I take responsibility. This is a fundamentally empowering position to take and it is the position that leads to the greatest learning and the greatest effectiveness. It is not about blame. It is not about who did what to whom. As you deepen your inner game of leadership you'll come to realize that such questions are of little value. Blame keeps you in a disempowered state, feeling you are a victim of forces larger than yourself, and you learn nothing about how to get more of what you want.

At a certain point in personal development most people become interested in learning about the impact they have on others and modifying their behavior to have the impact they want. Fewer people, however, develop to the point where they understand they are responsible for the impact others are having on them. I am the one making myself think, feel, and want what I do in reaction to you. This perspective is the mark of a truly differentiated person and is a powerful stance for learning about yourself. Here's a hypothetical example.

A young man joins our office. He is bright, outgoing, self-confident, and playful—at least that's my experience of him. Jeanette sees him as arrogant, self-absorbed, and not serious enough. Who is having the right experience? Is he responsible for the very different experiences of him Jeanette and I are having?

If he is a learner, he will be interested in understanding the impact he is having on Jeanette and me, and will learn from that. For example, he might learn to notice when his playfulness gets in the way of serious work. If Jeanette is a learner, she will take responsibility for the impact he is having on her and learn, for example, what predisposes her to label his behavior as arrogance instead of the many other ways in which that same behavior could be experienced.

Much more often, however, Jeanette will believe that the young man is responsible for the impact he is having on her—it's his fault and he needs to buck up. If she is a "good manager" she will give him some "constructive feedback." If she is a "bad manager" she will just treat him poorly without telling him why. Either way, Jeanette learns nothing and won't be able to bring out the best in this young man, who will probably just feel confused by the feedback and simply get the message that he is not OK. He can then either try to fit in, losing his creativity, confidence, and motivation, or get rebellious and lose his commitment, cooperation, and concern for the system.

Differentiation comes from realizing that what we see in others is mainly ourselves, reflected back to us. This is critically important to understand, especially with people to whom we have a strong emotional reaction. The fact that there is an emotional reaction means that I am fused with the person in some way, that I am not separating them from me. If I'm the boss I can probably get them to stop what I'm reactive to. I can try to avoid being around a person I have a negative reaction to. If I need to work with this person, that is clearly a difficult and ineffective strategy, but I can at least try, as Marv did with Holly, to minimize all contact. I can demonize them in my mind, adding to that negative trait others which allow me to feel morally superior to the person. From here I can imagine punishing or banishing the person, making them go away or changing them.

Usually it's precisely because my negative emotional reaction is so strong that I find it most difficult to take a learning stance toward my experience. Surely I'm not responsible for my experience in this case? Any reasonable person would have the same negative reaction, wouldn't they? To make sure, I search out others whose opinion I value and describe the things that are bothering me. I'm usually able to get them to agree that the other person really is bad or deficient in some way. Validated in my belief that the other person is the source of my negative experience, I can then safely stay in my current point of view. And learn nothing. And be totally ineffective in dealing with that person. And even get in my own way of getting what I want.

If two people who are having a negative reaction to each other use the skills in this book to have a learning conversation, an almost magic transformation will occur and their patterns of interaction will be inalterably changed. (Even if only one of the two people does that their relationship will change.) Each will discover ways in which they are confusing you and me and probably find out something new about themselves. It is almost always a profound learning experience because it is so rare and so tough to do.

The Boundary Between Past and Present

As I explained in the first chapter, and will describe in more detail in the next, our moment-to-moment experience is created both by things outside of ourselves and things inside of ourselves. It's because of these inner things that people who encounter the same situation have different experiences. A lot of the inner things that affect how we generate percepts come from our past. How we experience the present is more or less conditioned by our past and so we all have some problems confusing the present with the past.

Of all the aspects of differentiation, I think untangling the past from the present is the most difficult to learn on your own. I have been immensely aided by others who have helped me notice when my reactions and perceptions to the present seem "off." Maybe I am having strong feelings that are out of proportion to the situation. Maybe I'm having too little reaction to what is happening. Maybe the story I am making up has little relation to the actual facts. All of these responses are clues that the experience I am having is based as much—or more—on my past as on the present.

Most of the clear leaders I have met and worked with have spent some time exploring and learning about themselves. Generally, this means learning about the baggage they are bringing with them from the past. They do this so that they can learn to separate it from the present, not let it unconsciously affect how they experience the present or motivate their behavior. Increasingly, in my work with executives, I try to include sessions with a partner who is a psychotherapist to increase the leaders' awareness of the deep forces that are operating inside them. Let me give you an example of how important that can be.

Jeremy was the whiz-kid founder of a fast-growing start-up company. One of the seasoned members of his board insisted that he get some help with his leadership skills, and I was hired to help him. In my contract with Jeremy I said that I wanted to work with him on both his "outer game" and his "inner game." To work on his inner game, he would meet for one hour a week with me and a partner, where he would work on deepening his understanding of the forces inside himself, increasing his awareness and control over himself. He agreed. What I didn't tell Jeremy was that my partner was a very skilled psychotherapist, as the word therapy tends to scare people. But Jeremy figured that out after a few weeks.

We had been working this way for about three months when members of Jeremy's management team approached me with concerns they had about promises Jeremy was making that he could not keep. For example, while on an overseas trip Jeremy had agreed to send a joint venture partner 5 million dollars, which the company, in a cash flow crunch, simply didn't have. They could not understand why he was making such foolish and unnecessary promises, and were angry and scared about the long-term consequences for the company.

I confronted Jeremy with the issue during a psychotherapy session, and over the next three sessions, using techniques to access his deepest feelings and motivations, he came to realize that he made these promises to older men because he was trying to please them. He realized that the real person he was trying to please was his father. In his interactions with older men he respected, he was confusing his need to find a way to thank his father for all he had done (the past) with the transactions he was having with his older business associates (the present). Jeremy got clear about his desire to thank his father and what, exactly, he wanted to do to express that to his father. He developed a realistic plan to do that and we moved on to other issues.

The impact of this on his behavior and the organization was dramatic. Over the next two weeks Jeremy terminated three major joint venture relationships that weren't really that good for the company. He had realized he was in them simply because he wanted to please older men he was confusing with his father. He stopped making promises he couldn't keep and got a lot sharper in the negotiations he was currently in.

You can see in this example not only the problem caused by lack of clear boundaries between the past and the present, but the belonging-individuality paradox still at work. It is ever present. Jeremy was fused with the older men he was doing business with and not able to say no to them because of the separation anxiety he would experience—but the source of that anxiety was separation from his father. His desire to please them was a manifestation of his desire for belonging. They were surrogates for being in relationship with his father. It was only when he got clear about his unconscious motivations that he could be more choicefully self-defining in his encounters with such men. Developing a plan for how to deal with the real issue, his relationship with his father, helped to reduce any separation anxiety that might be created in future interactions with father figures, so he could operate more rationally and with more clarity.

Paying close attention to your here-and-now experience and noticing when the situation just doesn't seem to warrant your reaction is one way to figure out when the past is intruding on your present. But nothing substitutes for spending time working with someone who is skilled at helping people strengthen those kinds of boundaries.

Summary

In this chapter we've looked at one basic difference between those who can provide leadership in the new organizations and those who can't. People who are too fused with or too disconnected from the people they work with are not able to use the skills that create the interpersonal clarity needed for organizational learning. Their behavior is motivated by unconscious anxiety that comes out of the belonging-individuality paradox. The things we do to avoid anxiety can be quite detrimental to organizational success. If you are being reactive, you can't provide much leadership.

Differentiation is about being choiceful. It is a foundation upon which the skills of clear leadership come alive. People can learn to talk the talk of clear leadership, but without some real differentiation they can't often walk the walk. Differentiation requires healthy boundaries, where the person is clear about the difference between what is inside her and what is outside of her and between her past and her present. It requires a willingness to be a learner, to want to understand how you create the impact you have on others and how you create the impact they have on you. Unless you are willing to learn from your experience, you can't help others learn from theirs. Finally, differentiation comes from choosing both individuality and belonging, searching for ways to have both simultaneously. A person using clear leadership is self-defined enough to be clear about his experience and what he intends to do. At the same time he is connected enough to others to be able to see the consequences of his actions and be open to changing as he learns.

Leadership and the
Four Elements of Experience

In this chapter I will get very detailed and a little technical in describing what experience is. This may seem far away from the hustle and bustle of organizational life, but I promise that if you learn to be fully aware of your in-the-moment experience, your interpersonal competence will increase significantly. This model of the elements of experience is a key tool in three skills that follow: the Aware Self, the Descriptive Self, and the Curious Self. You need to be aware of your experience before you can describe it and you need to know what experience is in order to use your curiosity well.

The Basics of Experience

The percepts (building blocks of perception) we generate are the basis of our experience. Percepts are images and urges that, for the most part, are below our level of awareness. They are the primary material we construct our experience out of. We are constantly generating a stream of percepts, with or without external sensory stimulation. Percepts are generated from information we are gathering from our five senses. These are the external sensory input that result in experience. But these external stimuli are rarely turned, in pure form, into experience. Instead they are mixed with percepts that come from inside the mind, internal input. These are things like your personal history and upbringing, your education, your culture, your current beliefs, attitudes, and values, and things like your current mood, how well you slept, what you ate recently, and other facets of your biochemistry. Our percepts are also strongly affected by our mental maps: the ideas, beliefs, and concepts we use for making sense out of external stimuli. These internal stimuli cause the same external stimuli to produce different experiences in each person.

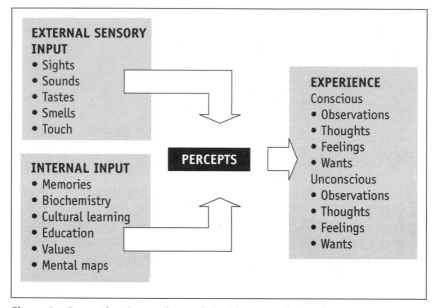

Figure 2 • Perception Generation and the Elements of Experience

Experience itself can be broken down into a set of elements that comprise it. They are generated out of the stream of percepts we create in response to internal and external input, as shown in the diagram. You are probably not that interested in unraveling the secrets of how internal and external inputs form percepts and get translated into experience. So I will start from the assumption that this is happening and go on to explore the consequences of that for organizing and leadership. If you believe that each of us takes what happens to us and creates out of that a unique, personal experience, then you hold one of the basic assumptions needed to use clear leadership successfully.

The next key assumption is that experience can be both conscious (you are aware of it) and unconscious (you are not aware of it). If you have not come to this understanding already you may find the idea of unconscious experience a bit difficult to grasp at first. Isn't experience, by definition, something you are aware of? I used to think so until I learned just how much of my experience was out of my awareness. There is a continuum of unawareness that ranges from experiences I am simply not paying attention to, on one end, to those I have no capacity to become aware of, at the other end. These are still my experience because they are happening inside of me and are affecting me, sometimes more powerfully than my conscious experience, but I am just not aware of them. For example, some people have a hard time being aware when they are angry. If you ask them, they will tell you they are not angry, but the muscles in their jaw are clenched and will hurt if poked. If you press hard on those jaw muscles the anger that is unconscious will often become conscious. A person's unconscious anger will influence their behavior, even if they are not aware of it, perhaps even more powerfully because of the lack of awareness. The anger might come out in sarcasm or saying hurtful things, excessive aggressiveness, punitive acts, or warped decisions.

As summarized in the following diagram, your observations, thoughts, feelings, and wants are the four elements of your experience. I call this model the experience cube, and it is a basis for learning to be an Aware Self, a Descriptive Self, and a Curious Self. The experience cube below shows the four elements of experience and demonstrates that there are parts to each that we are more aware of, close to the surface, and parts to each that we are less aware of, deeper down in the shadows.

This model of the four elements of experience is a road map to your experience. You can use it for deepening your awareness of your own experience and for focusing your curiosity into others' experience. How you use that awareness to create exceptional teams and organizations will be described in later chapters. Here I want to focus just on what experience is.

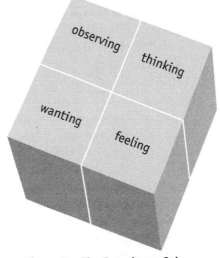

Figure 3 • The Experience Cube

The Elements of Thinking and Observing

Thinking involves all the cognitive processes. These include thoughts, judgments, interpretations, beliefs, ideas, visual images, speaking to oneself, and daydreams. Like each element of experience, thinking is set off by percepts that, in turn, are generated from internal stimuli and external stimuli. It is very important to learn the difference between these observations and the thoughts that we normally leap to. Observations are what we actually see and hear. Another name for them is sensory data—the information we collect from our five senses. No one sees and hears purely, like a video recorder. Our observations are shaped by internal stimuli and so they are an outcome of the perception-generating process. But they are different from the inferences we then create—our thoughts. We often confuse observations (what we see and hear) with our thoughts, and that is one of the causes of interpersonal mush.

An exercise I use to help people make this distinction is to have two people role-play a scene in which a subordinate is trying to get the boss's attention and the boss ignores the subordinate. Afterward, I ask people what they saw. Most of the people report out their interpretations and judgments (thoughts), such as, the boss was distracted with something, the boss was rude, the subordinate was anxious, and so on. Occasionally, a few people will say what they actually saw (observations): the subordinate knocked on the door, the boss did not look at the subordinate, the subordinate gave the boss a stack of papers. You see the difference? In the first set of interpretations, people made a leap from what they actually saw to stories they made up about the boss (he's distracted) and the subordinate (she's anxious) and to judgments they made (the boss is rude). In the second set, descriptions of the external stimuli are given without any interpretations or other thoughts added to them.[1]

To be able to properly describe your observations, you have to give a description of what anyone in your position would have actually seen and heard, with as little of your personal biases mixed in as possible. Understanding and being aware of the difference between your thoughts and the observations that go into them is crucial to being able to learn from your experience and create learning relationships. Good managers and team members must continuously be able to separate out what they actually see and hear from the interpretations they make so that they don't get blinded by their own stories.

I am not advocating that you stop making interpretations and judgments about what you see and hear. In the first place I don't think it is possible and in the second I think a part of interpersonal competence is being able to make accurate interpretations and judgments (while keeping in mind that they may be incorrect and need to be validated). What I am advocating is that you become as aware as possible about the actual sensory data (observations) your interpretations are based on. This will do three things for you that will help you be more effective at leading and working with people:

1. You will be able to see how much or how little data you have for your thoughts and ideas and avoid getting too far out on a limb when you haven't got that much to go on.

2. You will be able to tell others what the actual data is that led you to the interpretations you are making. This is a key piece of your experience that will help others understand you. It is indispensable for having learning conversations.

3. You will be more likely to see data that is contrary to your interpretations, and therefore stay open to thinking about things more clearly and accurately even after you have developed a satisfactory story.

Thinking is a lot about the internal dialogue, the part of me that talks to me in my head. Because so much of our thinking is done through language, language is a critical influence on how we think, and therefore on our experience. Many people have heard that the Inuit (Eskimos) have many more words for snow than exist in English. As a result, their experience of snow is far richer and more varied. The Hopi people did not have a future tense in their language and therefore could not think about the future. From their point of view no one could know the future and anyone who tried to talk about it was crazy. Words are not passive conveyers of meaning, but are active in constructing how we experience our world. People use words strategically to evoke one meaning over another. *Pro-choice* evokes a very different experience from the word *abortion*, just as *pro-life* evokes a very different experience from *anti-abortion*. The judgments and interpretations we make are highly colored by the words we habitually use to think with. As a vocabulary expands, so does the possible range of thinking.

More About the Element of Observing

What actually gets noticed, paid attention to, observed, is widely different for different people. It is so different that some theories treat it as a basis of personality. One person can walk through a house and be able to report out on the blend of color in the carpet and furniture, as well as the intricacies of the floor plan. Another can walk through the same house and have a hard time remembering the color of the walls. As far as we know, each person's eyes, as sensory organs, are having the same retinal cones affected by the same stimuli, but in each of us that information gets retained differently. Some people are just more aware of the sensory data that is coming in than others. For others, the information is still there somewhere in the mind—it just isn't conscious.

No one really knows how much we depend on nonverbal cues when we are communicating with people, but everyone guesses that it is a lot—more than on the verbal content. In our interactions we are making more meaning out of our observations of others than out of what they are actually saying. Whether we are aware of it or not, we are constantly looking at what people are doing with their hands, their facial expressions, how they move, where they look, and so on, to create our story about them and about what they are saying. Becoming aware of yourself doing that is the first step toward separating what you actually know from all the stories you are making up.

Good observation skills are the ability to mentally record and play back what is said and done with as little bias as possible. For most people it takes effort and practice to develop them. Many find it difficult to both fully participate in interactions and observe them as well. To be a clear leader you need to be able to do both. You have to be able to watch yourself and others at the same time as you are acting in order to be able to learn from your experience. This observing function is really just about awareness. The data are always there; the awareness, less so.

Without good observation skills you can't give people useful feedback, you can't explain the basis of your thoughts and judgments, and you can't confront others effectively. Why that is will become clearer as you read this book. The ability to observe what is going on inside of you (I'm having this thought, I'm making up this story, I'm feeling this emotion) and outside of you, moment to moment, is the goal. When you can do that, you can describe a key part of your experience to others.

The Element of Feeling

Feeling is composed of two things, sensations and emotions. They are both feelings because we actually feel them in the body. Emotions have sensations associated with them. If you can't feel it in the body, it is not an emotion. But emotions are different from sensations because they have a judgment about your state of being associated with them. Emotions have an explicit message connected to them whereas sensations don't. For example, if I feel love the sensation is a warmth around my heart. But knowing that I am feeling love tells me a great deal about my relationship with the object of that feeling, while warmth around the heart says nothing more, in itself, than that. If I feel anger, there is a tension in my jaw and, if I'm really angry, a slight nausea in my stomach. Again, anger as an emotion has a lot more connotations than a nauseated stomach.

Let me begin by describing sensations and their role in experience and then move on to emotions.

Body Sensations

Body sensations are the part of our experience that many people know the least about and pay the least attention to. Body sensations are things like heat and cold, pain and pleasure, tension and release. They are very basic to our experience and have a strong impact on our actions. For example, when we sense pain we react quickly, often without any thought, like pulling a hand away from a burning stove.

Unless you have been trained to pay attention to your body though a discipline such as dance, yoga, vipassana, chi gong, or somatic psychotherapy, chances are you've been trained to ignore your body and push it out of awareness. When I first started listening to my body I was amazed to discover how much unconscious pain I had—muscles that were sore that I was numb to. If you want to find out if you have unconscious body pain, get a therapeutic massage. If you are like most people you will find that some muscles in your body are in a good deal of pain that you are numb to until someone touches them. I'm not talking about deep, hard massage, I'm talking about pain from a light, soothing touch!

Pushing body sensations out of awareness seems to start in infancy. It's as though the sensations in our bodies are too big for our little bodies, and they overwhelm us. There is a joke that the average 20-year-old

man has no sensation between his neck and his groin, and there is a
lot of truth in that. In the rough-and-tumble of sports and school,
boys (and increasingly girls) learn to control their reactions, to not
show physical or emotional hurt, to always appear cool. We learn to
sit quietly in our seats for six or more hours a day from the age of six
onwards. Doing this requires numbing out to what would otherwise
be incessant bodily sensations that would get us into trouble.

In our society we don't have a language of the body, and there
doesn't appear to be any point in listening to it except to notice when
we are ill. Then we take our body to a doctor and ask him to listen to
it for us. But it turns out that body sensations are the most primal
form of experience, contain lots of important information, and have a
big impact on how we think, what we want, and what we do. They are
the only basis we have for validating subjective truth. It is difficult for
most people to be certain what they feel or want. Some people, if asked,
can quickly tell you how they are feeling. Most people, however, never
learn how to know or label their feelings outside of a narrow range.

When I was 20 I learned that I was expected to have feelings and
I learned what feelings were appropriate to have in what situations.
Girls liked that. I even went to classes and workshops where we talked
about our feelings. But I didn't learn to pay attention to my sensations,
to my body, so I didn't actually learn what I was feeling or wanting.
Somewhere in my late twenties I realized that in many situations I knew
what I didn't want but didn't know what I wanted. So I started listening
to my body and found out I was having lots of sensations, feelings, and
wants that were not getting registered in my experience but were still
affecting me.

Let me give you an example of someone whose unconscious sensations were causing him to act ineffectively.

---

*Shauna worked for Milo and respected his abilities and his competence
as a manager. They worked together for a number of years and developed a real sense of closeness and caring. After the first couple of years
Shauna found herself occasionally leaving interactions with Milo feeling
bad. At first she wasn't sure why that was, but as she paid more attention to it she came to believe that whenever she was feeling particularly
close to Milo he would put her down in some subtle way, as if he were
trying to create less closeness between them.*

*One day, right after Milo had pointed out a problem with Shauna's work
(even though the work had been hailed as a success by the client), she*

confronted Milo with her suspicions. Milo could not believe that he was doing anything more than offering constructive feedback when it was warranted. He did not believe he was trying to create distance, and there was no logical reason for it. On Shauna's part, however, the more she tried to get Milo to look at the behavior she was concerned with, the more it happened. When I entered the picture as a consultant it was getting to the point where Shauna was seriously considering leaving, even though she loved her job and felt that otherwise she and Milo were a good team. "It just batters my self-esteem too much and I don't think it has anything to do with improving my performance," was how she put it. Milo was upset at Shauna's "touchiness" and had come to believe that she wanted more out of the relationship than just work, and that was what she was really complaining about.

I was most curious about the adamancy with which Milo dismissed, out of hand, Shauna's experience. When people have no curiosity at all about something that others see, and dismiss it aggressively, that is usually a good indication that something unconscious is going on. In this case I suspected that Milo was unaware of some part of himself, so I suggested we try an experiment, which they both agreed to. I asked Milo to stand in one part of the room and Shauna to stand at the other end. Then I asked Shauna to slowly walk toward Milo and asked Milo to notice if there was any change in his body sensation, and to ask Shauna to stop when that happened. We did this, and as Shauna came within about 10 feet of him Milo cried "stop." I asked what had happened and he said that he now felt like his guts were twisting. I asked Shauna to slowly back up and Milo was amazed when the sensation went away after Shauna had backed up a few feet. We tried having her move back and forth a few times and each time the sensation would reappear when Shauna got within 10 feet.

At this point the implications of this were raining down on Milo's aware-ness and he became angry with himself for having been so out of touch and for having this unconscious reaction to Shauna. Wanting to break through the twisting feeling, he asked Shauna to walk right up to him. This caused his throat to close down so much he began to choke, and she backed off.

Milo learned that he had been reacting to the unconscious sensation of his guts twisting when he felt too close to Shauna and realized that his "constructive feedback" had been his unconscious way of reducing his discomfort by pushing her away. Now aware of the sensation, he was *simply able to ask Shauna for "space" (literally) when he needed it instead of putting her down, which she was more than happy to give him. Interestingly, as he learned that he could ask for and get as much space as he needed, the gut-wrenching sensation slowly went away.*

What I am trying to help you understand here is the power of body sensations and the extent to which they unconsciously compel our actions. These sensations do not exist randomly. In this case you will recognize that Milo was unaware of the intimacy anxiety he was feeling toward Shauna or of what he actually wanted. But his sensations told the story. Sensations contain very useful information about what is going on inside of us. Some people learn to listen to sensations that offer warnings, like a grumbling in the stomach, a pain in the neck, tension between the shoulders, and so on. Sometimes they are not even that aware of the actual sensation but have a "nagging doubt" that can't be put into words.

By learning to listen to the body we can learn to become aware of the unconscious aspects of our thoughts, emotions, and wants. We can learn if the stories we are making up about ourselves are true or not by developing an awareness of the internal B.S. detector built into our bodies. Subjective truths that we have been keeping unconscious often first come into awareness through sensation.

Emotions

Emotions are sensations with a message. There are hundreds of emotional words in the English language, but in my classes the average person has a hard time listing 20 when given a few minutes to do so. If you want to see how rich your emotional map is, put down this book and in the next two minutes list all the emotional words you can think of.

How many did you get? Now test them to make sure you actually listed emotions. Some people confuse judgments and feelings. They might say something like, "I feel OK." Where, in the body, does a person feel "OK"? This is actually a judgment (thought) about how they are feeling, not an emotion. Maybe they feel happy or excited or amused—three very different emotions that someone might judge "OK." Sensations like cold, hot, hungry are different from emotions, though those words are sometimes used to describe emotions. The hot I feel from the sun is a sensation. Feeling hot when I dress up is an emotion. Check to see how many of the emotions on your list are also on the emotional word chart at the end of Chapter 5. If they aren't on the chart, use this challenge: Where in your body do you feel this emotion? You may have to wait until the next time you are feeling it to know.

Having whittled down your list, how many valid emotions did you actually list? If you got more than 15 you have a significantly richer emotional vocabulary than the average college-educated North American. Sure, people will recognize hundreds of emotional words, but it's not the same as having them handy on your feeling map. Without the words, it is very difficult to describe our emotions to ourselves or each other.

Perhaps you know emotional words but don't think you actually feel them in your body. You have a sense of when you feel happy and angry but mostly you're not aware of having much feeling. This is a common experience for men unless they have had their capacity to feel activated. One of the things Robert Bly (who created the "men's movement" in the '80s) contends is that men generally only learn how to feel their emotions by having a close relationship with an older man who has learned to feel his emotions. That was true in my life. The birth of a child can also activate feeling in men, but the full spectrum only comes to those who are initiated in some way into their feelings. Bly also says that women don't seem to need that kind of initiation and that women cannot initiate men into their feelings.

The same circumstances that lead us to be numb to our body sensations lead us to be unconscious about a lot of our emotions that are too big for our small bodies and would overwhelm our experience. We try to not feel them, and many succeed. In some families, only certain emotions are allowed. It can be OK to express anger but not OK to express intimacy, OK to feel happy but not OK to feel sad. The permutations might be endless. We tend to be aware of those emotions that we learned were OK in our family of origin and unconscious about the rest.

Emotions have an enormous impact on our experiences, and therefore on the decisions and actions that occur in organizations. In some organizations there is a culture that does not view discussion of feelings as legitimate. In my view that is a sure way to maintain an ineffective climate for managing people. It's bad enough that so many people are operating on unconscious feelings. This in itself makes feelings a force outside of awareness and choice. To then try to socially banish discussion of them is a double whammy. People have emotions, and those feelings powerfully affect what they say and do. To attempt to ignore them is simply to push them underground and make them much more difficult to manage.

When decisions are not being implemented it is often because they violate people's feelings. How about the strategic plans of major corporations that call for radical changes that just get ignored? One company I've worked with developed a strategy that called for wide-spread implementation of empowered (leaderless) work teams. It never happened. Executives who verbally agreed to this part of the strategy had very mixed emotions about it. They were uncomfortable with leaderless groups, but it wasn't OK to say so because logically these looked like a good thing. So they officially agreed on the strat-egy, and then communicated plans that didn't get followed. Everyone felt just a little crazier, not sure what to believe and what to do in the future, and who knows what the opportunity costs were for them. When feelings are acknowledged and integrated into problem-solving and decision-making, better plans are created that people will imple-ment. That's about as "no-nonsense" as you can get.

I believe that the hallmark of emotional growth is the ability to fully feel one's sensations and emotions without being overwhelmed by them; to be able to contain them without diminishing them and so be aware of what they are while still acting rationally and purposefully. For me this meant learning to feel my anxiety and take the risks any-way; learning to feel sorrow while taking aggressive necessary action; learning to feel my real caring for someone while saying things that I knew would disturb them.

The Element of Wanting

The fourth element of experience is *wanting*—the desires, intentions, motivations, aspirations, needs, and wishes you are having moment to moment. I believe that each of us is born with a clear sense of what we want at any moment. Just watch young children—they know exactly what they want. The process of growing up in our society, however, leads many of us to lose awareness of our wants. As children there are many things we want that we are told we can't have, often for good reasons. To survive, we have to learn to repress our wants and do things like sit quietly in classrooms all day long while we'd much rather be doing something else. Learning to delay immediate gratification has many very good consequences, but it also has the negative consequence of making us less aware of our current wants. In addition, in our consumer society we are inundated with messages about what we should want, confusing us even more about our real wants. By the time we reach adulthood most of us are so confused about it that we are often much clearer about what we don't want than what we do want.

Awareness of wants is one problem. Expressing our wants is another problem. Some people have been taught that it is selfish, or impolite, to express their wants. Others have learned that it causes problems in relationships when they talk about their wants, so it is better to just say nothing. In both cases, these are normal adaptations to being around people who react negatively to our wants. In the previous chapter I explained the problem of fusion. When I am fused with you I am compelled to respond to what you say you want. It's not OK for you to just say what you want and leave it at that. The person fused with you will think he must either (1) give you what you want, (2) help you get it, or (3) convince you that you don't want it or that it is not good for you. Under these conditions people learn that if they say what they want then they have to contend with the reactive person's response.

For example, a parent whose self-identity is fused with his child's behavior, who can't afford to give his child everything she wants, will try to get the child to stop having wants (or at least stop asking for them). But, you see, the problem here is not the child's wants but the parent whose boundaries are so fragile that he has to repress the child from expressing her wants to feel OK about himself. The parent's lack of boundaries is the problem, and this gets passed on to the child, who is now confused about her experience. In organizations, how can a manager effectively motivate and lead people if she doesn't know what they want? But the fused manager will feel so compelled to respond to people's wants that she'll try to avoid hearing them in the first place by giving the message that expressing one's wants is not a good thing.

If a person feels personally rejected when he doesn't get what he asks for, he may decide it's better not to express his wants. Not expressing his wants is a way to defend against feeling rejected. This is a different kind of fusion. Here the person's boundaries between what he wants and who he is have gotten mixed up. When a person has healthy boundaries he is able to separate who he is from what he wants. He is able to separate other people's reactions to his wants from their reactions to himself. He is able to hear what the other person wants without believing that he is now responsible to deliver it, and to say what he wants without believing that it is the other person's responsibility to give it to him.

In organizations, and any other kind of relationship, people rarely get what they want unless they are clear with themselves and each other about what they want. If people are not getting what they want, then they are unlikely to give their motivation, commitment, loyalty, and hard work to the team or organization, so expression of wants is vital. You cannot negotiate good deals, develop win-win solutions to problems, assign tasks to motivated people, or effectively resolve conflicts unless everyone is clear about what everyone else wants. It is as simple, and as difficult, as that. One rule of clear leadership is that people have to say what they want. The second rule is that they may not get it. Clear leaders know that they have to get clear about what people want and let people know that just because they want something doesn't mean they'll get it.

One terrible trap I have seen managers put themselves in is to allow people to say only what they *don't* want, while still making the manager responsible for satisfying them. I've seen this most in union-management relations, where the union will say, "You are management—you propose and we'll tell you if we like it." This is a great way to drive yourself crazy. But it is not all that uncommon, because making up stories about what other people want is a daily occurrence in most organizational interactions. I have found that managers will ask subordinates what they think, and may even ask what they feel, but will forget to ask what they want because they assume that, now that they know what the others think and feel, what they want is obvious. Well, sometimes it is and sometimes it isn't. I am still often surprised by what people say they want after I think I already know. Trying to satisfy people's wants, when you've made them up, is just as good a way to drive yourself crazy as letting them tell you only what they don't want.

Finally there is the problem of thinking that my wants are not OK, that to want what I want is in some way wrong, illegitimate, immature, or whatever. Let's face it, there are lots things we want that we don't give ourselves. I may want to not get out of bed and go to work, but I do anyway. I may want to buy a totally impractical little red convertible or you might want to buy a little black cocktail dress that will only get worn twice a year, but we don't. It's not bad to want them, but that's not the same as having them. All of us are going to censure some of what we tell others about our real wants and motivations, if just to avoid embarrassment. In organizations, this can get dangerous, however, if nobody is saying what they really want in order to go along with others. Jerry Harvey tells a now famous story of a family that one dusty day drove 100 miles to Abilene to go to a diner for lunch when no one really wanted to go there, simply because no one wanted to offend anyone else and so no one said what they really wanted.[2] This "Abilene Paradox" can happen because people are afraid to say what they want, or it can happen because people really care about each other and are willing to go along with what the others appear to want. In Jerry's story, nobody wanted to go; they ended up there out of good intentions but lousy skills. Nobody was telling the truth of their experience out of a desire to avoid looking selfish and to respect the story they had made up about the others' wants.

The clear leader knows that she needs to understand the wants and motivations of the people she works with, the suppliers she deals with, and the customers she serves. The clear leader recognizes that she must lead in creating the climate where people tell each other the truth about their wants, hopes, and motivations by telling the truth about her own wants. The clear leader recognizes that people are only going to be as forthright with her as she is with them. So the clear leader has to think hard about censoring her wants, especially if she doesn't want others to censor them back. And it is good to let subordinates know that she is human, has childish or impractical wants, and can express her wants without expecting to get them, too!

Summary

The experience cube is a model of experience and, as you'll see in the next three chapters, a very useful tool for clear leadership. Observations are the actual sensory data we are collecting. Thoughts are the interpretations, ideas, judgments, and beliefs we are having. Feelings are the body sensations and emotions we are having, and wants are the desires, motivations, and aspirations we are having. My belief is that in every moment each of us is having observations, thoughts, feelings, and wants. The sum of these is our experience.

Some of these you are aware of and some of these you aren't. Learning from experience requires people's ability to access and describe to each other their full range of experience. The first place that starts is awareness.

PART TWO

The Four Selves
of Clear Leaders

The Aware Self

Gaining Self-Knowledge

Many self-help books and, lately, leadership books talk about the need for self-awareness—but what does that mean? In this book my intention is to make that as concrete as possible. The crucial step in self-awareness is the ability to know what your moment-to-moment experience is. All other forms of real self-awareness flow from this.

Why is awareness a basic skill of clear leaders? Because in organizations everyone is having a different experience. In order to communicate, cooperate, and develop agreement people need to understand each other's experience, and it is through exploring differing experiences that people come to understand and change problem patterns in organizations. But first you and others must be aware of what your experience is.

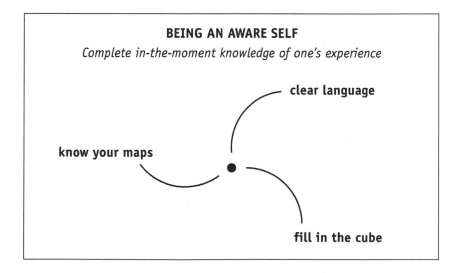

BEING AN AWARE SELF

Complete in-the-moment knowledge of one's experience

clear language

know your maps

fill in the cube

The skill of being an Aware Self has three components. One is the ability to know your moment-to-moment experience. I call this filling in the cube. The second is using clear language when you think and talk, language that clarifies who is having what experience. The third is the ability to know the difference between your mental maps and the world those maps describe. I'll begin by reviewing issues in becoming aware of different parts of the experience cube. We'll then move on to investigate patterns in how we speak that mystify our experience to ourselves and others, and look at how to correct that. Finally I'll discuss how our experience is shaped by the architecture of our thinking and why awareness of that is crucial for leading organizational learning. At the end of the chapter I will offer some ways to practice increasing your awareness.

Filling In the Cube

One image I like is that we all have four containers (the four elements of experience) that we walk around with. At any moment we can stop and dip into a container to see what is there. Different people are able to dip into different cubes to different depths. Some of us can dip into a couple of containers quite deeply and then barely know where to find the others. Others can skim along the top of all four containers easily but can't dip too far. There are endless variations to how aware people are of their experience, but I think we all have pretty much the same containers and I think we can all learn how to dip deeper into each one of them.

Part of the problem of awareness is simply paying attention. The more people pay attention to all four parts of the cube, the more aware they become of their experience. The more you pay attention to your moment-to-moment experience, the more you will learn just how much of your experience is out of your awareness but affecting you nonetheless. I used to be completely unaware of my anxiety. I was so unaware that after especially important and difficult business meetings I would notice my hands shaking and not know why. There were some positive consequences to my lack of awareness; for example, I took a lot of risks that I didn't recognize as risky and some paid off. There were a lot of negative consequences as well. For example, I would treat people I cared about abruptly and carelessly when I was anxious, without noticing I was doing that. People around me would notice something was up when I was anxious, but if they asked me about it I would just say, "I'm fine." I wasn't aware of how this reduced their confidence or trust in me, and they would be left to make up their own stories about what was really going on. Ultimately, some people sensed that there was something about me that couldn't be trusted and would not be willing to follow me. They were right. I wasn't aware of important motivations and feelings affecting my actions.

Each person has a different level of awareness in each element, and each person has a different speed at which they become aware. At one extreme are those who are fully aware of what they think in the moment. At the other are those who need time to be by themselves to figure out what they think. Some people know what they are feeling as they are feeling it. Others have a vague sense that some feeling is present but can't label it. And the same is true of observations and desires. In each element of experience there is a continuum of awareness, and we all vary in each area. The skill of being an Aware Self is to be fully aware, right in the moment, of what you are observing, thinking, feeling, and wanting.

Thinking

Thinking tends to be the most developed element of experience among business people, as it is the one we pay the most attention to in school and the one that has most legitimacy in business culture. People tend to be more aware of what they are thinking than what they are feeling, observing, or wanting. Yet even so, there can be thoughts that are outside awareness, particularly if these thoughts are in some way threatening to us. The things I don't want to think about are still rattling around in my head, just outside my immediate awareness. They tend to be fodder for dreams, which is why dreams have been called the "royal road to the unconscious." But dreams are difficult to interpret accurately. In the end it is easier to screw up your courage and be willing to face the thoughts that are impacting your experience even if you are keeping them from your awareness.

How do unconscious thoughts affect your experience? Let me give you an example.

Sheila was a manager who had some unconscious judgments about herself that impacted her experience in ways that decreased her effectiveness. She thought she wasn't really competent but kept this thought away as much as possible. As a result, she would notice any sign of others' incompetence. It is quite common for people to keep a thought about themselves unconscious by thinking it in relation to others. It's as though making the judgment about others is an escape valve, allowing the pressure of the thought being kept out of awareness to dissipate. I described this process of projection in Chapter 1.

Sheila didn't say a lot about it, but she experienced that wherever she worked people just weren't very competent. She often thought that she had to clean up behind her subordinates and do their work for them because of their lack of competence. Her bosses, similarly, were disappointingly inadequate. She came to believe that the only person she could rely on was herself. Others, of course, always had a vague sense that they were being put down by Sheila, but she had no idea of that. Why should they feel that, when she never said anything about it? You can imagine all the ways in which this pattern reduced her effectiveness as a manager and led to her eventual burn-out (and, during her recuperation, the beginning of self-awareness).

An unconscious thought, feeling, or want can be a very powerful determinant of our experience and, because it is unconscious, be outside our choicefulness. Sheila was creating the experience of living in an incompetent world, but she didn't see it that way. She did not recognize her choicefulness. In her mind she had the terrible misfortune of having to work with people who were incompetent, and she had lots of examples to support it. Yet someone else in the exact same situations could have paid attention to all the times when people did competent things, and to their accomplishments. If Sheila had been aware of her unconscious thought that she was incompetent, then she could have acted choicefully in several ways that would have been more effective for her and for the people who worked for her. First, she could have gotten more precise and realistic about her own level of competence, discovering what she was competent at and what she needed to develop. She could then have worked at developing the skills in which she needed to truly believe she was competent. Second, if she had been conscious of her self-judgment, she probably would have become aware of all the judgment she was laying on others and been more choiceful in looking to see what their strengths and skills were in addition to their deficiencies. Third, she could have come to understand why she was judging herself so harshly when her results clearly showed that she was competent.

Why Sheila kept this thought unconscious is a subject for psychotherapy and doesn't need to concern us here. I have found that people don't need to learn *why* they make some part of their experience unconscious in order to become conscious of it. I will give some techniques for increasing your awareness of your thoughts at the end of this chapter. For now what is important is that you understand that a portion of your experience is composed of thoughts (beliefs, values, opinions, judgments, cognition, and so on) and that some of your thoughts can be out of your awareness but still part of your experience.

Feelings

Awareness of feelings can be difficult for some. A way to repress feelings (I know about this because I used to do it) is to close down the diaphragm, that area in the center of the body just below the rib cage. This stops the feelings from traveling upward into the chest and into awareness. When a person is repressing feelings in this way their diaphragm is sore, but usually that sensation is out of awareness until you poke the diaphragm. One consequence of this is that repressed, strong feelings put force on the closed diaphragm, which causes the spine to subtly torque, which in turn leads to lower back pain. For years I would get lower back pain (I attributed it to a basketball injury—a satisfactory story), which I don't get anymore. I wonder how much of the lower back pain in our society is caused by repressed feelings.

The effect on organizations of repressing feelings is just as debilitating. Even when individuals are aware of their feelings the organization may not allow disclosure of them. "Decisions and plans should be based on sound analysis of facts and logic, not emotion and feelings" goes the mantra of organizational repression. The clear leader knows this is complete nonsense. Feelings are a key part of our experience, which in turn shapes what we see, think, and do. People may talk about logic and analysis, but what they actually do is based as much on their feelings as on anything else. By not talking about them all we do is keep them out of awareness, where they can't be discussed and dealt with choicefully. Perhaps the most powerful feeling that rarely gets talked about in organizations is anxiety.

The Role of Anxiety

From observing hundreds of groups make and avoid making decisions I have come to the conclusion that the strongest force in organizational decision-making is the avoidance of one feeling: anxiety. The profit motive pales in comparison. I have seen decisions taken where millions of dollars have been left on the table or wasted so that people would not have to deal with issues that made them feel anxious.

Common examples of anxiety avoidance are not confronting non-performing managers or departments, not exploring new ideas that are outside of people's competence or comfort zone, silencing views or perspectives that challenge the current accepted view of things, and avoiding making decisions when there are strongly held differences of opinion. A common form of anxiety that we seem to want to avoid at all costs is *embarrassment*. The rule appears to be, "Don't embarrass yourself and don't embarrass others." Those who consistently break this rule don't get very far in traditional organizations.

On the one hand, causing unnecessary embarrassment or anxiety is not very effective for working with people. That doesn't mean tolerating complacency, however. Clear leaders are people who provide a nonanxious presence—they have their own intimacy and separation anxieties under control and therefore don't amplify anxiety in the system. But this does not mean they smooth over issues and concerns that need to be addressed for the system's good. A willingness to look squarely at and confront anxiety-provoking issues is required for interpersonal clarity. This, in turn, requires the leader to be able to tolerate his own anxiety—to be differentiated from it, not acting out of it but aware of it and acting rationally in spite of it.

Anxiety is a particularly difficult issue for successful people because many of them are not aware when they are anxious. Learning to be unaware of anxiety has some very useful consequences for a young, ambitious person. Anxiety can be paralyzing. Anxiety can stop us from taking risks. Anxiety can make us tongue-tied, cause us to lose our wits when we most need them. We can look courageous to others when really we are just unaware of our fears. The brashest, most confident, most seemingly self-assured people are those who typically get ahead in business. Anxiety doesn't look good, and visible anxiety makes others get in touch with their own anxiety, which is doubly unwelcome. As a consequence, we have a disproportionate number of senior managers in organizations who lack awareness of their own anxiety.

The downside of this lack of awareness is that anxiety affects behavior in unconscious ways. These managers don't even know that they are acting out of their anxiety, or, more precisely, their desire to avoid anxiety. This has two very negative consequences for managing people. One is that such managers are not acting rationally when they think they are. The other is that they tend to become increasingly disconnected from the people who work for them. The reason they become increasingly isolated is that unconsciously anxious people manage their anxiety by pushing away any source of anxiety. If a decision causes anxiety, it gets put off. When someone is creating anxiety for them, they do something to make the person want to go away. All of this is done without awareness so the managers don't even realize what is going on. Even those who think of themselves as people oriented and as nice people will act this way out of unconscious anxiety. They become, as described in Chapter 2, disconnected.

Here's a typical scenario: a subordinate is giving his unconsciously anxious boss an update on a project. There is bad news. The boss is getting anxious as she hears the bad news and, without being aware of what she is doing or why, begins to tell the subordinate how to fix the situation without really understanding it. Each time the subordinate tries to tell the boss that he has already tried her fix or give her more information she interrupts again with more problem-solving. After a while the subordinate just stops telling her what he really thinks and feels and wants. After assuring his boss that everything will work out he leaves feeling frustrated, unsupported, and demoralized. The boss, oblivious to what has gone on, thinks she has done a good job of getting her subordinate back on track. And the interpersonal mush is thicker than ever.

Feelings affect what we think and want and motivate us to take actions. Whether it is anxiety or any other unconscious emotion, we need to make sense of our actions to ourselves and will search for sufficient external justification for actions that are really being motivated by feelings. When I put off a decision because it makes me anxious, I come up with what seem to be good reasons to put off the decision and ignore the anxiety. For example, when I avoid dealing with someone to avoid the anxiety, I can rationalize that I am too busy to deal with them right now; I have other issues that are more pressing; it's Friday afternoon, I'll leave it for Monday; I don't really have rapport with that person, maybe so-and-so should deal with it; maybe I'm blowing this issue out of proportion, I'll just sit tight and watch it for a while to see if I really need to deal with it. And so on.

Like other aspects of experience, as long as they are out of awareness, feelings exert a powerful influence that we have no choice over. What happens when we acknowledge emotions we have that are getting in the way of rational decisions and actions? We're able to act more rationally. By naming the feeling, we reduce its power, and we can take it into account in making decisions, which are then more likely to actually get implemented.

Wants

Bringing wants into awareness can be difficult for some people. I described some of the reasons that happens in the previous chapter. We can be unaware because of simple lack of attention. We can be unaware because part of us doesn't want to know. And some people can be unaware because they lack the resources to know what they really need. At a critical stage in infancy they rarely got what they needed and so never developed the ability to know what they truly need. These people don't know what they want until they get what they think they want and then see how they feel about it. If you are damaged in this way learning to know what you want requires therapy by someone skilled in very early childhood developmental healing. But anyone can increase his awareness of his wants by assuming that at every moment he is having wants and then paying close moment-by-moment attention to what is motivating him.

Some normal human motivations are socially acceptable and some aren't. It's the unacceptable motivations that are most likely out of awareness. I'd rather not notice the part of me that wants to always win an argument, that's greedy, that's vengeful. I pretend that if I'm not aware of those parts of me I won't act out of them either. So I won't notice when the greedy part takes more than I need just so I'll be sure to have enough, or when I'm arguing just for the sake of winning. As I become aware of these wants I get more control over my actions. I notice when I'm taking more than I need and then choose whether I want to leave some for others or be greedy. Knowing what I want doesn't stop me from wanting it, but it does make it easier to choose my actions.

One of the consequences of uncovering all my less-than-perfect motivations, and coming to accept them, is that I develop compassion for myself, and in turn I develop more compassion for others. And then it becomes easier for others to own up to their less-than-perfect motivations in my presence. We can acknowledge the realities and limitations of our wants and needs and make choices that we'll probably follow through on.

A great technique for learning what your real motivations are is to look at your results. Since you are creating your experience, and other people are having different experiences in the same situation, there must be a part of you that wants to have this particular experience. If you are constantly winning at something there must be a part of you that wants to win. That seems obvious to most people. If you are constantly failing at something there must be a part of you that wants to fail. That seems less obvious, yet in my experience it is nonetheless a subjective truth. Why would someone do something wanting to fail? A very interesting question.

Early in my work life I had a string of lousy bosses; at least, that was how I described it. More accurately, I had a string of experiences of bosses whom I did not get along with, who seemed incompetent to me, whom I felt contempt for and who ended up firing me. After I'd had the same experience three or four times it occurred to me that maybe it wasn't them—maybe there was something I was doing that caused me to have an experience of what seemed like incompetent bosses. After I rooted around in the bottom of my wants bucket for a while I discovered that I wanted to be the star in every authority's eyes. I wanted my bosses to immediately realize how great I was, and I wanted to feel warm and close to them. When I got this from managers I became a great employee, but when I didn't I quickly pulled away from them and started looking for reasons to lessen their authority and importance in my mind. Because they did not immediately see and embrace my competence, I wanted to believe that they were incompetent. I didn't want to work there anymore. And that was the result I created.

Some people have, I think, taken this perspective too far. They will say such things as "If you have cancer you must want to die." I believe that people create their experience out of what happens to them, but I also believe that things happen to people that they wouldn't choose. The flip side of "I create my own experience" is "shit happens." But it is a great aid to awareness to take the point of view that I attract what I get into my life and that if I want to know what my wants are, I need to look at what I am getting.

A critical aspect of wants in organizations is that of things I want from you—things I want you to do, say, feel, and want. I want people who work with me to have certain kinds of experiences. Most learning conversations get to a point where people talk about what they want from each other and from themselves. Just because I want something, however, doesn't mean I have to get it. Knowing I want you to be having a certain kind of experience, describing it to you, and being choiceful about how I act if I don't get it is completely different from being fused with you. When I'm fused I'm not really aware of what I am doing; I am simply reacting to my bad feelings and getting you to try to change what you say or do. There is no awareness in fusion. Clear leadership requires being clear about what I actually need—what are the absolute must-haves to continue working with these people in this organization—and the difference between these needs and what I want. The more awareness I have of my needs and wants, and the distinction between them, the more I can ensure that my wants don't get in the way of our working together. So I may still want to be the gleam in every authority's eyes, but I know I don't need it. I can work just fine with someone who doesn't think I walk on water. And because I am clear about what I do need, I'm more likely to create experiences where I get that.

Awareness is the first step, and our awareness is shaped in many ways by our language. A person's awareness is increased when she stops using common errors of language that mystify her experience. Her thoughts become attuned to differences between subjective and objective reality and her wants become clearer. This leads us to a second aspect of being an Aware Self.

Clear Language

There is something about the way we are taught to talk about our experience that leads us to confuse what is inside with what is outside. It leads us to mystify ourselves and others and it reduces our awareness of creating our own experience. It is interesting to me that this seems to be a cross-cultural phenomenon. From what I can tell, people with different languages and very different cultures do similar things. What we do is talk about things inside of us as if they were outside of us.

For example, if someone enters a room and feels cold he is most likely to say, "It's cold in here." Coldness is a sensation, an inner experience. I have canvassed rooms of people and found that some are cold, some are hot, and some are neither. The feeling of cold is inside the person. Notice how this common way of thinking and talking takes the origin of the experience out of the person and puts it in the room. What is inside is described as being outside. Since language shapes how we think, we are actually confusing ourselves into thinking that what is inside is outside. When I think "it's hot in here," or "it's tense in here," or "it's fun here," I have confused inside and outside. I have lost clear boundaries between what is in me and what isn't, and so I am less differentiated. If our language assumes that our experience (hot, tense, fun) is everyone else's experience, that will be how we think about it. We won't even see it as our experience, but rather as a quality of the place or group, and we'll assume that others are having the same experience. In effect, we are treating a subjective truth as if it were an inter-subjective or objective truth.

One way we confuse inside and outside that really contributes to interpersonal mush is saying "you" when we really mean "I." Many people do this, and they not only confuse the people they are talking to, they confuse themselves. Here's an example of an engineer I interviewed talking about his disappointment over the effect his new machine designs had on product quality:

"When you go and see what they've done in that factory you just want to cry with the mess they've made. We really worked hard to improve the machines and ensure a leap in quality improvement, but you look at their attitude and just have to shake your head. You think to yourself, 'If I were running the plant I could really make a difference,' but it's not up to you and there's nothing you can do about it. We tried but it's out of our hands."

Obviously, the speaker is the one who just wants to cry about it. You-language is so prevalent that most of us have learned to translate it when we hear it. But who is this "we" that worked hard to improve the machines? It turns out it was the speaker, but that was not obvious until I asked. When I use you-language to talk about my own experience I confuse myself into thinking that my experience is generalizable, that given the situation everyone else would have the same thoughts and feelings. A less common but similar problem is people saying "we" instead of "I." It's confusing trying to follow who is having what experience. Every time I say "we did such and such" I confuse myself about who did what (not to mention the people listening to me).

One effect of inappropriate you-language is that it makes it harder for people to engage with each other. If Jean is sitting at a meeting and Natalie says something like "It's so tough when you're on the road every week, it really wears you down" and Jean doesn't have that experience, what happens? What happens is that the only obvious way to engage in that conversation is to begin by disagreeing. To enter into a conversation with Jean, Natalie would have to talk as if she were in conflict with Jean when, really, it's simply that they have different experiences. Jean has presented her subjective truth as an objective truth. Most people just let it pass, not wanting to start a disagreement. By using you-language a person makes it more difficult for others to engage and be curious about her experience.

You-language is so ubiquitous and seems so natural that even people watching themselves on videotape, trying to learn not to use it, will miss seeing when they are doing it. Here are some common examples of you-language, we-language, and it-language:

It depends on how you look at it . . . when it really depends on how I look at it

I can see we need to take a break here . . . when really I need to take a break here

It's scary to tell the boss the truth . . . when really I'm scared to tell the boss the truth

We're unhappy with your performance . . . when really I'm unhappy with your performance

Why do we talk in ways that mystify ourselves, that make what is inside seem to be outside and mix up different kinds of truth? One reason is that we don't have to take responsibility for our experience. If it is outside of ourselves, we don't have to hold ourselves as choiceful. When I say "it's tense in here" I don't have to take responsibility for the tension I feel. I don't have to confront the possibility that there are other people who aren't feeling tense and ask myself why I am if they aren't. Rather than making a statement about myself, which makes me feel a little vulnerable and exposed, I seem to be making a statement about the situation.

Another reason is that you-language and we-language helps us to avoid responsibility for our opinions and judgments. The engineer in the example above did not have to look at whether he had really been effective in his attempts to improve product quality because, from his way of confusing inside and outside, anyone in his situation would see that it was the plant's fault. By talking about how "we tried our best" he could even avoid a sense of personal failure by spreading it around to a "we" that didn't exist. When I say "it depends on how you look at it" I am taking the focus away from myself or my way of thinking.

This way of confusing things appears to help people to manage the individuality-belonging paradox because they avoid saying things that might separate them from others without giving up their individuality. You-language allows me to state strong personal judgments in a way that is less threatening to my membership in the group. When I tell my boss "it's scary to tell the boss the truth" I am saying something that could threaten my relationship with others, especially my boss. Saying it in this depersonalized, externalized way seems much less threatening than saying "I'm scared to tell you the truth." But like all forms of fusion, it only appears to be helping by reducing anxiety. Instead, it actually makes things worse because it creates interpersonal mush. The first statement (it's scary to tell the boss the truth) mystifies my interaction with my boss by apparently making a general statement about the way things are. It does not appear, on the face of it, to be a statement about my experience. We could debate its objective truth, but that would be irrelevant because what I really mean is that I'm scared to tell you, my boss, the truth, but I am saying it in code. Maybe my boss will figure it out and maybe he won't. Maybe I won't realize that not everyone is scared to tell the boss the truth, and probably we'll never even get close to discussing why I find my boss, the person, scary to level with. Only the direct statement, "I'm scared to tell you the truth," brings real interpersonal clarity and promotes a conversation where we tell each other the truth of our experience and can learn together.

When we use language that clarifies we don't confuse objective, subjective, and inter-subjective reality: we keep them distinct and so we make it easier to create clarity and to create agreement with others. Sometimes I hear someone disagree with someone else's experience. I am always surprised when I hear it. One person will be talking clearly about his own subjective truth and another will literally say "I disagree." They don't mean "I don't believe that is your subjective truth," they mean "that is not my subjective truth," but again they are confusing the nature of subjective truth. Usually what is going on here is that the person who is disagreeing has made a leap in their thinking—they are disagreeing with the story they have just made up. In their own mind they have taken the other person's "I" and turned it into "you" or "we."

Correctly thinking and saying "you" when you mean "you," "I" when you mean "I," "it" when you mean "it," and "we" when you are really referring to a group you belong to, really helps to avoid problems created by confusing different types of truth. It is one of the simple yet powerful clear leadership skills, skills I see being used by effective leaders and professionals in empowered organizations. It is easy to describe, but for many people it is difficult to do and takes a lot of practice and coaching to master. Using clarifying language increases your awareness and reduces the interpersonal mush you are creating around you.

Know Your Mental Maps

Maps are the outcome of learning from experience. Soon after birth we begin to develop internal representations of the external world. Some of these are about how to get what we want. How do I get fed? How do I get praise and attention? How do I avoid punishment? Some maps are about what things are. Who am I? What is good and bad? What am I good at? Answers to these questions form just a few of the hundreds, perhaps thousands, of maps we use. Part of what we call growing up is developing a set of maps that allow us to successfully navigate through life. Different theorists have called these maps concepts, theories, formulas, paradigms, schemata, and software. You may have read Peter Senge's book on organizational learning in which he refers to them as mental models. I like to call them mental maps or just maps for short. Like any map, they are not the same as the territory. They are a symbolic representation of the territory, but, in the words of the great semanticist Alfred Korzybski, we often confuse the map for the territory. This is why understanding one's maps is a significant aspect of the Aware Self.

Every time we enter a new situation we begin building a map of it. When we are first developing a map we are pretty conscious of what we are doing. Whether it's learning how to solve business problems, deal with problem employees, or get good job interviews, we learn as much or more from our failures as from our successes as we slowly build maps that help us to succeed at what we are trying to accomplish. Once we get a map that works for us, and we use it over and over again, it tends to recede into the background, out of awareness. After a while we don't even recognize that we are operating from a map.

A well-ingrained map is the platform for our awareness and sense-making. The stories we make up about people are not random. They come from the maps we have developed about people in general acting in the situation we are making sense of. These are often called biases or perceptual filters. They have a profound effect on our experience, which can be tempered by awareness. When we don't have a map we feel confused, our sense-making is more tentative, and we seek out other opinions. When we have a well-ingrained map we apply it automatically, without even noticing that we are doing that. That process is part of what we need to become aware of. Good maps are great because they help us operate effectively. We don't have to relearn everything from scratch. They are our wisdom. But maps also cause problems because they focus our attention. We tend to see only what is on our maps and miss what isn't. When the map is invisible to us, and we confuse it with reality, it distorts our perceptions and can cause us to see people doing things they didn't do and hear them saying things they didn't say, and cause us not to see things they did do and not to hear things they did say.

Maps shape our awareness for good or ill. It's hard to be aware of something you don't know exists. If it's not on your maps, you don't know to look for it. When you learn a new map your awareness changes too. This book has described a number of maps already, and will describe more as you go on. If you've never thought of interpersonal mush before, or its impact on an organization, now you will. If you haven't paid much attention to the negative consequences of you-language you may start to see them now. That's how maps work; they are an aid to awareness and a block to awareness.

One of the significant things about many maps that people create about each other and their organizations is that they have resulted not from having checked out the validity of the ideas, but actually from having avoided checking out the validity of the ideas. What does that mean? Let's say that I see my new boss get very upset at someone who is disagreeing with her, so I make up a story that she doesn't like it when people disagree with her (of course there could have been many other reasons why she was upset the one time I observed it). Am I likely to check this hypothesis out by disagreeing with her and seeing what happens? Not unless I'm self-destructive. Am I likely to ask her directly about it? Not in the normal atmosphere of interpersonal mush. More likely, I will avoid disagreeing with her and instead watch to see what others do. I'll notice they don't disagree with her either (how often does someone disagree openly with a new boss?). I might talk to others about my story and they may confirm that they, too, avoid disagreeing with her. Perhaps I will, at some point, feel a great need to disagree with her and think up some elaborate strategy for subtly getting her to see a different point of view. If I'm successful, this will only reinforce my map that one can't disagree with her outright, that one must be very subtle.

Karl Weick was the first to describe how organizational reality can be created this way. He pointed out that a surprising number of people's maps don't come from testing ideas about reality but exist because people have avoided the tests that would disprove them.[1] A lot of the "way things are around here" is that way only because people are afraid to try doing things differently. This observation helps to explain why innovations in social processes tend to come from newcomers—they don't know that's not how things are done around here. One of the characteristics of many of the clear leaders I've met is that they tend to break these unwritten rules, and almost always get away with it. One clear leader who was a first-line supervisor in a pretty stuffy traditional organization was trying to get managers interested in a new technology. He called up and invited the general manager of another division, who was a champion of this new technology, to come to the plant and give a talk on it. Other managers were aghast! A first-line supervisor does not call a divisional general manager! Meetings were held by senior managers in the plant to discuss damage control. Should someone call him and apologize or should they bluff it out? What retribution would the plant suffer from this affront? Well, the general manager came, thanked people for inviting him, and gave a great talk. No one in the plant could remember ever having called a divisional general manager for anything before.

Not checking out the validity of our maps is just another form of interpersonal mush. Whether it's about people, tasks, or processes, the maps of people who work together can be inaccurate, invalid, out of sync, dissimilar, or at cross purposes. So we need to put our maps on the table, look at them together, see what is causing us problems, and change our maps when that is appropriate.

If it were only that simple I wouldn't need to write this book. What makes it difficult is that (1) we are not aware of all of our maps, (2) we have an emotional investment in our maps, and (3) we have a tendency to forget that our maps are not the territory. People differ around what kinds of maps and what kinds of conversations cause them anxiety, but everyone has a comfort zone beyond which displaying and discussing their own maps makes them uncomfortable. You could say that the leadership of organizational learning is mainly about containing the anxiety created by exposing and exploring each other's maps, and you wouldn't be far off. It's also about helping people uncover and understand what their maps are in the first place. I'll describe a technique you can use to do that, called cardwork, in the chapter on the Descriptive Self.

If I think my map is the reality I won't be interested in hearing about alternative maps. Others will see me as having strong opinions about the way things are. If I'm the boss I'll probably make it uncomfortable for others to describe alternative maps—thus decreasing organizational effectiveness and increasing interpersonal mush. Another problem is that people can identify with their maps and hold on to them pretty tenaciously. When I identify with my maps, I confuse who I am with them. One of the reasons for resistance to change is that change often requires a new map for success. When the environment changes so that the maps that people are identified with no longer work, many will first try to change the situation back so that their old maps will continue to work. Attempts to call for *more* rules and regulations in groups, organizations, or nations are almost always motivated by this kind of resistance: Please recreate the old world we know how to succeed in. I think the big reason for holding on to maps so strongly is that they reduce anxiety for us. Uncertainty makes us anxious. Maps get rid of uncertainty.

Three Kinds of Maps

There are three kinds of maps that I refer to again and again in this book. The first is the stories we make up about each other. We develop maps about each of the significant people we work with that include how they think, what they want, what they like and dislike, their biases and hot buttons, and so on. We've already explored this one in a lot of detail. Your stories of people are open to a lot of distortion, bias, and inaccuracy, so it's very important not to confuse your maps of them for the territory and to stay open to being surprised by who they really are. When you are an Aware Self you stay open to seeing new parts of people that aren't on your map.

A second kind of map I call an identity map: It identifies what things are. At work people have identity maps about what the goals are, who has what role, what those roles are, what success is, what quality is, what customer satisfaction is, and so on. I have a map of clear leadership: it's composed of the four skills I'm describing in this book. For the most part, identity maps gain their validity because a large enough number of people hold the same map. Identity maps are an example of inter-subjective truth. Whether or not my map of a team's goals is accurate depends on how similar my map is to other people's goal maps.

Here is another place where people can create problems for themselves if they try to treat these kinds of maps as objective truths, as if quality or success could be calibrated and measured like the density of a molecule. It is possible to create measurement systems for specific ways of defining quality or success, but that only gives them the veneer of objective truth. The nature of either depends on the group of people defining it. For example, in one company success means increasing return on investment; in another, it means increasing market share. As I write this book conventional maps of business wealth, which seemed like objective truth, are being turned on their head by web-based companies that have hardly made a profit, have few hard assets, and are worth more than General Electric. An Aware Self needs to be aware that his identity maps are not objective truths, and inter-subjective truths can change when we're not looking.

A third important kind of map consists of the ideas we have about cause and effect: how to make things happen, how to accomplish tasks and goals. Chris Argyris and Donald Schön coined the term "theory of action" to describe these kinds of maps.[2] I have a theory of action map about how clear leaders provide leadership—that's part of what this book is about. If I am trying to provide leadership to an empowered team this map guides my actions. Every goal-oriented action you take is based on some theory you have of how that action will lead to that goal. You may be fully aware of your theory or you may not, but it is there. If we are trying to accomplish a goal together, it's helpful to be operating from a common theory of action.

Muriel was the founder of an unusual and successful retail store that had grown so large (25 employees) that she found it was now controlling her life more than she wanted it to. She had been trying to "get a life" for a few years and had come to the conclusion that she needed to change her management style when she hired me to help her out. It turned out that every time she had hired someone to run some part of the store, before long she was back involved. Sometimes she had to reverse decisions that the new manager had made, making people confused and upset. She had tried promoting people from inside the store and hiring people from outside the store but she had not been able to find anyone who seemed competent to take over any facet of the store.

It would have been easy to make up a story about Muriel not being able to let go of control, and many of her employees had. I began by working with Muriel on redesigning the structure of her organization and reengineering some of the store's work processes. Of course, all these work processes had just evolved, willy-nilly, over the years, and there hadn't been a lot of thought about how they might be designed to work most effectively. We thought that maybe by doing that she could identify areas that could run themselves without her involvement. Attempting to understand the work processes forced Muriel to become explicitly aware, for the first time, of what she was actually trying to accomplish. Obviously the store was there to make a profit, but that wasn't Muriel's main goal, nor had it ever been. Muriel had never been interested in being a successful retailer. She had always wanted to see herself, and her store, as a resource to the community. As this got clearer, the logic behind her actions and her problems with what had seemed to her to be incompetent managers became clearer.

The key was Muriel's identity maps and her theories of action. Managers hadn't worked out because they weren't operating from the same theory of action as Muriel. For example, if a manager's theory of action was that the way to succeed was to increase profit he was operating from a different map than Muriel. Muriel had a modest amount of money she wanted to make, and an amount she wanted to be able to reinvest back into the store. After that, there was a part of her that felt guilty making a profit, as if she were ripping off her clients. Providing a valuable service at the lowest possible cost was an important part of her theory of action, and unless a manager understood that, his actions would not seem right to her.

Muriel wasn't aware of what her theories of action were, so she couldn't explain them to others. All she knew was that people didn't seem to do it the way she wanted it done. Once she could describe her theories of action and identity maps she was able to train people that she could turn over parts of the store to and refocus her energies on what was most interesting to her.

When we work together to achieve some outcome, our effectiveness is dependent on our ability to describe, compare, and learn together about our identity and theory of action maps. If we are unaware that we have maps that guide our actions we are likely to confuse our maps with reality. In Muriel's case, she confused her maps with people's competence. Since she couldn't describe her map, she and others couldn't learn together. There was just a succession of failed managers.

Muriel owned the store and had the right to decide what the goals were. She had a success map that needed to be shared with her subordinates. And she had developed a set of ideas, theories of action, for how to accomplish those goals. Her theory of action for how to manage employees was somewhat unique. Her theory of action for how to select products for the store was entirely idiosyncratic. Once she became aware of *what* she was trying to accomplish (identity map), people who worked for her could start to devise new and better ways to accomplish it (theories of action). By seeing and believing that her new managers were operating from her success map, she got a lot more flexible about how they went about doing things and it became clear that Muriel did not have a problem letting go of control.

People need to be aware of their maps, especially those maps that need to be in alignment with others' maps in order for people to work together. It helps the organization when its authorities have clear maps about what they want the team, department, or organization to do. We call this clear mapping vision. This vision is an identity map, and to be effective the leaders probably need to hold onto it against the inevitable attempts of others to change their minds. This is what I see clear leaders doing. But when it comes to theory of action maps, clear leaders are much more flexible and willing to learn and change. Managers with strongly held theories of action can stifle creativity and innovation if they think their theory is the way to accomplish some outcome. This tendency to confuse the map for the territory probably explains why a period of innovation often comes in the wake of a change in management.

Espoused Maps and Theories in Use

Every moment at work I am having an experience. My maps are an input, part of what creates that experience. They are also an outcome; I create and modify my maps based on my experience. Most of this cycle of map–experience–map is taking place behind my awareness. I don't usually pay much attention to how my maps are creating my experience or being modified by it. It is as natural as breathing. Because, for the most part, my maps are outside of my awareness, I have imperfect knowledge of them. At any moment if you asked me "Why did you do such and such?" I can probably give you a rational answer. But that doesn't mean it's a valid answer, and therein lies one of the biggest impediments to organizational learning and the reason why learning to pay close attention to your experience is so important.

Almost 25 years ago Chris Argyris and Donald Schön identified one of the key blocks to organizational learning. They pointed out that there can be a big difference between what people describe as their theories of action and what their theories of action really are. They called this the difference between people's "espoused theories" and their "theories in use." Our espoused theories are what we tell ourselves are the reasons for our actions, while our theories in use are the real reasons. Our theories in use are our real mental maps, the actual basis for our experience and actions. Our espoused maps are the stories we make up to explain our actions to ourselves and others. Sometimes our espoused maps and maps in use are the same, sometimes they overlap, and sometimes they have little resemblance to each other. There are many reasons why we might be unaware of our theory of action maps, ranging from psychological defense to simply not paying attention. For our purposes the reasons aren't that important. You just need to understand and acknowledge that you can't always be sure if the map you think you are operating from is really the map you are using.

It turns out that most people have an intuitive sense of this already. It is not all that unusual to question, in our own minds, whether other people really know why they do what they do. As you listen to someone give what sounds like a rationalization for their behavior you might occasionally find yourself making up a story about what the real reason is. Maybe you think they are not telling the whole truth, or perhaps you think they don't really know themselves. If the latter, than you are making a distinction between their espoused theory (their story) and their theory in use (what you think the real reason is).

This is one key reason that normal attempts in organizations to discuss and change problem patterns often fail. Even if people are willing to describe their maps, other people may not believe that those are their real maps in use. There is no way, in an intellectual discussion, to know for sure. More likely than not, people keep their doubts, and the stories they make up about their doubts, to themselves. Rather than clearing out the interpersonal mush, abstract discussions about why things happen the way they do can just create more.

This is where learning to be able to track your experience moment to moment proves to be invaluable. By working at being an Aware Self in the here and now you sidestep the problem of espoused maps and increase your awareness of your real subjective truth. Through paying close attention to your experience you find out what your maps in use really are. Let me give you an example.

Rose was the CEO of a small rural hospital and Chuck was her second in command. The hospital had been in the community for more than 50 years and there was a feeling of family among the staff. The hospital was part of a larger chain that was going through the same cost crisis all health care providers were experiencing in the United States. Rose was 15 years younger than Chuck, but he respected her visionary abilities in a time of great turbulence in the industry. For Rose's part, she respected Chuck's experience and operational acumen. They considered themselves a great team, but things had started to go sour over the past few months. Chuck began to notice a disturbing pattern. Even though he and Rose agreed that the hospital had to run more efficiently to survive in the long run, Rose was forgiving departments that ran over budget. Each time she did this he pointed it out to her and described his concerns about the implications of her actions. His theory of action was that people were going to have to feel some pain to start getting serious about operating more efficiently. Rose didn't disagree. She shared the same map. But each time she found some contingency money to shore up a blown budget she had a good reason. Chuck thought each explanation was reasonable but found the overall pattern troubling. When he tried to discuss it with Rose she agreed with his maps and his theory of action but then went ahead and did something different. At the time I was consulting to the headquarters staff and interviewing senior managers throughout the larger organization. When Chuck described his concerns about Rose to me I suggested that I might be able to help them have a different kind of conversation about this issue. I talked with Rose about it and she didn't see what good it would do, but she was concerned about her relationship with Chuck getting worse and agreed on the chance that it might make things better.

We met in Rose's office and I started by asking Chuck to describe his experience. He talked about the four incidents that had occurred in the previous six months. I asked Rose just to listen as I asked him to describe what he felt in the moment as he talked about this. He described his fear for the organization and his confusion about Rose's behavior. As I probed further he got in touch with his resentment that she came off looking like the "good guy" and he got stuck being the "bad guy," holding the line on budgets. He felt saddened and hurt by her behavior, almost as if she were betraying him, which he quickly added was "nonsense" but was part of the baggage he was carrying around. I asked him what he wanted and he said that he had thought what he wanted was for Rose to hold the budget line, and he still did, but now he realized what he wanted even more was to feel, once again, that he and Rose were on the same team.

I then turned to Rose, who was visibly affected by what she had heard. She quickly launched into an apology, assuring Chuck that she had no intention of betraying him and hadn't realized the impact this had on him. Before she got too far into this, I asked her to stop for a second and just pay attention to what she was sensing in her body. She paused for a few seconds and said, "I have a sinking feeling in my stomach." I asked her to look at Chuck, who was sitting across from her looking sad and glum, and to notice what was going on inside her at that moment. "What do you want right now?" I asked. "I want to take his hurt away. I want to fix it and make it all better," she replied. I then asked her if the sensations she was having were at all familiar, if she could remember having them before. She paused for a few seconds, looking down at the floor, and then snapped her head up and said, "Yes. I feel the same way when a department head who's gone over budget is sitting in that same chair [pointing at Chuck] with the same sad look on his face."

Rose was bright, and the implications of her insight from paying attention to her here-and-now experience were immediately apparent. "Oh my God," she said, "is that what I'm doing?" It was clear that Rose's espoused theory of action, which matched Chuck's theory in use, was not her theory in use. At that point she became embarrassed and wanted to disown the compassionate (fused?) part of her and promise never to do it again. However, I insisted that we look more closely at the positive intent behind her past actions and try to understand what her real theory of action was. It turned out that she had a map that said part of her job as CEO was to get resources for people and departments. She also had a map that said maintaining the family atmosphere in the hospital was important for patient care and overall effectiveness. She didn't want people to feel "unnecessary and arbitrary pain" if they didn't have to. The need for cost-cutting was so apparent and overwhelming that she hadn't been aware that she was holding contradictory maps.

Chuck agreed that maintaining the sense of "all being in this together" was important to the overall effectiveness of the hospital and agreed that their previous theory of action (induce enough pain to get people to change) might negatively affect that. He also agreed that her past rationalizations for supporting cost overruns had each had some merit. But the pattern would have to change if they were going to improve their cost control. Chuck and Rose found themselves caught between the contradictory assumptions of managing organizational effectiveness through teamwork, cohesion, and sense of belonging on one hand, and through impersonal controls and hard discipline on the other. Because they couldn't come up with one theory of action that fit all situations, they agreed that in the future Rose would not forgive a budget overrun without first fully consulting Chuck, and together they would find a decision they both agreed to on a case-by-case basis.

Rose and Chuck could have gone on for a long time having logical, rational discussions about the best way to run the hospital, but nothing would have changed. Rose was not aware that her map in use was different from her espoused map. Each time she acted differently from her espoused map she had a great reason for it. That's how sense-making works. We can always come up with sensible, logical explanations for past behavior, but that doesn't mean our explanations are valid.

When you learn to track your here-and-now experience, moment to moment, you get around the problem of espoused maps. You put aside rationalizations and explanations and just focus on what is actually going in you, here and now. If you do this sincerely and pay attention to your sensations as well as your thoughts, the real feelings and motivations that underlie your actions become apparent. Your real maps get put on the table and real learning and change can occur. That is the promise of the Aware Self.

Exercises to Develop Your Aware Self

At the end of each skills chapter is a section for people who would like to increase one or more of their clear leadership skills. Most of these exercises require a practice partner. Since these are skills of leading and working with people, that's probably not surprising. In fact, if you are going to try and develop these skills without finding a teacher I strongly encourage you to do it with one or more other people who've read this book and want to develop their skills as well. At the end of the book I describe how to set up a clear leadership practice group and where to get further resources.

Knowing Your Experience, Here and Now

1. Sit across from your partner and, for an agreed-upon period of time, notice your moment-to-moment awareness. Say whatever you become aware of as you become aware of it. Start with a one- or two-minute time frame where one person just talks out their stream of consciousness while the partner listens. Then switch roles. As it becomes easier, increase the amount of time until you can go on indefinitely.

   It may help if you preface each statement with "Now I'm aware . . ."

   Often when people first try this exercise they begin with their observations (e.g., "Now I'm aware of the green color of the walls. Now I'm aware of the chair you're sitting in. Now I'm aware of the hum coming from the lights"), but after they've exhausted that they have to turn inside for awareness.

   The partner's job is to listen and notice which of the four elements of experience the person is mostly aware of. Point this out to the speaker when he is finished. Practice bringing all four elements into awareness.

2. Another exercise is similar to the above, but you focus on a specific element of experience for an agreed-upon period of time. In this one the partner asks you for your awareness of that element and then you answer. They thank you and then ask again. Again, start with a one- or two-minute time limit and increase this as you get better at it. Here's an example:

   Partner: What are you feeling [observing, thinking, or wanting] now?

   Person: Irritated.

   Partner: Thank you. What are you feeling now?

   Person: I'm not sure.

   Partner: Thank you. What are you feeling now?

   Try to avoid getting stuck in long periods of silence. Say something and move on.

Developing Your Observer

The ability to record and play back exactly what you and others said and did has tremendous payback in all sorts of ways. You are much better able to learn from your experience. The ability to be recording at the same time that you are fully involved is key. To develop this skill you simply need to practice it. Two or three times a day, after you have been in a meeting or interacting with another person and have a few minutes to yourself, go back over the meeting or interaction and try to recall exactly who said what, and in what sequence. If you are like most people, you will be surprised at first by how little you can actually remember. It seems that simply the intention to learn how to do this, and constant practice, make the difference. Over a short time you will find that you are remembering more and more. Once you can leave a one-hour meeting and then play back what happened and in what sequence, you've mastered this skill.

Knowing Your Real Wants

To do this exercise you will need to be alone in a place where you can talk out loud without anyone hearing you. Think of some outcome or result that you don't really like. This could be a problem pattern you are in with someone at work or in your life, or some specific interaction you had that left you upset. Ask yourself, "Why did I create . . . [fill in the blanks]?" and then say, out loud, the first thing that pops into your head. It is critical that you not censor or prejudge whatever pops into your head; just say it. The reason you need to do this alone is that you will find that the reason is something you are not proud of or are embarrassed by. That's why it's unconscious in the first place. The reason you need to say it out loud is that if you don't, it will quickly recede back into the unconscious, where it came from. Like dreams, unconscious content rapidly fades from memory, but if you say it out loud it stays in memory.

For example, Richard found himself constantly leaving interactions with a co-worker feeling angry. Over time he had come up with a number of explanations for his anger, all of them having to do with the co-worker's inadequacies. He had to work with this person, who was effective and influential in the organization, so he resolved to just mellow out and not get so worked up. But that didn't help. Having just taken a course in clear leadership he decided to see if he could figure out what his part in this situation was, so he closed the door to his office and asked himself out loud "Why do I always get so angry around Sam?" What immediately came out of his mouth was "Because she's a stupid fucking girl." Whoa! thought Richard. Where did that come from? Richard prided himself on his sense of equality and on treating people the same regardless of gender or racial differences. He wouldn't be putting Samantha down just because she was a woman, would he? But because he'd said it, he decided to try it on a little longer and see what it felt like. That's when he noticed that around Samantha he had the same ambivalent feelings as he'd had toward some girls in high school whom he was attracted to and who used to scorn him. Richard realized that he was a lot more attracted to Samantha than he'd allowed himself to realize and that his anger was his way of defending himself from being scorned by her. His unconscious want had been to protect himself from feeling put down. Once he realized that, his anger went away and he could be choiceful about what he wanted: a really good working relationship with Sam.

If you accept that you create your own experience and sincerely ask yourself in this way why you are creating a certain experience, you will almost always get an answer.

Increasing Your Awareness

Undoubtedly, the most effective way to learn about yourself without the aid of a skilled therapist is journalizing. Ira Progoff is a great teacher who has written books on how to use journals to increase self-awareness, and if you are interested in trying this you should get one of his books. Through journalizing, you basically keep a written record of your experiences, observations, thoughts, feelings, and wants on a regular basis. Then every now and then you go back over what you have written and analyze what the underlying themes and patterns of your experience are. This can be a great aid in uncovering what you really think, feel, and want in life.

Using Language That Clarifies Rather Than Mystifies

The only way to practice this is to try to use appropriate pronouns and then get feedback on how well you are doing. Watching yourself on videotape is very helpful. Probably your best option is to ask your partner to point out each time you use pronouns inappropriately. It's much easier to notice other people using mystifying language than to notice it ourselves.

If there is someone at home or work who thinks quickly and is willing to be a "spotter" for you, make an agreement that they point out whenever you are using mystifying language.

A way to do this is, whenever you say "you" or "we" or "it" instead of "I," your partner asks "who?" It will take a few weeks, but your language will really start to change and you'll notice an impact on your sense of differentiation too.

Knowing Your Mental Maps

The technique I use for understanding my own and other people's maps is called "cardwork." I describe this in detail in the next chapter so I'll leave exercises for it until then.

Summary

In this chapter we have looked at the skill of being an Aware Self. We have looked at how being able to describe your moment-to-moment experience is the key to self-awareness. We've looked at how to become aware of your experience by breaking it down into four elements. Knowing your experience means knowing what you observe, think, feel, and want moment to moment. For most of us, a great deal of our experience is unconscious, outside of our awareness. That doesn't mean it doesn't influence us. Instead our unconscious experience influences us in ways we have no choice over. Increasing the skill of self-awareness is about becoming more aware of what is going on in each element of experience and how your maps are influencing that.

The Aware Self uses language in a way that clarifies, for herself and others, where the origin of her experience is. She avoids mystifying her experience. Through clear language she increases her awareness. And she is aware that her maps are, at best, inter-subjective truths whose validity depends as much or more on what other people think as on any "objective" truth. She knows that her maps are influencing her awareness and tries to avoid being blinded by them by keeping them in sight and not confusing them for the territory. She knows that it can be difficult to know what her maps really are and that she can make up satisfactory stories but that they may not be valid—another person can believe one thing is motivating her while something else really is. Moment-to-moment awareness of experience is the only reliable guide to what your real theory in use is, and to understanding what is really going on.

Why develop our Aware Self? There are many reasons. Perhaps the most important is that awareness equals choice. Without awareness we are pushed around by forces that are outside of our choicefulness. Becoming aware of your experience is a route to being more differentiated if you, like many people, tend to be fused with your feelings or wants. Most adults realize that we are not our observations or our thoughts, but some people forget that they are not their feelings or their wants either. When I confuse the boundary between myself and my feelings then I am controlled by them, and other people will be scared of my irrational actions. When I am my wants I am self-centered and driven by needs for gratification. Differentiating myself from my experience (being separate from it but still connected to it) makes it easier to be less reactive and more choiceful in how I respond to others. It helps me to differentiate myself from other people.

The Descriptive Self

Communicating Honestly

Clearing out the interpersonal mush and creating interpersonal clarity requires everyone to get clear about their own experience, others' experience, the maps they are all using, and the differences among their maps. This requires, as discussed in the previous chapter, the skills of awareness. Another necessary set of skills are those of being a Descriptive Self. The ultimate skill of being a Descriptive Self is being able to describe your maps and experience to others in a way they can hear and understand. To help you learn this skill I have divided it into the four aspects shown on the card below. These are transparent, not intimate; statements, not questions; describe impact before you react; and describe experience, not judgments. In this chapter I will elaborate on each.

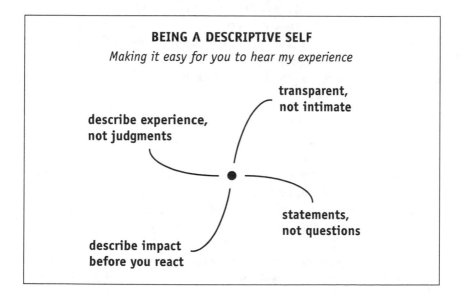

BEING A DESCRIPTIVE SELF

Making it easy for you to hear my experience

transparent,
not intimate

describe experience,
not judgments

statements,
not questions

describe impact
before you react

Four Aspects of the Descriptive Self

Transparent, Not Intimate

Being a Descriptive Self is not about being intimate with people at work. It is not about telling your life story, exposing your life secrets, or "letting it all hang out." It's not about being close and intimate. It's not about being "open" in the conventional sense of the word where you tell everything that is on your mind. Being descriptive means just that, describing to others what is going on in your head so that they have more accurate information to base their sense-making on. You can choose to be friends with people at work or not, but that has nothing to do with the skills of clear leadership. Friendship is not the issue. Being pleasant or charming is not the point. Clear leaders don't needlessly upset people, but they are not charm school graduates either. If I had to use one word to describe their commonality, it would be integrity, or maybe sincerity. They may not always be nice, but they are sincere. You can trust them to level with you.

When first learning these skills many people find the distinction between transparency and intimacy difficult to grasp. Being transparent, telling other people your subjective truth, sounds like a very intimate thing, but the way I am using it here, it is not. Another distinction some people find helpful is the difference between the *here and now* and the *there and then*. When you are being descriptive you are talking about your *here-and-now* experience. *Here* means that what you are talking about is related to the people who are listening. *Now* means that you are describing what is going on in your head at this moment. *There and then* is when you talk about people or events that are not related to the people who are listening to you. Here's an example:

I was working with a group where one member, Mark, was taking a big risk by telling the truth about his desire to influence and give leadership to the group. This was a touchy subject but very important to the members, who were rapt with attention. At that point he was being transparent as he described his excitement, his ideas, and his wants. Then he started to talk about why he felt driven to be influential, about leaving the country of his birth and finding it difficult to provide for his family in this new one. Mark was visibly distraught as he disclosed his concerns. At that point he had shifted from being transparent to being intimate, and the effect on the group was dramatic. People stopped listening to him and some physically pulled back. They began making up myriad stories about why he was saying what he was saying. I was able to stop Mark and ask people to describe the stories they were making up about him at that moment. These ranged from thinking Mark was trying to get support for his leadership through emotional blackmail to thinking he was trying to get others to display their own softer emotions. Actually, Mark wasn't sure why he had gotten so personal and thought it really wasn't relevant to the points he was trying to make. Hearing that helped people get back on track and start listening to Mark again.

Telling people about what you did on the weekend or about your kids or your past, being warm and friendly and intimate, is generally irrelevant to a learning conversation. What is relevant are the thoughts, feelings, observations, and wants going on in you that help the other person understand your experience as it pertains to the issues you are dealing with. So the proper attitude is transparency, not intimacy.

There is an important distinction between expressing and describing one's emotions. I bring this up here because people often confuse expression of feelings with intimacy. When I *describe* an emotion I tell you I am feeling it without acting on the feeling. When I *express* an emotion I act out the intensity of the feeling itself. For example, I might express my anger (if I'm really angry) by pounding tables, slamming doors, and throwing things. When I express a feeling in this way, the emotion is controlling me and this can be dangerous for interpersonal relations. Under the grip of a strong emotion I might very well do things that I later regret. Other people get cautious when I'm gripped by a strong emotion. It can cause fear and anxiety. They become more focused on trying to calm me down than on getting clear about our different experiences. Expressing emotions is very different from telling you, as calmly as I can, that I am angry. By calmly describing my feelings I give you important information that you need in order to understand the rest of what I am saying and doing. That is transparency.

Statements, Not Questions

When you are describing yourself you use statements. When beginning a "problem" conversation with a subordinate many well-intentioned managers are likely to ask questions instead of making statements.

Sometimes they even appear more skillful doing so. Certainly, a person asking questions seems to be listening more than a person who just makes statements. Leaders need to listen, but there is a time for listening and a time for talking. Questions are good when you are listening. To be a Descriptive Self, however, requires declarative statements.

For example, "Do you support our plans or don't you?" seems to be a straightforward question, but what kind of sense-making will it generate in the receiver? One person may interpret undertones of distrust. Another might begin trying to imagine why the question was being asked in the first place. A third might think that her reservations about the plans were clearly not welcomed. Questions lead to more clarity all around when they are preceded by descriptive statements. For example, "Yesterday you seemed really committed to our plan when you were describing it to Sally, but today you keep hedging on your commitment. I'm feeling confused. Do you support our plans or don't you?"

Some people use questions to hide behind. As long as I am asking you questions I don't have to reveal myself. Some use questions rhetorically. They really are making a statement but mask it as a question. The most notorious of these are the "Don't you think . . ." types of questions. The person who asks "Don't you think . . ." often means "I think you should . . ." but feels less vulnerable and, perhaps, less pushy phrasing it as a question. To the person hearing it, however, it has a different impact. The person who gets the "Don't you think . . ." question hears the implicit judgment in the question and is well aware what the "right" answer is. I think these kinds of questions actually create a certain amount of distrust toward the person asking them. It is far better for a person to simply state what his belief is and then ask the other her opinion than to ask rhetorical questions.

Some managers have concluded that when they talk first they don't find out what others really think. They've learned that their authority can cause people to pretend to agree with them when they really don't. These managers have learned to ask people questions before making their views known. This is a perfectly valid thing to do when you are interested in people's ideas and opinions about a task or a problem, but does not work if you are trying to create interpersonal clarity. Most people find describing their experience to others risky, especially if they are in an organization where this has not been common in the past. In a risky situation the manager has to go first, or she is not leading. A manager cannot expect subordinates to answer questions about their maps or experience if she herself has not fully described her maps and experience and answered their questions first. Therefore a leader needs to go first in making statements about what is going on in herself before asking others questions about what is going on in them. It is even better, in a learning conversation, to preface questions with declarative statements describing why the question is being asked. This is less important in a relationship of equal power where leading with curiosity may sometimes work better.

When someone asks me a question, especially my boss, sometimes I make up a story about why they are asking me that question, what they are really trying to find out, and what possible danger might lurk behind the question. Letting people in to what is going on in your head before asking questions reduces the amount of inaccurate sense-making they engage in and helps to contain the anxiety they may be creating for themselves. Before asking a question, tell them why you are asking it. This also models the kind of descriptive, "telling the truth of my experience" information you want from them.

Describe the Impact Before You React

In any conversation there are two things going on simultaneously, the *content* of the discussion and the *experience* of the conversation. When you say something to me you have an impact on me beyond simply the content of your statement. When I am being a Descriptive Self I describe the experience I am having as we talk, before I react to what you just said.

What do I mean by the difference between the content and the experience? Below is a quasi-fictional dialogue between two people at work having a normal phone call. I say quasi because it was related to me by one of the people; I'm making up what was going on in the other person's mind. Sue is leading a cross-functional team in which Frank, who reports to Bob, is a member. Here is their conversation.

Sue: *I'd like to talk with you about how we're managing the ABC project.*

Bob: *Sure, what's on your mind?*

Sue: *I think we agree that this is a really important project for the long-term success of the company.*

Bob: *Yeah, probably true.*

Sue: *So it deserves our best attention and resources.*

Bob: *And your point is . . . ?*

Sue: *Well, I've had more complaints about Frank not doing his part properly and I really think we need to do something about it.*

Bob: *What's the problem this time?*

Sue proceeds to describe two instances in the past two weeks when other parts of the organization noticed discrepancies in Frank's figures. Also, Frank is late with some of his reports.

Bob: *OK, I'll have a talk with him. I'm sure there's a good explanation for these problems.*

Sue: *Well, I appreciate that, but, you know, this isn't the first time you and I have had this conversation and I was wondering if you'd consider some alternatives.*

Bob: *Like what?*

Sue: *Well, I know that your department has other priorities right now. Perhaps you'd consider just taking Frank off the project and transferring the work to me.*

Bob: *That's an interesting proposition. Let me think on it and I'll get back to you. I think I should at least talk to Frank first, don't you?*

Seems like a normal conversation that could happen in any organization, right? But what was the impact they were having on each other as this discussion took place?

Below, in the right column, are some of the reactions each is having during the conversation.[1] The reactions come from the story each is making up about the other. In this example, Bob doesn't express many of his reactions. If he did, he would be more honest, but probably at the expense of making Sue angry and alienated. Most of Bob's reactions are judgments and, as discussed in the next ground rule, judgments don't aid learning conversations. Reactions are when I just sound off with whatever is on the top of my head, like my judgments. Behind these judgments, however, is the experience Bob is having, the story he is making up, that is leading him to those judgments. That is the "impact" that he needs to be able to describe if he is going to learn from this experience with Sue. The same holds true for Sue.

What was said by...	And what was going on inside...
Sue: *I'd like to talk with you about how we're managing the ABC project.*	Bob: Oh yeah, what's bugging you now? I can just feel myself tensing up because every time you are on the other end of the phone I have more problems to deal with. I'd sure like to just once have a different conversation with you.
Bob: *Sure, what's on your mind?*	Sue: You seem in a good mood today. Maybe I can finally break through with you around Frank. I feel like a runner poised for a race. I really want to come up with a long-term solution to this problem and I know you are starting to get bugged by me and I don't want that.
Sue: *I think we agree that this is a really important project for the long-term success of the company.*	Bob: Yep, she definitely wants something from me. I can feel my guard going up. I just hope it isn't about Frank again. The guy is two years from retirement, I'm stuck with him and damn it, people who put in 35 good years deserve to be treated decently.
Bob: *Yeah, probably true.*	Sue: Uh-oh, he's getting defensive. How can I get him to be open about this? Sometimes I feel so helpless to make a dent in his attitude.
Sue: *So it deserves our best attention and resources.*	Bob: Oh shit, it is about Frank. What's he done this time? I just feel nauseated at the thought of having to give him grief one more time. I've got more important things to do than deal with this crap.
Bob: *And your point is . . . ?*	Sue: Yep, definitely not with me now. I guess I just better plunge in and try to make this work.
Sue: *Well, I've had more complaints about Frank not doing his part properly and I really think we need to do something about it.*	Bob: I wonder if you've really had complaints or if they are just your complaints. What have you got against Frank anyway? Sure he's a little slow, but he's a decent guy and tries his best.
Bob: *What's the problem this time?*	Sue: Well, at least you asked. Maybe you're becoming more open to looking at this issue. I feel a little ray of hope. I really want you to see how serious this is.

What was said by...	*And what was going on inside...*
Sue: *(Proceeds to describe two instances in the past two weeks when other parts of the organization noticed discrepancies in Frank's figures. Also, Frank is late with some of his reports.)*	Bob: So there are a couple of numbers off, big deal. Those should be double-checked anyway, no matter who does them. I'm actually feeling relief that it's such a little deal. I wish you would just chill out. Not everyone is as much of a perfectionist as you.
Bob: *OK, I'll have a talk with him. I'm sure there's a good explanation for these problems.*	Sue: Oh no. That's what you said the last two times and things just don't get any better. I don't think you really understand the potential this project has to make a huge impact in our profitability. OK, try Plan B. I hope you go for it.
Sue: *Well, I appreciate that, but, you know, this isn't the first time you and I have had this conversation and I was wondering if you'd consider some alternatives.*	Bob: I know you'd like me to put someone else on this project but I can't. We are totally understaffed and it would take someone at least two weeks to get up to speed. But I don't expect you to take no for an answer. Why don't you just learn to work with Frank? He's got strengths as well as weaknesses. Use them.
Bob: *Like what?*	Sue: I know you don't have the manpower to replace Frank and because you supervise him he doesn't really feel any of the heat I would put on him to get results. My first choice is that you would transfer him to me but I know that you would never consider that, so I am willing to use my Saturdays and come in and make sure that work gets done correctly. Don't you understand that every time we issue an incorrect report the credibility goes down, and that ultimately the project will have no impact if that happens?
Sue: *Well, I know that your department has other priorities right now. Perhaps you'd consider just taking Frank off the project and transferring the work to me.*	Bob: Whoa, hold on there. I'm not sure I want to be completely out of the ABC project, and anyway, my department is responsible for those numbers. Just what is your game here anyway? Can I trust you or are you trying to climb over my back? You don't seem that type to me but now I feel I have to watch myself around you.

What was said by...	**And what was going on inside...**
Bob: *That's an interesting proposition. Let me think on it and I'll get back to you. I think I should at least talk to Frank first, don't you?*	Sue: You're not buying it. Shit. I've got to find some way to contain the damage Frank is doing. I know you are stuck with Frank but I wish you wouldn't fob him off on me. If you insist on doing that, at least give me some authority to make sure he does the work right. This is so depressing.

In order to have a learning conversation, some of the stuff going on in that right column needs to be said. Not all of it; that would be openness. But some of it. Bob and Sue have a problem pattern. They keep having conversations about Frank, but nothing happens—that's the pattern. No doubt in Sue's mind Frank and Bob are the problem. In Bob's mind, Sue is the problem. Actually, the problem is that they are not leveling with each other about their experience or their beliefs about the situation, so the pattern doesn't change.

When someone describes the impact, they disclose their here-and-now observations, thoughts, feelings, and wants in a calm, dispassionate way. They do this in a way that does not attack, criticize, or blame you. Instead of reacting to you, they put their experience on the table for both of you to look at. Before responding to the content of the conversation, they describe the experience they are having as a result of what they just heard. Then they respond to the content. When both parties do this, the sense-making that is causing the problem pattern becomes visible.

In day-to-day conversation we don't need to describe what is going on in the right-hand column to each other. It would take too much time and probably drive people crazy. But when we need to have a learning conversation we have to describe the impact the other person is having on us in the here and now—as it is happening. That is the only way for the other person to get an accurate picture of what is going on in us. Otherwise they just make it up based on the inaccurate story they have that is probably causing the problem pattern to begin with.

For illustration, here is an example of a snippet of a learning conversation that Bob and Sue might have if they described the impact each was having on the other before reacting to the content of the conversation:

Sue: *I want to have a learning conversation with you about our pattern of talking about Frank and nothing much changing.*

Bob: *I agree that we have a problem pattern, but the impact of you bringing it up is that I can feel myself getting tense and guarded as we start this conversation. I guess part of that has to do with how many times we've been around this and how I feel about Frank. I think ABC is a good project, and I want to help you out, but not at the expense of Frank's dignity or the other work my department has to do.*

Sue: *I find myself getting tense and guarded too, but I also feel a little relief and some hope hearing you level with me. I can understand that you don't want to jeopardize the other work you must do and I want to find a solution that doesn't do that, but I want to feel assured that you do support the ABC project and see that there really is a problem here. I'm a little surprised by what you just said about Frank and I guess I don't really understand how you feel about Frank. I'd like to understand that more.*

Bob: *When I hear that you respect my need to get my department's work done I feel myself relax a bit and realize I've been thinking that you only care about your project and don't really care about my problems. Maybe that's not true. As for Frank, he's worked here for 35 years and made a real contribution to this company. He's only got a few years left until retirement and I don't think those should be a living hell for him. Sure he's a little slow, but he's also got a lot of experience and wisdom. I don't think you've really tried to get to know him or his strengths. I would like you to put more effort into making the project work with Frank, and I wish you would deal with him directly and stop putting me in the middle.*

Sue: *I respect your attitude toward Frank. I agree we shouldn't treat people who've put a lot of good years into the company poorly, but I don't think we can allow our success to be jeopardized by them either. I'd like to make the project work with Frank or whoever. I believe he is competent to do the job but I don't seem to be able to get his attention. The reason I call you is that he reports to you and seems to only care about what you tell him. Really, I'd rather not have to go through you, but I thought you wanted to keep control over Frank. I've thought the real problem is that I don't have any authority over Frank's time and so he doesn't pay as much attention to the project's needs as I want him to.*

Bob: *Oh, I'm getting a different picture of the situation now. I thought you just thought Frank was incompetent and wanted me to replace him. It's true that I have Frank working on some other things now and he may not be clear about the importance of ABC. It sounds to me like we are going to need Frank to participate in a three-way conversation to really work out a solution. But before we do that I wonder if you and I need to get clear about anything else that's gone on over this. . . .*

Does this seem like a normal conversation at work? Probably not. It's not supposed to. For the most part people don't have learning conversations at work. That's why the interpersonal mush is so thick. But clear leaders are able to create these kinds of conversations, even with people who don't know anything about the ground rules of being Descriptive Selves.

I'd like you to notice two things about the conversation. Before Bob or Sue responds to the other's content, they describe the impact on themselves of what the other person just said. For example, before Bob responds to Sue's question about his feelings toward Frank, he tells her the impact her statement about not jeopardizing his department's work had on him. This is what I mean by "impact before react." In a learning conversation I describe the here-and-now impact you just had on me—the experience I created from what you said—before going on to say what I want in response. In this way, each person is able to track, moment to moment, the experience they are both having and ensure interpersonal clarity. As I showed you in the previous chapter, it is often through looking at the here-and-now experience that people are having with each other, moment to moment, that new insights into the really thorny problem patterns emerge. Focusing on the here-and-now experience is the best path to finding out what our unconscious experience is.

The second thing I want you to notice is that Bob and Sue are using the four elements of experience to describe their experience to each other. In almost every statement they describe what they are thinking, feeling, wanting, and, if appropriate, observing. They share their maps of the situation. That is what being a Descriptive Self is all about.

Describe Experience, Not Judgments

The ground rule of describing experience, not judgments, is a key to what makes this approach to organizational learning improve people's relationships and patterns of interaction. It is what makes this different from the human relations approach of being "open and honest." For many years as I was training to be an organization development consultant I would attend courses where I was told that it was better to be "open and honest." Usually after a couple of days I would decide, "OK, I'll be open and honest; let's see what happens." Invariably I would upset people and quickly retreat back to being careful of what I said. What I've come to realize is that when I said what was on the top of my mind, it was usually the judgments I was making up about people and their behavior.

If you go back to the original conversation between Bob and Sue you'll see what I mean. Bob and Sue have a series of judgments about each other. Imagine if they were "open and honest" with these. . . .

Bob: *Oh no, you again. You only call when you have problems.*

Sue: *You are already getting defensive and you don't even know what I'm calling about. There've been more complaints about Frank's work.*

Bob: *I'm not being defensive. You just always call me to complain about Frank. Have there really been complaints or are these just your complaints? What have you got against him anyway?*

Sue: *Me! What is it with you and Frank? I know you're stuck with him, but why do you keep running away from these problems?*

When I describe my judgments I talk about *you: you* only call when you have problems, *you* are getting defensive, what have *you* got against him, why do *you* keep running away. In effect I am talking as if my story about you is the truth instead of *my* truth. This is a crucial difference. Implicit in your judgments is that I am right or wrong, good or bad. When I hear your judgments of me I want to argue and defend myself. Instead of getting more clarity, we just end up hurling our judgments at each other without ever inspecting the stories we are making up that lead to those judgments. More than likely we walk away hurt and angry and our relationship will be in worse shape than if nothing had been said at all.

I think this is one of the main causes for the prevalence of interpersonal mush. We learn time and time again that if we tell "the truth" (i.e., let me tell you what I *really* think) we make other people upset and things get worse instead of better. But really, what is going on here is a lack of understanding of just what the truth is and a lack of some simple skills in how to say it. My experience, and the judgments I create from it, are my *subjective* truth, not yours. When I hurl my judgments at you I am acting as if my subjective truth were some kind of objective or inter-subjective truth, which of course it is not. My judgments are just the outcome of my sense-making, and if you were working from the same perspective and information that I have, you might make the same sense of things too. So I need to show you the stories and information I am using to make sense with. And I need to do it from the attitude that this is simply my truth and is probably different from your truth. When I do this, instead of making you upset I make myself understandable.

When I describe my experience I talk about *I*. I am acknowledging that my thoughts are based on a story that I have made up and that my story may or may not be accurate; it's just my story. Sure, my story is going to contain judgments about you, but when I am describing my experience I couch these as things going on in my head that I am letting you see so that you can correct me if I'm wrong. I use the experience cube to guide me: only when I've described my observations, thoughts, feelings, and wants have I fully described my experience. Here are some examples:

Judgment	Experience
At this rate you aren't going to have the report done properly on time.	I haven't heard from you once this week (Observation) and it confuses me (Feeling), as I don't understand how you can make progress on the report without discussing it with me (Thought). I want to be assured that you will have the report done properly and on time (Want).
You're ignoring me and trying to control this meeting.	I have some ideas about what we should do and how we should do it (T), but the last two times I've tried to raise them you've interrupted me (O) and it's starting to annoy me (F). I think we all have equal say in how this meeting goes (T), and I would like to know that you will listen to and consider what I have to say (W).
I don't think you are giving your best effort.	The story I'm making up in my head about you right now is that you aren't putting your best effort into this; am I right? (T) No? Well, let me describe to you what I'm seeing that is making me think that way (W) . . .

As you can see, when I describe my experience I don't assume what your thoughts, feelings, and wants are, I check them out. I show you that I am aware that my maps about you are just my current story and demonstrate that I am willing to change those maps if you are willing to tell me your truth.

Describing Maps

Part of the skill of being a Descriptive Self is being able to describe your maps to other people in ways that are simple and understandable. There are a number of approaches to map-making available today that range from the disciplined and rigorous (like fish bone diagrams or systems thinking) to the intuitive and creative (like mind mapping). Some excellent software has been developed for individuals and groups, and I expect to see even better stuff appear soon. Each has its uses and I encourage you to develop as many mapping tools as possible. A number of years ago Tom Pitman and I developed an approach to describing mental maps that I find quite useful and I think fits the clear leader's needs to be able to clarify and articulate his maps and other people's maps in simple, direct ways. Research on schemata—what academics call mental maps—has often compared the schemata of experts with those of novices (for example, how do different people think about how to teach, manage people, fix a car, and so forth). The one consistent finding from this stream of research is that novices tend to have long lists of issues and activities that are not well integrated. Experts, on the other hand, tend to have much shorter lists, with items that are more abstract and integrated. While the theories of action of novices are literal and linear, the theories of experts are holistic, relativistic, and metaphorical. Cardwork is a technique for uncovering and describing the genius in each of us. It, in a sense, forces you to think like an expert. At the end of this chapter I'll give you a detailed explanation of how to create cards. Here I just want to explain the basics.

There are two kinds of cards—identity cards and theory of action cards. Every card is a complete map in itself. For example, this book is based on an identity card. It's my map of the skills necessary for leadership in empowered organizations. My card is shown on the next page.

In this card I have reduced the complexity of my map of leadership and interpersonal competence down to four spokes on a propeller so that I can explain it in fairly simple terms to you. Each spoke of a propeller can be turned into further cards. I have done that in this

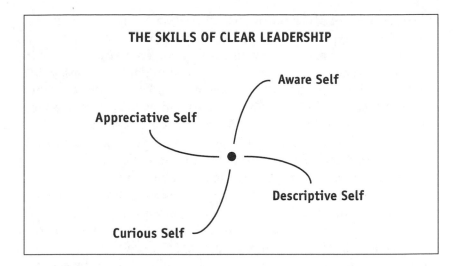

THE SKILLS OF CLEAR LEADERSHIP

Aware Self

Appreciative Self

Descriptive Self

Curious Self

book as well. Each skills chapter is based on my theory of action about how those skills create interpersonal competence, and at the beginning of each chapter the card that describes that theory is shown.

Clear leaders know what their theories of action are and can explain them in simple, direct ways to the people they work with. This is another very important part of being a Descriptive Self. If you manage others or are expected to give leadership to a team or work group I urge you to work out what your key theories of action are and talk about them to the people who work with you. A good basic set of clear maps on topics like "success," "teamwork," "quality" or "customer service," "dealing with conflict," "managing your boss," and "getting ahead" should be at the fingertips of any manager. Experiment with different variations on titles (e.g., success, we succeed, succeeding together), as these can bring up important differences in maps. Put them on the wall where others can see them. Keep updating them as you learn. Encourage others to come up with better maps. Learn together from your successes and failures. Keep working on becoming more aware of what your maps and your real theories in use are.

Exercises to Develop Your Descriptive Self

Describing Your Experience

A great way to practice this skill is to tell your partner about something that recently happened to you. Draw a picture of the experience cube on a piece of paper and as you tell your story put your finger on the element of experience you are currently describing. As you tell the story, move your finger to the element that you are in each time your story shifts. When you are describing your thoughts, opinions, judgments, and interpretations, your finger should be in the thoughts square. When you are describing feelings and emotions, your finger should be in the feelings square. When you are describing what you saw and heard, your finger should be in the observing square. And when you are describing your motives, intentions, desires, and needs, your finger should be in the wants square. Notice which square you spend most of your time in and which squares you spend less time in. Try to fully explore and describe your experience in each element. Your partner should point out when you have your finger in the wrong square and help you figure out what the right square is. Your partner can also ask questions to help you fully explore the squares that you've spent the least time in.

Describing Feelings

Feeling is the element many people have the most difficulty describing. It's easier to know we are feeling something than to know what to name it. There are hundreds of feelings, and learning to be able to name each can take a lifetime of introspection. For this reason it is useful to start with a basic handful of primary feelings. I call these primary feelings because so many other feelings are shades of intensity of one of the primary feelings. On the Emotional Words chart are 14 primary emotions and other feeling words that correspond to each primary emotion at varying levels of intensity. If describing feelings is difficult for you, begin just with these 14. Whenever you are wondering what to call your feeling, check out the list of 14 primary feelings and you can almost always find one that fits. After you find it easier to identify each of the 14 you can go on to more subtle shades and intensities. If you really want to work at this I advise you to type or write the 14 words on a piece of paper or photocopy the diagram and carry it around with you so that you can look at it when you are trying to figure out what you're feeling.

Describing Impact Before You React

Here's an exercise for learning the difference between reacting and telling your experience. Have your partner say something very controversial about you to you. If you think you can stand it, have them

EMOTIONAL WORDS

Primary	Related Feelings
Friendly	Appreciative, caring, concerned, warm, loyal, loving, lustful, attracted, curious, interested, respectful, brotherly
Happy	Content, elated, glad, ecstatic, up, cheerful, inspired, joyful, complete, bemused, marvelous, fabulous, peaceful, satisfied, moved, giggly
Anxious	Afraid, scared, terrified, frightened, worried, bothered, troubled, concerned, threatened, nervous, doubtful, suspicious, horrified
Surprised	Confused, puzzled, doubtful, amazed, fooled, tricked, betrayed, shocked, dumbfounded, perplexed, lost
Angry	Irritated, mad, enraged, disturbed, furious, frustrated, disappointed, annoyed, pissed off, petulant, defensive, unsatisfied, resentful, righteous, indignant
Desirable	Beautiful, feminine, pretty, flirtatious, sexy, handsome, hot, wanted
Shy	Timid, bashful, introverted, hesitant, tentative, unsure, unclear, tremulous, small, weak, insignificant
Alone	Isolated, abandoned, cut adrift, anchorless, displaced, stranded, lonely, solitary, detached, disconnected, separate
Embarrassed	Ashamed, aghast, abashed, remorseful, guilty, regretful, shamed, de-faced
Hurt	Wounded, wronged, broken, pained, sore, harmed, crushed, beaten, defeated, destroyed, used, abused
Tired	Rushed, busy, worn out, harried, used up, sleepy, passive, languid, apathetic, sedentary, lazy, bored, indifferent, lethargic, flat, wooden, stilted

EMOTIONAL WORDS CONTINUED	
Primary	**Related Feelings**
Confident	Competent, strong, assured, composed, proud, skilled, able, fit, ready, poised, sure, certain, convinced, courageous, brave
Energized	Charged, alive, feisty, energized, motivated, enlivened, playful, raring to go, extroverted, bursting, bubbly, coltish, giddy, swept up, vital, excited
Sad	Depressed, down, melancholy, sorrowful, disturbed, blue, tearful, nauseous, awful, grief, mourning, unhappy

say something that really pushes your buttons. When they do, say the first thing that comes to mind. Notice what kind of statement that is. Now have your partner say the same thing to you again but this time look inside, notice your experience, and describe what you are observing, thinking, feeling, and wanting in the moment. Here are some statements your partner could use:

- You're not very bright, are you?

- If I were you I'd just give up.

- The best thing we could do is just nuke those stupid (insert a group).

Describing Experience, Not Judgments

Perhaps the most difficult part of this skill is the ability to describe the experience you are having in relation to another person in the moment to that person. There is a lot of room for anxiety, vulnerability, and embarrassment in doing that, so it is something you really do need to practice before you launch into a learning conversation with someone you are having a problem pattern with.

A good way to first practice this is to work up to it with your skill practice partner. Begin by spending a few minutes having a discussion about what you both think about the idea of having skill practice partners.

Then move onto describing your experience of each other as skill practice partners. Then, and this is what you are working toward, describe to each other what your experience of each other is right at this moment, in the here and now.

Notice what thoughts, feelings, wants, or sensations you didn't say. Notice why you didn't say them. Tell that to your learning partner too.

Once you have done this a few times and feel comfortable with it, use the awareness exercise from skill 1 but do it in relation to each other. For an agreed-upon length of time (up to five minutes a person) describe your stream of consciousness beginning with the phrase "Right now as I experience you I . . ." Say it over and over. Work your way around the experience cube systematically. (e.g., Right now as I experience you I observe . . . ; Right now as I experience you I think . . . ; Right now as I experience you I feel . . . ; Right now as I experience you I want . . .). As you get more comfortable doing this, just let your experience come out of you naturally.

Using Cardwork to Describe Maps

Cardwork is about making your identity maps and theories of action explicit so that they can be described, discussed, and tested. It's also a way of getting clear about other people's maps. It's a great way to practice getting clarity about theories of action even if you don't explicitly use it at work.

Flow diagrams and critical path charts are one way of capturing a theory of action. They depict a series of activities toward some end. Cardwork is quite different. Well-constructed cards have the following characteristics, depicted in the card below.

I use 3 x 4-inch blank cards and construct them in the following way:

Five or Six Parts: A theory of action card has a title, a subtitle, and three or four phrases (never more than four) connected by a spinning, propeller-like image.

Complete in Itself: The title describes what this theory of action is about. The subtitle captures the outcome of successful action. The phrases provide a complete theory of how one reaches that outcome.

Spinning in All Directions: The phrases each capture a crucial facet of how one accomplishes the goal, task, or action, but they do not have to be in a linear, step-by-step sequence. Each phrase can itself "spin" and have more than one relevant meaning.

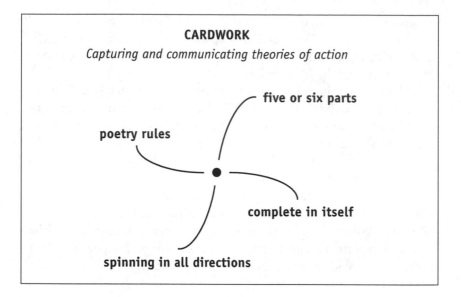

Poetry Rules: The title, subtitle, and phrases are constructed to evoke as many possible associations as are useful. Use wet, sticky, metaphorical language as opposed to dry, precise, intellectual language. A rule you can use for knowing when a card is completed is that, reading from the top right, it sounds like a poem. For example:

CARDWORK

Capturing and Communicating Theories of Action

Five or six parts
Complete in itself
Spinning in all directions
Poetry rules

I have found cardwork very useful in trying to understand my own and someone else's theory of action or identity map. An identity card is constructed the same way as a theory of action card but doesn't have a subtitle. Helping to make someone else's card usually leads us both to much deeper insight into their maps and helps to build good working relationships.

To practice, start by using cardwork to identify some of your own theories of action. A few good cards to start with are "leading teams," "influencing others," and "satisfying customers." Pick a title. Then decide what the outcome of effective action is. If you are doing a card on "leading teams," what do you think great team leadership produces? That is the subtitle. Next, brainstorm all the things you think are required from a leader to produce that outcome. Once you are finished brainstorming, go back over the list and whittle it down. Combine similar ideas and eliminate redundant ones. Do this until you have whittled it down to no more than four key points. Arrange these so the card reads more or less like a poem and then draw your card. If you find this useful, you may want to make a list of all the areas at work where you must be operating from a theory of action and make yourself a "deck" of cards.

Here's my current Leading Teams theory of action card:

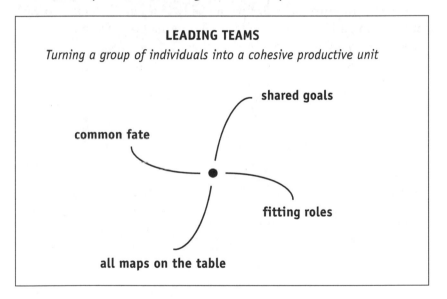

LEADING TEAMS

Turning a group of individuals into a cohesive productive unit

shared goals

common fate

fitting roles

all maps on the table

Summary

Being a Descriptive Self is describing your thoughts, feelings, wants, observations, and maps in a way that helps others see what is going on in your head so that they can give you information you lack in order to develop a more accurate story. One of my colleagues, Joan Mara, does a great demonstration to illustrate the proper attitude toward being a Descriptive Self. First she has people play-act a snowball fight.

Snowball fights are like hurling judgments. People try to nail each other while trying to avoid having anything land on them. By the end, all the snowballs are lying on the ground, melting. Contrast that with a game of catch. When people play catch they throw the ball so that the other person can catch it. That's what you have to do as your Descriptive Self—toss the ball to others in a way they can catch!

Part of the skill of clear leaders is knowing when others need them to be Descriptive Selves, when others are most likely to be making up inaccurate stories. Times of stress, uncertainty, and confusion are when people are most likely to make up negative stories, so those are times for leaders to get really descriptive. It's a useful habit for managers to ask people, "What do you think I just said?"—especially when the relationship is new and people are operating from different maps—and then repeat what they said until the person hears it accurately. By speaking as Descriptive Selves we replace interpersonal mush with interpersonal clarity, but only if we are listening to each other. Being a Descriptive Self is only one-half of a learning conversation. Being a Curious Self is the other.

The Curious Self

Helping Others Communicate

6

Clear leadership requires a balanced ability to be descriptive about yourself and curious about others. Being curious is an openness to hearing what goes on in other people's heads. The mastery of the Curious Self is the ability to get other people to be Descriptive Selves with you about their maps and experience. One of the things I have noticed about effective leaders is that they are naturally curious. They are always open to learning and will take whatever opportunities they have to gather different people's observations and opinions. Everyone has some curiosity, but disconnection and fusion and reactions to unconscious anxiety can push a person's curiosity away. Everyone can increase their curiosity skills, and once more I have broken this skill down into four aspects to make it easier to

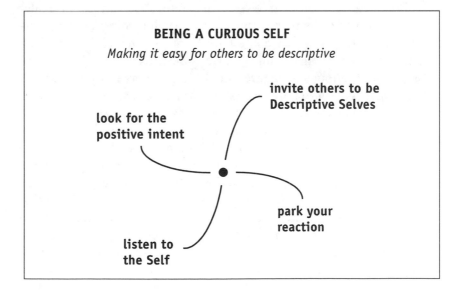

BEING A CURIOUS SELF
Making it easy for others to be descriptive

invite others to be Descriptive Selves

look for the positive intent

park your reaction

listen to the Self

understand. They are: invite others to be Descriptive Selves, park your reaction, listen to the Self, and look for the positive intent.

Invite Another's Descriptive Self

Being a Descriptive Self is not all that common. In addition to lacking the skill of it, people have had painful experiences that have made them wary of being descriptive. Most people have to be convinced that you are sincere about hearing their experience and can be trusted with it. It's difficult to demand that someone tell you the truth of their experience. It's easy for them to conceal what they really think, feel, or want, and how do you know what they aren't telling you? Telling the truth of your experience is a voluntary activity, and people are more likely to do that if they believe that what they say is going to be treated respectfully and with some dignity. Dignity—now there's a word you don't run into much in management textbooks. Dignity is about being treated as if you deserve to be here (in this group, this organization, this world). We strip people of their dignity when we point out their "flaws" in a way that threatens, at least in their mind, their social identity and, by extension, their memberships. I will say more about this in Chapter 10 in the section on shame. The hallmark of being a Curious Self is that others sense a real openness to hearing their inner experience in a way that won't diminish it or them.

Pouncing on someone else's inaccurate observations or faulty logic will just shut them up in the future. So will turning learning conversations into a win-lose contest where we try to figure out who's right and who's wrong. Being a Curious Self is *not* about being curious just long enough to figure out the other person's problem. It's about being willing to fully understand, as best they can tell you, what their experience is—to stand in their shoes and look at the world as they see it so that you can make sense of their sense-making. To invite another's Descriptive Self into the room, you have to be willing to acknowledge that whatever their subjective truth is, it's valid for them.

For many people, being a Descriptive Self is a vulnerable act. The proper mind-set when you are asking another to be descriptive is that of a gracious host inviting them to an event that they are going to enjoy. A written invitation tells you when, where, why, and who, and that's a good model for being a Curious Self. When and where you ask someone to be descriptive can be important in getting their truth.

A time and place where they don't feel pressured or threatened is obviously best, especially with people who are not used to being descriptive with you. Many people want to wait until they are alone, one to one, before having a learning conversation. That makes sense in terms of reducing the threat factor, but there can be a price, and people need to consider when it may be better to have learning conversations that are witnessed by others who are affected. The strongest teams are those where people can talk out their issues with everyone present. The ground rule is that the only people who can fix relationship problems are the people in the relationship. You and I can't fix your problem pattern with Bob. Only you and Bob can. And if the issues involve three or more people, they all have to participate in a conversation that turns mush to clarity.

It's also useful to tell people why you are curious—lead with being descriptive yourself. When people are reluctant to open up, help them see the benefits of being descriptive. Tell them what you get from it, why you want more of it, and what you would like from them. If you want them to be descriptive more than once, however, they had better enjoy it, or at least not suffer from it. They will need to test how trustworthy you are before they really let it all hang out. They will test to see how well you actually listen, how much you accept what you hear without reacting to it or getting fused with it, and what you do with the information once you have it.

Before going any further I want to clear up a possible confusion here. While I don't think it's effective to demand that another be descriptive, I do think it is possible and appropriate for managers to say that using clear leadership skills are a job expectation. Managers are responsible for outcomes. If they believe that those outcomes are best accomplished using the skills of clear leadership, they are as entitled to demand that as they are any other performance parameter. But if authorities abuse their power and/or abuse information people give them, then people will close up and interpersonal mush will reign.

Park All Reactions

Somebody says or does something that gets a reaction out of me. I react—usually by saying something with an edge to it. They react back. Maybe we have a discussion. Maybe we have an argument. Maybe we just disconnect and go away nursing our reactions to each other by ourselves. The key thing that happens when I act on my reaction is that I stop understanding you.

There are probably a lot of reasons why people react before they fully understand another person. Some of the more common are (1) an unconscious separation or intimacy anxiety that just got triggered, (2) a feeling of embarrassment, (3) a desire to correct the other person's misperceptions. In each case there is a knee-jerk reaction where I find some way to stop the other person in their tracks and try to get them to change their experience—change their perception or their judgment, their feeling or want. It's easy to see in others, harder to notice in ourselves. When we first start trying to have learning conversations a common mistake is to listen to the other person's experience for a minute or so and then, without hearing their whole experience, start to describe what we see differently. The Curious Self stops and hears the other person out *fully* before pointing out where he has a different experience.

Notice that almost all reactions are preceded by a story we just made up about the person or event we are reacting to. As we listen to people we are constantly making up what their experience is, what they really think or feel, their real motivations, what they know and don't know. Our reactions are often a result of the story we just made up. All that inner turmoil from a strong reaction might be based on a completely inaccurate story! The most useful response when you notice yourself reacting to a story you are making up is curiosity. Be still and pay close attention. You need to catch the part of you that is reacting with a fight-or-flight response to the anxiety and just *park* it.

The tendency that we all have to react to something a person says before we fully understand them is most pronounced when they are telling us their experience of ourselves. I hear them say something about me that is not part of my truth, and I want to correct them right away. But if I haven't fully listened to them, there's a good chance that my "correction" will be off the mark. Even if I'm right, I have still cut them off before I have gotten the full story, and having been "corrected" once they may not be willing to continue talking. Parking your reaction is noticing that you have stopped listening and want to interrupt the other person—and not doing it. Since listening to another person's experience of you is common in learning conversations, learning to park your reaction is really important if you want to be able to invite others to be descriptive.

Learn to park your reactions and you will create a lot less interpersonal mush.

Listen to Others' Selves

Lots of companies and programs in management offer a module or two on listening skills. Usually, these focus on something called active listening, and the main skill they teach is learning to paraphrase back what people are saying to you. Taking these courses for the first time is usually a good lesson in how difficult it is to really listen to others. Listening is not a simple or passive thing. It takes concentration and effort. Paraphrasing back what people are saying forces you to pay attention, not let your mind wander, and ensures that you understand the meaning, not just the words, of what others are saying.

Active listening is a technique, and like any technique of listening it rests on an understanding of why listening is so difficult and an intention to work at listening to the other. Some of the difficulties of listening are caused by our mental maps. When it comes to listening, maps create three problems. First, we listen for what is on our maps and tend to not hear what isn't. If I am trying to tell you about something that isn't on your map you will have to listen extra hard to hear it. Otherwise it will more than likely pass you by. The second problem is that many of us have "listening maps," things we are listening for when interacting with others. As a professor I am aware that I have a listening map I sometimes use when a student comes into my office. I'm listening for "the question"—some question they have about the course material they need me to answer for them. If it is just after I have handed back an assignment I have a different map—I'm listening for the change in grade they want. When I am using this listening map I am not really paying as much attention to what they are saying as to wondering what "the question" is. As soon as I hear it, or anything that sounds remotely close to it, I stop listening and work on my answer. I care about my students and try not to do this, but I am aware that I sometimes fall into this trap of listening *for* instead of just listening openly.

I'm sure if you think about it you will discover that you have all kinds of listening maps. You probably have listening maps for subordinates; when one comes to your desk, what are you listening for? You probably have listening maps for your boss. You may have listening maps for specific people at work. You probably have listening maps for other people in your life as well. These maps are not necessarily bad. We have them, like we have any map, because they've been proven accurate enough in the past to be useful. But when we decide to enter into a learning conversation they get in the way. A conversation creates learning when it adds something to my map that wasn't there before. If I only pay attention to what is already on my map I can't learn anything new.

The third problem occurs when we enter a conversation with a map of where we want the conversation to go and how we want others to respond. We spend a lot of time talking to ourselves (thinking) instead of listening to the other person. This is particularly true when my purpose is to persuade you. Instead of listening to you I am preparing my next persuasive argument while you talk.

In a learning conversation we need to put our maps aside and just listen openly. We are not there to persuade each other of anything. We are there to clear out the interpersonal mush and get to interpersonal clarity. The willingness to put aside your maps and inner dialogue and just listen openly is more important than any technique anyone can show you.

Three Levels of Listening

Assuming that you are willing to listen openly, there are a couple of techniques that can really boost your ability to have productive learning conversations. I call this listening at all three levels. At the first level you listen to the other person talk about something—usually her story about some event or issue. At the second level you are listening to the person's experience of it, using the experience cube to guide you in making sure you really understand her experience. At the third level you are listening to her experience of herself. At this level, you are exploring her personal maps with her to really understand her and her experience.

Level 1: Active Listening

Active listening is the ability to understand the meaning within what a person is saying and to communicate that understanding to the person. When you listen actively, you hear not only the person's words, but also the feelings, attitudes, and unexpressed meanings behind the words. By expressing this level of understanding, you help the person better express his thoughts, feelings, wants, and observations and help him feel listened to. It also gives you an opportunity to put yourself in that other person's shoes and understand his world. Active listening is critical to a learning relationship.

How do you do it?

- Face the person and maintain comfortable eye contact.

- Be aware of the other person's body language.

- Listen for the meaning behind the words.

- Don't confuse content and delivery. Assume the person has something to say even if she is having trouble saying it.

- Try to put yourself in the other person's shoes.

- Don't key in on one thing the person says and miss the whole message.

- When you find that your short-term memory is full, stop her and summarize what you have heard. This will empty your short-term memory and you can continue to listen.

- When you summarize, tell the person as completely as you can what you heard her telling you, but don't just parrot back her words.

- Don't add or subtract from the other person's message.

- Check that the person feels understood, and then check out any hunches about things she has left unsaid.

Level 2: Listening to the Other's Experience

When we listen at level 2 we inquire into the person's thoughts, feelings, wants, and observations using the experience cube as a guide. As you listen to the other person, are you able to describe all four elements of his experience? If not, then you need to ask questions about the missing elements. Initial questions are simple ones: What did you observe? What did you think about that? What did you feel during it? What did/do you want? This is the beginning of listening to the person's experience of a situation.

In addition, you need to listen to the important maps that are a part of the person's experience. It is especially useful to listen for the person's purpose and his theories of action. Questions about purpose and theories of action are a little tricky. Purpose refers to the overarching wants the person attaches to the situation and situations like it. Questions need to be sensitive to the person and the nature of the experience being related. Something like "In the big picture, what do you want out of situations like that?" can be used in many listening situations.

Theories of action are the maps people have of how to get what they want. Here we are listening to the person's ideas of how to act in the world and, in particular, in the situation being described. These questions have to be carefully worded so that the other doesn't feel defensive or think he is being judged. A question like "Why did you think doing A would cause B?" can be perceived as a negative judgment (e.g., only an idiot would think A would cause B). Phrasing of such questions needs to communicate a belief in the other person's competence and a sincere curiosity about how he thinks about his actions. A question like "When you did A, what did you expect to happen?" helps you understand his theory of action.

When you are listening at level 2 you go beyond actively listening to what the other person is telling you to helping yourself and the person get clear about his experience and the maps that are helping to create that experience. By the time you have finished listening you should be able to fully describe his experience.

Level 3: Listening to the Self

At level 3 we are asking the person to describe what she observed, thought, felt, and wanted about herself in relation to it. Use the experience cube to guide questions, but instead of asking about her experience of it, ask about her experience of herself. The basic questions here are "What did you observe about yourself?" "What did you think about yourself in this experience?" "What did you feel about yourself in this experience?" "What did you want from yourself in this experience?" Often, this quality of listening leads the person to new insights about herself. This is one of the subtle ways clear leaders help people solve their own problems. They don't take on people's problems, but they also don't turn people away, insisting that they go off and solve their own problems. Instead, clear leaders listen to their subordinates in a way that leads them to new insights about themselves and the problems they're facing. Let me give you an example.

In a course where I was teaching change techniques to organization development consultants, I was listening to an OD consultant talk about her best experience of being a consultant. My focus was on helping her to learn more about how to be an effective consultant. We started at level 1, with her describing a client system that she had worked with and the work that she did. As we moved to level 2 she described how different this experience had felt from other consulting work because she really felt a partnership with the client system—a sense of belonging that she had not experienced many times before. At this point she had not told me anything that she hadn't thought about before. When we moved to level 3, however, she got in touch with her belief that an OD consultant should not be looking after their own needs when working with a client system and that in this case she had allowed herself to have needs too. This turned out to be a very emotional revelation to her, as she discovered that it was really OK for her to have needs and get her needs met while working in a client system and that, in fact, doing so led her to be more effective as a consultant. At this point my listening had helped her to generate new insights into her role as a consultant—insights that reframed her experience and led her to a different map of how to be effective. And I had never given her a word of advice.

Level 3 questions are more intrusive and more personal, so it is up to you to decide whether that level of information is useful or needed in the learning conversation you are having. When I teach this material to managers, a number always voice their concern that these questions are too personal, too touchy-feely, and will generate a negative reaction in others. But when they try it out and listen to someone, practicing level 3 skills, they almost never get that reaction. Instead they're told how wonderful it was to be listened to so well, how interesting and thought-provoking the questions were.

To have learning conversations, you don't need to listen at level 3, but you do need to listen at levels 1 and 2. That means that by the time the other person is finished you should be able to paraphrase back their experience in all four quadrants of the experience cube and understand the relevant maps they are using.

Look for the Positive Intent

This is one of the best techniques of people I've observed who really live clear leadership. When they are trying to make sense of someone else's actions, they try to understand what positive intent might have motivated those actions. It is part of the appreciative mind-set I describe in the next chapter. Others sense this and feel more willing to be descriptive and tell their truth.

Much of what we do is the result of a series of mostly unconscious calculations in which we trade off what we want, what others want, and how much we and they want it. For the most part, we seek to find ways to satisfy our needs without stepping on others and, if possible, help them satisfy their needs too. These actions are guided by our maps, and if our maps are bent or faulty, our outcomes will be bent too. Sure, people sometimes have less than good intentions, and some they may never be willing to describe. But I have found that even actions that might repulse me are often motivated by intentions I find praiseworthy—it's the person's map for how to accomplish those outcomes that leads to actions I don't like. If I focus on understanding the map and the positive intentions, I open up a space where the other person is much more willing to tell their truth.

Ferd, a supervisor in accounting, was an old-timer with a long memory and high standards, who let people know, with no quibbling, when they made a mistake. Alana, an HR manager, happened to be there on unrelated business one day when she observed him berating a young, cowed employee. She was angered by the emotional abuse she witnessed and had a number of negative judgments about him and his behavior. She was also curious, however, about what kind of experience led him to act that way. She followed him back to his office, knocked on the door, and asked if he had a minute. Ferd looked at Alana suspiciously, no doubt thinking that she was going to give him a lecture about his behavior, and motioned to a chair. Then she said something like this: "I was watching you out there and it occurred to me that you must really care about the quality of work coming out of your department." His face took on a bemused look; he took her measure and then said, "No, that's not it. I just want so much for them, the young ones, and they don't know how tough it really is. But after they work for me for a while they get it, and they move on to better positions." It turns out Ferd had managed the department for a long, long time, and believed he had been dead-ended early in his career because no one had pushed him. As he talked about how much he wanted for the "bright-eyed innocents" who came to him in entry-level jobs, he pulled out a list from his files of everyone who had ever worked for him and where they now were in the company. He choked a little as he looked over the list, as if each name were some precious creation of his that he had loved and nurtured, taking great pride in those who had advanced far. Alana left with a very different story about Ferd and no lecture to offer.

I believe that if Alana had gone into that conversation focused on her negative judgments, wanting to change Ferd before understanding him, she would never have found out what was really behind his actions. It was a tender, heartfelt thing he shared with her, and people don't do that when they are being judged negatively by others. Clearly

Ferd's theory of action—the best way to "toughen up" his apprentices—might not be yours or mine. But that is a different issue from thinking Ferd is a bad, troubled, or evil person.

When I inquire with others to help us both learn about our parts in problem patterns it is always much easier when they believe that I see their positive intentions. My curiosity is not as threatening. In the face of probing questions about their experience, some people can feel quite threatened, fearing that the questioner is looking for what is "wrong" or "flawed" with them. This will close a person down. When I demonstrate an openness to seeing the good intentions behind "bad" actions, I make myself an ally to the other person. I will return to this theme in the next chapter, on being an Appreciative Self.

Exercises to Develop Your Curious Self

Listening to the Other's Experience

Listen to your partner describe some recent experience. Use the experience cube as a guide in asking questions to ensure that you fully understand what his experience was (level 2). Try to understand any important identity maps and theory of action maps that are relevant to this experience. Once he is finished telling you about his experience, describe it fully back to him. If you have listened well you should be able to summarize all four quadrants of the experience cube.

As you are listening, notice when you are starting to lose track of what your partner has already said. That is when you should stop him and paraphrase back what you have heard to that point. It's amazing how that helps you retain all the information you have heard and makes you able to absorb more.

Notice when you stop listening or when you want to offer your opinion or help him fix a problem. Do not offer any of your thoughts and feelings. If you are having reactions, park them. Just listen.

Your partner's job, in addition to telling you about an experience, is to give you feedback on how well you are able to fully paraphrase back the meaning of whatever he was telling you. Your partner should also give you feedback on how welcoming your listening was. Did you make him want to open up or did you make him want to be less open? How did you do that?

Listening at Level 3

Once you have mastered listening at levels 1 and 2 go on to practice listening at level 3. You partner should pick something to talk about where she is trying to get more clarity or trying to come to some decision. Troubling issues, opportunities she's not sure about, confusing experiences are good things to practice on. Your partner should focus on getting clearer about what her experience really is.

Begin by listening at levels 1 and 2, but look for opportunities to ask level 3 questions that begin, "How do you think about yourself . . . ," "What do you observe about yourself . . . ," "How do you feel about yourself . . . ," and "What do you want for or from yourself . . ."

Again, you should be able to paraphrase back, at all times, what your partner has said. Completely avoid giving any advice or opinions for the duration of the listening exercise.

Your partner's job is the same as in the previous exercise, with two further pieces of feedback. She should tell you which questions really helped her increase her clarity or deepen her understanding of her experience, and she should tell you if she ever thought you were giving her advice or making implicit judgments.

Seeing Positive Intent

A way to increase your ability to see the positive intent behind other people's actions is to begin by listing the things people you know do that really bug you. This could be people at work or in your personal life. Once you've got a list with at least five different people on it, go back over the list and invent as many possible explanations for their behavior as you can that you find reasonable or acceptable. Now comes the hard part—go talk to those people about their experience of their actions. Remind them of a specific time you saw them act the way that annoys you (without telling them it annoys you). Check out whether any of your ideas is correct. Ask questions to find out what their experience and maps were when they acted that way.

Using Cardwork to Understand Other People's Maps

Once you've gotten the hang of making your own cards (as described in the last chapter), make a few cards for your partner; that is, make a card that depicts one of his theories of action. Being a cardmaker takes some good listening, trying hard to understand how the other sees the world, and not letting your own beliefs and ideas intrude. First, decide with your partner what the card is about. For example, the card may be on something like "cutting costs." That becomes the title. Then help your partner get clear about what the outcome of effective cost cutting is from his point of view. This could be something like "spending less money without sacrificing service." That becomes the subtitle.

When making someone else's card you have to take an appreciative stance, assuming that the other has a genius for how to accomplish the goal or action. Interview your partner about his theory of action, keeping a running list of all the fragments and images the person uses to discuss his map. Allow yourself to use your intuition to ask questions about the beliefs and ideas your partner may not be conscious of, and bring these together into words and phrases that capture and communicate batches of these fragments.

Once your partner feels he has said all he can, you craft a card, using the rules of cardwork, that best captures his theory of action. Go back over the list of ideas, eliminating the nonessential, consolidating common ideas until you have no more than four points. Draw a card and give it to your partner, and ask whether the card accurately captures his theory of action. Either the card is accepted or you work with your partner to craft a card that is acceptable. The "poetry rules" part of cardwork is perhaps the least important. It is not about trying to make clever rhymes. However, every time I have used cardwork with managers, it is the person whose card has rich images and evocative phrasing that has the biggest impact on others. What is important is that the subtitle describes the outcome of successful action and that there are no more than four phrases for how that is accomplished. Most importantly, the card really must reflect your partner's map, and not have your own mixed in.

At work you do not have to formally make someone's card, but you do have to know how to ask them questions to find out what their maps are. Practicing making other people's cards is a great way to develop that skill. Leadership is a lot about influencing people, and you cannot influence someone if you don't understand their maps. Sam Culbert has written an excellent book on the intricacies of understanding and influencing personal maps, and I encourage you to read it.[1] In the meantime, cardwork is a simple and effective way to think about and check out other people's maps.

Summary

The Curious Self is interested in getting the real story—what the objective facts are in a situation—understanding another person's subjective truth, and understanding the impact her own actions are having on other people. All of these truths are necessary to get to clarity. The mastery of the Curious Self is the ability to make it easy for others to be Descriptive Selves—to be willing to tell you what their subjective truth really is even when they aren't too proud of it. The Curious Self listens fully until she can describe the other people's experiences as well as they can. In addition to good listening skills, it takes an attitude of invitation—making the opportunity to be descriptive look like a painless thing.

The biggest obstacle to being a Curious Self is our reactivity, the tendency to want to respond and correct before the other person has finished telling their truth. Learning to notice when you are reacting, and parking that reaction until the other person is finished, increases the likelihood that they will tell you their complete truth. Parking your reaction is indispensable to a learning conversation.

Finally, the truly skillful at being curious know that they are more likely to really understand behavior they find annoying if they search for the positive intent behind it. Demonstrating that you are interested and willing to see the best in people makes them a lot more willing to tell you the truth of their experience and, as we'll see in the next chapter, can create a kind of clarity that amplifies the best in ourselves and our organizations.

The Appreciative Self

Inspiring the Best in People

7

Interpersonal clarity is the prerequisite for effective cooperative action. It improves communication, problem-solving, decision-making, conflict management, and teamwork. As I hope I have convinced you by now, without interpersonal clarity no group of people working together can come close to achieving their potential.

But there is one other thing I see exceptional leaders in empowered organizations doing that seems to be an important ingredient to their magic. Put simply, they focus more on what's working and what they want more of, and less on problems and what they want less of. Taking a cue from Dave Cooperrider and Suresh Srivastva, I've come to call what they do an appreciative stance toward management and change.[1]

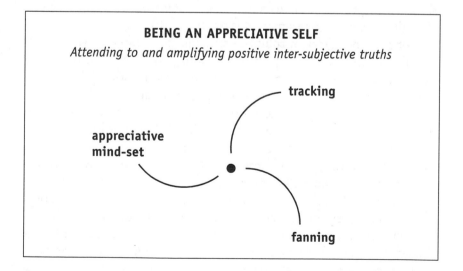

BEING AN APPRECIATIVE SELF

Attending to and amplifying positive inter-subjective truths

tracking

appreciative
mind-set

fanning

In traditional organizations many managers see themselves as "problem-solvers." Authority to act on problems rests in the hands of the few, while the many are there to gather information, make suggestions, and execute the solutions arrived at by the few. The best problem-solvers are promoted up the hierarchy and in many organizations "management" is synonymous with "problem-solving." Management schools have been, I think, justly criticized for training MBAs mainly in how to apply problem-solving formulas. There are a number of deficiencies with the "manager as problem-solver" model that is contributing to the demise of bureaucratic organizing. One is that such organizations make suboptimal use of their biggest operating expense, their payroll. Instead of using the minds of everyone to achieve and sustain competitive performance, most people are used as the hands and feet of the organization while only a comparative few are used for their brains. This separation of problem-solvers from solution implementers creates a number of other problems. One is increased resistance to implementation from those who have had no say in the "solutions." "Those who plan the battle don't battle the plan," as the saying goes. Another is that the "problem-solvers" tend to be a few steps removed from the actual problems they are solving. Research has shown that solutions tend to be more efficient and more effective the more "variance is controlled at source"—that is, the more people close to problems are the ones solving the problems. Finally, the separation of those who report problems and then execute solutions from those who actually solve the problems considerably slows down processes of adaptation and innovation. In today's rapidly changing business environment this traditional form of leadership takes too long to find the right solutions and get them implemented.

These are some of the very reasons that new, "empowered" organizations are being created. These organizations "flatten the hierarchy" precisely so that those solving problems and making decisions are close to where the problems are. In theory, everyone is a problem-solver and local adaptations to local problems occur rapidly. In practice, however, these new organizational designs are still often managed with traditional leadership styles, so the results are far below those that are produced when people use clear leadership.

The clear leaders do a lot less problem-solving than traditional leaders. They rely on the people doing the work to solve problems. Instead of focusing on problems, they focus on solutions. They are continually looking for instances where things are going right: where quality is increasing, where customers are being satisfied, where internal processes are being managed seamlessly, and where wealth is being created. They get clear about where things are working well and they work to amplify it. They focus on increasing what is already working well. Instead of trying to compensate for weakness, they build on strength. Instead of criticizing and punishing people for their failures, they praise and reward people for their successes. Instead of worrying about what to do with the processes or people that aren't working well, taking what is working well (and the bulk of the workforce) for granted, they wonder about what to do with the processes and people that are working well. By managing people through appreciative processes, they use less energy to have a much greater, positive impact on people's motivation and organizational performance.

I call this set of behaviors being an Appreciative Self. There are two skills that underlie appreciative processes: tracking and fanning.[2] Using them requires an attitude toward life I call an appreciative mind-set. In addition to differentiation, it is the platform upon which the skills of clear leadership rest.

Appreciative Mind-Set

The first step in being an Appreciative Self is developing an appreciative mind-set. As it turns out this is not that easy for many people. We are all heirs to a deficit mind-set that may have increased in Western culture in the past century.[3] Our society trains us to see the glass half empty, to notice what is broken, lacking, needs fixing, and isn't good enough. In organizations a lot of the drama of management is taken up by the identification and quantification of the gap between what is and what should be, the actual and the ideal, the goal and current performance. We are fixated on problem-solving. As soon as current performance gets close to the goal, we more than likely move the goal line. As a result much of the time in organizations people live in "gap land," that place of "not good enough." Some try to put a positive spin on it with words like "challenge" and "opportunities," but most people see that the ground their managers stand on when they use those "inspirational" words is gap land. So they feel the gap, not inspiration.

Most people understand the critical role of self-esteem in the lives of people who accomplish and succeed. Without self-esteem even the most talented fail. We know that if we constantly criticize a child, telling her she isn't good enough, setting standards she cannot meet, and never lavishing our praise upon her, she will develop an inferiority complex. What happens to a team or organization that gets the same message? What happens to people when most or all of their organizational life is lived in gap land? I've come to believe that organizations also develop inferiority complexes, and when that happens there is no chance of outstanding performance. One large company I consulted with had been very successful in the past but had spent the last 10 years continuously missing the standards and goals its executives set. This company was going through a major transformation in its industry. They had lost market share and wealth but had made numerous positive changes that no one was focusing on. Instead there was a pervasive sense of inferiority. People were even embarrassed to tell their neighbors what company they worked for. In meeting after meeting in this company I encountered a phenomenon I came to call "pulling the rug out from underneath ourselves." For the most part meetings were full of cynicism and doubt that the company could do anything right. Every now and then a group would start to get excited by an idea of something positive they could do, and then someone would voice the collective doubt that they really could pull it off and the energy would instantly deflate. It was a very difficult atmosphere in which to get any positive momentum going.

When all we do in our organizational life is go from one crisis to the next, one problem to another, work becomes drudgery, or worse, paralyzing. The only time action is mobilized is when you have a serious problem. You can't create a climate of continuous learning and improvement in a problem-oriented culture. Such cultures develop a "don't fix it unless it's broken" map, for good reason: they have so many already broken things to fix.

One CEO of a large telecommunications company put it like this:

[Appreciative processes] can get you much better results than seeking out and solving problems. That's an interesting concept for me—and I imagine most of you—because telephone companies are among the best problem-solvers in the world. We troubleshoot everything. We concentrate enormous resources on correcting problems that have relatively minor impact on our overall service and performance. . . . [W]hen used continually and over a long period of time, this approach can lead to a negative culture. If you combine a negative culture with all the challenges we face today, it could be easy to convince ourselves that we have too many problems to overcome—to slip into a paralyzing sense of hopelessness. . . . Don't get me wrong. I'm not advocating mindless

*happy talk. . . . We can't ignore problems—we just need to approach
them from the other side."*[4]

What happens when we let go of a deficit mind-set and develop
an appreciative mind-set? The most general thing is that we start to
see our organizations primarily as people and human relationships
with limitless capacity and potential to achieve whatever the human
imagination can yearn for. Social systems are not like natural systems;
they don't follow natural laws. In modern society we are trained to
think of social systems as natural systems, as complicated sequences of
cause and effect. If you do A, B, and C then D will follow. In business,
economists and financial experts, in particular, like to think this way.
But most of us intuitively know it's not true. Post-modern philoso-
phers have been pointing out the differences for most of this century.
Although scientists have been trying to discover laws of human nature
since the 19th century, about the best they've come up with is "a
behavior rewarded tends to be repeated."[5] And notice it is only
"tends," because sometimes rewarded behavior isn't repeated.
Organizations are not based on objective truths but on inter-subjective
truths—they exist the way they do because of the web of agreements
among the people inside and outside them. Are we good or bad? Are
we successful or unsuccessful? Are we in conflict? The answers to
these and a thousand other questions are inter-subjective truths. We
can collect objective data to try and help us figure out what is true—
but the results of our research only become true in an inter-subjective
sense once the people they affect believe they are true.

This is one of the reasons why spectacularly successful managerial
innovations in one company that are simply copied in another place
almost never yield the same results. There are no simple or complicated ABC formulas that always work because we each create our own
experience, and people co-create the social systems they live in. What
gives social systems their reality are people's shared maps. The only
limit to what is possible is our collective imagination. When our collective imagination changes, the world changes. Here's an example
you may already know about.

---

*When the ecology movement started it was seen as anti-business. Business-
people thought "ecology nuts," and in particular "ecological warriors,"
who pulled off daring and dangerous stunts to stop environmental*

damage, wanted us all to return to living in peasant agrarian societies. Ecologists, on the other hand, tended to see business people as greedy, short-sighted lunatics who were relentlessly damaging the support systems of "spaceship earth." There was almost no meeting ground. These people had nothing to discuss; they were enemies. One VP of future planning for a major wood products company was overheard saying, as late as 1987, "This ecology thing will just blow over."

Something happened that changed all that. It happened in 1987 when the World Commission on Environment and Development published its report Our Common Future, *better known as the Brundtland Report. The report set out a concept, with a new phrase that became a new map that almost instantly changed the relationship between business and ecologists. The new idea that expressed the yearning of the human imagination was "sustainable development." Within a year of the commission's report the social system that had existed was so dramatically changed that one very well-known organization of eco-warriors went into a crisis. For decades they had been screaming "Listen to us, listen to us," and now business and government, under the banner of sustainable development, was suddenly turning and saying, "Yes, we want to listen to you, what should we do?" This organization went through more than a year of internal conflict and soul-searching trying to figure out what its new role should be in such a radically changed set of social and organizational relationships. In the end it decided that it must continue outside the mainstream in a critical advocacy role, and left others to join the boards of companies and government planning commissions that followed this dramatic change in Western culture.*

At the beginning of the 21st century when telecommunications, media, and transportation have shrunk our world and we are continuously confronted with the enormous variety in human cultures, the average person has some recognition of the arbitrary nature of social systems. Most of our great-grandparents never traveled farther than 30 miles from where they were born. They didn't have TV to beam images of different cultures and ways of thinking into their living rooms. Almost everyone they met in their lives grew up believing the same things they did. No wonder they thought there was a "divine order" or "natural law" to human relationships. But the clear leader knows differently. She knows that people "see it when they believe it," that what people think about and the way people think about things makes all the difference in organizations. How we think has a direct influence on our sense-making, our experience, and ultimately our actions.

Since it is through our actions that we co-create the world, it turns out that our biases have a much more profound impact than merely clouding our perceptions. It is not just that someone who wears rose-colored glasses sees a rose-colored world. Research in many areas of human existence consistently shows that self-fulfilling prophecies happen, that what we believe will happen is more likely to happen because of our beliefs.[6] One of the most striking examples is the research initiated by Robert Rosenthal, whose studies have produced what came to be known as the "Pygmalion effect." In hundreds of studies conducted by dozens of researchers with children and adults, the same effect has been found. If you tell a teacher that a randomly selected group of people are the best at something in the course, by the end of the course they are the best! It doesn't matter whether you are teaching reading to children or marksmanship to army recruits, the results are the same. The teacher expects randomly chosen student A to be the best, and by the end of the course, on objective tests of achievement, he is. How does this happen? Potential explanations have been put forward but none proven.

This phenomenon also occurs in healing. The "placebo effect" refers to the fact that if you give any group of sick people fake medicine, about 30 percent will get better simply because they believe they will. The reality of self-fulfilling prophecies (literally, faith healing) is so accepted in medicine that tests of new drugs must contain placebos (fake drugs that look real) and be administered by people who don't know which is fake and which is real. Significantly more of the people getting the new drug than the fake drug must be cured for the drug to be considered effective. How about that! A significant number of people will get better if they think they are going to get better! Medicine is only now studying how that happens.

My point is that a leader's beliefs about the people, teams, and organizations he works in probably come true. If he is biased toward seeing the best in people, that's what he gets. If he is attending to the worst in people, he gets more of that. But taking an appreciative mind-set is not about having a Pollyanna view of people. It comes from having a map that acknowledges the power of maps for creating the relationships people have.

Your Thoughts and Feelings
Do Affect Other People's Behavior

The people I have had the most negative emotional reactions to in my work life have been the people who have taught me some of the most important lessons about myself. The most important lesson of all, however, has been that when I own the part of me (the split-off projection) that I am reacting to in the other person, he or she miraculously changes and becomes much easier to deal with. For example, there was one person I worked with who used to "make me" very angry. I often found myself at the other end of arguments with him over what our organization should do and how we should do it. It got so bad I found myself avoiding him and having daydreams where I would roundly defeat him. I finally applied my own medicine to myself and thought about what unfavorable words I would use to categorize him. Then I took those words and searched for a part of myself that is rigid, tradition-bound, and elitist, and it didn't take me long to find it. When I owned the part of me that I had been trying to deny, took back the projection, all my fusion with him went away. We stopped arguing and I discovered that we actually agreed on a lot of things.

Part of this kind of change, of course, is due to my change in awareness; my map changes, so my experience does as well. But part of this is also that the other person's behavior changes—and others notice it as well. It is as though my negative thoughts are part of the system that keeps their negative behavior in place, and when my thoughts change, the system changes and so does their behavior. Let me give you the example of the first time I put this idea into practice.

My partner and I were working with a group of 35 engineering managers and their direct reports at a five-day workshop that was the beginning of a long-term change effort. After the first three days I was totally frustrated and becoming hostile toward the people we were working with. My partner agreed that they were reluctant, resistant, always questioning our motives, argumentative, narrow-minded, and closed to our ideas and suggestions; but he was less emotionally affected by it than I was. He had worked with this client system longer and seemed to be taking it in stride. I, however, was fused and getting emotionally hooked by their behavior. Toward the end of the third day I found myself starting to sarcastically attack some of them. I realized that if I continued to do this

I would lose any chance of being effective with them, so I decided to try out some ideas I had been developing about how I could alter my experience. The next morning I got up an hour earlier than usual and put myself into a quiet, meditative mood. Then, one by one, I visualized what each of the 35 people looked like when they were five years old. As I got a clear visual picture, I imagined myself putting them in my heart and felt the loving feelings I can have for any sweet five-year-old. When I felt the loving feeling I went on to the next person until I had done this with each of them.

An hour later when the fourth day of the workshop started, the atmosphere in the room was completely different than it had been for the previous three days. Right from the start the group enthusiastically participated in the activities I suggested. They were open, interested, and completely receptive to our ideas. The day was a huge success and a turning point in our work with them. My partner and I were stunned by the change in their behavior. We had a hard time believing it was just from my morning exercise, but we could not discover any other reason for their change. Interestingly, the participants we talked to about this later either had not noticed a difference or agreed there had been a difference but could not name what it was.

Can I explain the change in this social system by conventional notions of cause and effect? No. So this and a variety of other experiences has led me to question our commonly held assumptions about cause and effect, at least as they apply to people, and to come to the conclusion that we somehow affect each other with our unspoken thoughts and feelings. There are a number of simple experiments I have since learned that demonstrate this. One of the simplest involves a group of people and two volunteers. I usually ask a strong man and a petite woman. The strong man sits with his back to the group so that he cannot see what I or the group is doing. He holds out one of his arms, parallel to the floor, and resists while the petite woman tries to force his arm down. Usually she can't. Then the group is asked to focus an emotion at the man, and on a board or flipchart where he can't see I write the word "hate." After five or ten seconds the woman is asked to try to push his arm down again. She can do it easily. The group's negative emotion, directed at him, weakens his bioenergy system. I then ask the group to direct another feeling toward the man and write "love" on the board. After five or ten seconds she once more tries to push his arm, which is now rock solid. I have done this with dozens of groups and it never fails. In fact, some men claim they can sense the change in emotions being directed at them. If you try this yourself it's important to make sure that you and the others have enough time to really feel the emotion you are directing at the sub-ject. And be sure to end with love, as you don't want the poor person walking around with other people's hate in them.

I suggest that a person's thoughts and feelings have an effect on other people and that, like the Pygmalion effect, the thoughts and feel-ings of those in authority have an even bigger impact on people who work for them. If you are a manager, you are probably having an effect on people who work for you simply by the way you think about them. Wait a minute, you may say. Doesn't this totally contradict what you were saying earlier about boundaries and keeping you and me sepa-rate? What about the "I'm responsible for the impact you have on me" stuff? From my point of view it is paradoxical but not contradictory. Both things are true: We each create our own experience *and* others' unspoken thoughts and feelings affect us. From the point of view of differentiation and learning the most useful map to use is that each person creates the impact that others have on him. From the point of view of leadership and positive influence the most useful map is that the mind-set leaders have affects their followers. These are just two maps; they are not "the truth"—which none of us knows. They are paradoxical, but that doesn't make them any less useful.

We Get More of Whatever We Pay Attention To

There is an ancient piece of wisdom that whatever we pay attention to grows. It's as though simply paying attention to something invests it with more energy. The appreciative mind-set chooses to pay atten-tion to things it can value, care about, be happy with, and want more of. It recognizes that inquiry into inter-subjective truth can either be a looking at the past, where we try to uncover the agreements we've had, or a looking to the future, where we try to uncover the agree-ments we want to have. The appreciative mind-set is more interested in the latter kind of truth.

This means, first of all, being clear about what you want more of. Sometimes that is easy and sometimes it isn't. People often begin by knowing what they want less of, especially from other people. "I want her to stop gossiping," "I want him to stop interrupting me when I talk," "I want them to stop filing nuisance grievances." OK, but what do you want *more of?* You cannot use the skills of the Appreciative Self to stop something, not directly. Appreciative processes are used to amplify things—to create inter-subjective reality by increasing the amount or frequency of something you want more of.

Second, for it to be a truly appreciative mind-set, you need to be calling to something that touches people's imagination, their aspirations and spirit. You may want one more widget produced, but that, in itself, isn't going to touch the hearts and minds of anyone. Opportunities to excel, make a difference, grow and develop, achieve our potential, be the best, live in community, make a better world, fulfill our dreams, gain new hope, surpass expectations, be a winner, enable the children, ennoble our spirit, be a part of a dynamic and caring team, be in real partnership with others, make a valued contribution—these are the kinds of things that an Appreciative Self pays attention to.

Jerry, a manager who was trying to develop his Appreciative Self, found himself stumped over a "problem person" who worked for him. Bernice had been in her job before he arrived and was protected by the union she belonged to. Jerry found her obnoxious and intimidating, with a minimal work ethic, and believed that she poisoned the whole atmosphere in the office. His attempts to give Bernice corrective feedback had met with sullen silence and no change in her attitude. He found himself stumped over what he wanted more of from Bernice. He tried out different ideas with me: "I want her to be nicer." "What's nicer?" I asked. He described what she would stop doing if she were nicer. "I want her to just do her job." "Does she do her job now?" I asked. Well, yes. "Actually she really knows her job but just doesn't care. That's it, I want her to care more." "What would it look like if she cared more?" But all he could come up with were things she would stop doing if she cared more. "You're going to have to work harder at figuring out what it is you want to see in her," I said.

Jerry was still trying to figure this out when, a few days later, he was in a meeting with his regional manager and his staff, including Bernice. His manager was describing a new service that they would begin to offer customers and his belief that they needed to transfer someone from another office with expertise to provide the service. Jerry said, "We don't need someone else. Bernice knows more about that than anyone we could transfer. Don't you, Bernice?" Bernice did not change her sullen expression but nodded her head, and the regional manager said, "OK, we'll start out with Bernice, but if you feel you need more support on this let me know," and the meeting concluded.

An hour later Bernice came back into Jerry's office with a list of ideas for how to launch the new service. Jerry was stunned; she had never taken initiative on anything before. He realized that an appreciative process had been set in motion. He now started to see the part of Bernice that wanted to be recognized as the best, as making a valued contribution, and he began tracking and fanning that part of her at every opportunity. Two weeks later when I saw Jerry he was buoyant at the change in Bernice. "She still uses coarse language and makes fun of me, but I have to say that she has really turned around in terms of her work. She actually stayed late at the office last week, and other people are noticing it too." Jerry hadn't realized what he was doing when he praised Bernice in front of his boss and her peers, but he had the where- withal to quickly capitalize on it because he was working on developing an appreciative mind-set.

Developing an appreciative mind-set is not something most of us can do overnight. I have met a few people who seem to be naturals at it. For most of us, however, it is a lifelong task to focus less on what's not right and focus, instead, on what is right. I'll offer you some techniques for developing your appreciative mind-set at the end of the chapter.

Tracking

Once you know what you want more of, then you start "tracking" it. The image here is of a hunter tracking game in the jungle. It takes constant attention, a light step, and seeing the clues hidden in the sur- rounding foliage. It is, most profoundly, the ability to see what you want more of as already being there. After 10 years of teaching man- agers (and myself) the skills of the Appreciative Self I've concluded that this is the toughest part: developing your ability to see what you want more of as already there in the people and systems you work in. Sometimes you just have to start with a leap of faith.

A team from Healthy World, a non-governmental organization, had entered the small, war-torn African country to get permission from the current ruler to allow them to begin inoculating children against diarrhea,

one of the major causes of infant mortality. There were reports that gov-
ernment forces were killing women and children in outlying villages, and
just before the audience with the ruler someone had put a videotape
into Jack's hands, showing a recent massacre. The irony of inoculating
children who might then be gunned down was not lost on Jack, the
team leader, and he decided to try and do something about it.

When he was given an audience with the ruler he explained their desire
to inoculate the children and asked for permission to do so, which he
was given. He then also asked the ruler if he would help to open the
first clinic to begin "saving the children of your country." The ruler
agreed to do that. Then, in a risky move, Jack asked for a videotape
machine and played the tape of the ruler's troops massacring women
and children. Nothing more was said except to thank the ruler for having
given his permission to "save the children of your country."

A few days later when the outdoor clinic was set up and mothers were
lined up with children to get the inoculations, the Healthy World staff
put the syringe in the ruler's hands and invited him to give the injec-
tions. As the long line of thankful mothers, joyful over the blessing they
were receiving at the hand of their ruler, moved past, the Healthy World
staff kept saying to him, "You are saving the children of your country.
Now you really are the father of your nation." The ruler so enjoyed him-
self he decided to cancel all his engagements and spent the next few
weeks traveling with the clinic throughout the country, personally inocu-
lating children and being reminded over and over that "now you really
are the father of your nation." The massacres stopped.

In this case, Jack and his staff looked for and found the part of this warlord that cared about the people he ruled. It wasn't something that people would have instantly seen in this man. In a sense, they had to take a leap of faith and look hard for every sign of compassion in him with the appreciative mind-set that there was a part of him that want-ed to be and could be amplified into "the father of his nation."

It's easy to track something when it already exists in abundance. One senior manager I know personally tours his far-flung operations twice a year. He spends one or two days at each location while man-agers and employees make presentations on the best improvements they've made in one of three areas: increased operating efficiency, customer satisfaction, and product improvement. His expectation is that the people who were personally involved in the improvements will make the presentations. If he believes there's more potential in an idea or a group of people, he will give them more resources to keep doing whatever they are doing. In a sense, he has trained his managers to do his tracking for him, and his personal attention and methods of amplification ensure a steady stream of improvements for him to fan.

But it can be difficult to track something when we don't see it there in the first place. This is the tough part of tracking and is what makes the appreciative process more than just positive reinforcement. The Appreciative Self begins with the assumption that whatever we want more of already exists, if only in tiny quantities. We begin by believing in the best in people and organizations. We have to get over the belief that our experience is "the truth" and assume we can have a different experience by changing our map. Numerous managers I've taught this technique to have discovered that when they start to look for something they didn't think was there, they start to see it. The more attention they pay to it (fanning), the more of it they get. Let me tell you one more dramatic story.

Tim, the consultant, flew in for his usual monthly two-day plant visit and as usual was met at the airport by Fred, the operations manager. Tim had been working at the plant for six months and was credited with having helped create a lot of positive change in work relationships, which was paying off in productivity and quality improvements. Fred, however, met Tim at the airport with a tale of doom and gloom. Two weeks ago the replacement for the regional vice-president, who was physically based at this plant, took up his new position. The new RVP, Eric, had a reputation throughout the company as ruthless, demanding, aggressive, manipulative, and very hard to work for. But as a plant manager in another region he had gotten results in more than one operation, and that had led to this promotion. Tim's clear leadership style seemed the complete opposite of Eric's style, and Fred thought that Eric would quickly pull the plug on Tim's consultancy. As they drove back to the plant Fred regaled Tim with stories of Eric's abusive behavior since his arrival. Things sounded very bad indeed. Tim decided to try to keep an open mind.

Once Tim arrived at the plant a number of people came up to him to talk about their despair over the changes since Eric had arrived. At 10 that morning the usual management meeting took place, but the atmosphere was even worse than it had been when Tim first started working there. Sure enough, Eric was bossy, sarcastic, and demeaning. People were completely closed down and no truth-telling was going on. Tim decided that he would not be able to do anything for them if he got caught up in their sense of helplessness and doom. Instead, he began tracking the part of Eric that wanted to be a wise, compassionate, and loved leader. He looked and looked, and noticed at one point in the meeting that Eric offered some good ideas about how to deal with a personnel problem. At a break Tim mentioned how wise and compassionate that idea was. Over the next two days Tim was in the presence of Eric six more times, and each time he ignored everything else about Eric and just paid attention to the part of him that wanted to be loved as a leader. Whenever he saw Eric do something that had the slightest wisdom or compassion he said something about it.

During lunch of the second day Eric sent a message to Tim that he wanted to see him before he left for the day. Everyone, including Tim, assumed that Tim was going to be given the pink slip and that would be the end of that. When Tim went to see Eric, however, something quite different happened. Eric almost broke down as he described to Tim his realization that he had gotten where he was by being ruthless, demanding, and aggressive, but that he was at a management level now where those characteristics would not be effective and that he was scared and didn't know what to do. He asked Tim to help him, and the work went on from there.

It seems obvious to me, and I'm sure it is to you, that if Tim had paid attention to what he didn't like in Eric's behavior he would have quickly been shown the door. Using an appreciative mind-set and tracking the best parts of Eric allowed that part of Eric to recognize an ally—someone who saw what others weren't seeing—and created enough trust in him to confide his doubts and fears to Tim. Let's face it, who are you going to go to for help and advice? Someone who sees the worst in you or someone who sees the best in you? The Appreciative Self creates followership by tracking the best in people and fanning it when he sees it.

Someone who is good at tracking is constantly looking for what she wants more of, without presuppositions of where she'll find it. A friend and I went to a conference where the leaders of two dozen hand-picked, successful NGOs had been invited to talk with academics about processes of change across political and economic boundaries. We were excited about our expectation that we would be able to witness some of the world's best trackers in action over the coming week. We ended up a little disappointed, however, at how little tracking we saw. But one image has always stayed with me and it says a lot about the difference between the trackers and the rest. Everyone would come into a large conference room between sessions for major speeches or to discuss what was being learned at the conference. Most people would walk in, find a seat, and sit down. But the really good trackers did not sit down. They stood up along the walls on the sides of the room. They were constantly wandering about talking to anyone and everyone. You might call this "good networking," and it is, except the trackers weren't just collecting contacts; they had larger game they were stalking. There was something each of them was looking for more of. I have since learned that I can often tell who the good trackers are just by noticing how much each person moves around in a crowd. Good tracking takes constant motion, looking for more and more of the thing being tracked, never assuming you know where you'll find it.

Fanning

Fanning means to metaphorically blow air on a small fire to turn it into a roaring blaze. You are fanning when you look for ways to increase what you want more of. You could call it positive reinforcement, though fanning strategies can be more inventive than that. But simply paying attention to what you want in itself tends to amplify it. There is some evidence that any kind of attention, even negative attention, tends to amplify whatever is being attended to. In many situations attention is a kind of reinforcement.

In a company-sponsored leadership training course where I talked about appreciative processes as one of a set of change-management options, a woman approached me at the break to tell me she finally understood what she was doing. Right out of high school she had begun as a clerk at a customer service center of this large company and after many years became the store's supervisor. The store, located in a major city, consistently ranked high on productivity and customer satisfaction (though she never understood why they got better ratings than others), and six months ago she had been promoted to regional manager of a small non-urban region with a dozen centers. The very next day she had an appointment with the president of the company to tell him how she had been able to propel the region from an 83 percent customer satisfaction

> *rating to 92 percent, something unheard of in the company. She said,*
> *"Thank God I took this course because I did not know what I was going*
> *to say to the man. But now I see it. I just pay attention to what they*
> *are doing well and ignore what I don't like. It's what I've always done."*

In my early years as a researcher and consultant, when I did lots of interviews and gave managers anonymous feedback, I found a number of common complaints, no matter what organization I was in. One of the most common was the reaction to the question "What do people get rewarded for around here?" Workers and lower-level managers would almost invariably laugh or shake their heads and say something like "Rewards?! You don't get rewarded for anything around here. The only time you ever hear anything is when something's wrong. If you do a great job well, that's what you're supposed to do and no one pays any attention. But as soon as there's a problem you sure hear about that!" No wonder that, in such environments, the simple act of noticing the great job people do daily can lead to leaps of improvement in quality and productivity.

Praise

In addition to just paying attention to what you want more of, you can fan through praise, blessing, and asking for more. *Praise* refers to appreciating something that has already happened. When we are praising we are calling attention to something that has already been done and appreciating it. For any fanning process to be effective, it has to be sincere. Many companies have "employee of the month" kinds of programs, which are intended to use praise as a positive motivator. Such programs, however, will just get chewed up in the interpersonal mush if the person or committee doing the praising is not really operating from an appreciative mind-set. If the praise is just the result of some impersonal mechanism (e.g., most widgets sold) it can act as an incentive for some people, but it is not an appreciative process. Poorly thought-through praising programs can sometimes have the opposite effect from that intended. I know of one company that tried to influence its managers to improve their employee relations by having employees vote for the best supervisor of the month. What happened was that the supervisor widely seen as the most lax and ineffective won the first vote and then there was a race to the bottom as some other supervisors tried to win votes by coddling the employees. This created friction between those supervisors who were willing to do that and those who believed they were trying to do their best for the company. The latter became more and more disenchanted and upset with employees who saw their fellows getting more and more coddled, and employee relations got worse instead of better.

Any sincere praise can have a fanning effect when it provides positive reinforcement, but praise can have a deeper significance. The great psychologist Heinz Kohut has shown that praise from someone we look up to is an indispensable way in which we develop a strong Self.[7] We continue to deepen and strengthen our Self all our lives, and I believe this kind of praise is just as necessary to adults as it is to children. For praise to have this kind of impact on adults, however, it must come from someone seen as a good authority. To describe what I mean by "good authority," we need to step back for a moment and understand the notion of psychological archetype.

Carl Jung, another great psychologist, coined the term *archetype* to describe bundles of image, affect, and intention that transcend time and culture. They are like templates that are hard-wired into the human mind. Jung's theory is that we are all influenced by a collection of ancient urges, desires, and inclinations. At most times in the history of humankind these have been talked about through myths and stories. These urges and desires tend to have a coherence: the urge to overpower, for instance, goes with the urge to protect. When we see a person who tends to overpower we may also notice a willingness to protect others. These bundles of qualities get personified into the characters who populate our myths and stories. In this case Jungians would talk about a *warrior archetype*—a template with common characteristics that appears as a soldier or hunter or knight in the stories and myths of all human cultures.

What makes Jung's and his followers' arguments so compelling is that the same images and stories reappear time and again, in all economic levels of society and in all cultures. They can be seen in all human art, poetry, scientific discoveries, and religion, and in our patterns of thought and feeling. It is as though the human race projects these deep structures onto things that we create. The stories and images that tap this structure most clearly are the ones a society retains and tells itself over and over. Some stories seem to be closer to the source, and as such they offer advice and wisdom on what it means to be human and how to lead a life worth living.[8]

Robert Moore, a Jungian scholar, theologian, and psychotherapist who has studied myths and legends, has identified a deep part of the unconscious mind that has needs, feelings, and potentials, which he has

Bad Authority	Good Authority
Seeks adoration and being the center of attention	Adores others and makes them the center of attention
Self-serving	Serves the people
Has a vision of own greatness	Has a vision of the great society, culture, organization
Blames others	Takes responsibility
Holds on to power	Steps aside when it is appropriate to do so

come to call the "King archetype."[9] The King archetype is very instructive for learning about leadership. It is as though our beliefs and feelings about the difference between "good authority" and "bad authority" are hard-wired into us as human beings. I have found the study of "ritual kingship" the best map for understanding the kind of leadership people want to follow and the kind they do not. Listed above are some of the key differences in the stories of the "good king" (good authority) and the "shadow king" (bad authority) that seem to exist in all cultures through the ages.

I believe there is a yearning today in Western culture for the good king and queen, for leaders we can trust to put the needs of the whole ahead of their personal interests, who are more interested in their vision of the great team, organization, or society than in their own personal grandiosity. There seem to be so few of them in business and government that when one comes along her power to elicit followership appears truly astounding.

One of Moore's important insights is that a core function of the King and Queen archetype is to give others praise and blessing. The bad King (or Queen) demands that he be the center of attention, that he be seen as the smartest, the strongest, the quickest, the best. From the shadow king's point of view his employees are there to admire and adore him, to praise and bless him. Such leaders, however, create deep and suffocating interpersonal mush around them, stifling the potential of the people they have power over and leaving a toxic work environment in their wake.

The good Queen (or King), however, makes others the center of attention. In her presence others feel bigger, smarter, stronger, more able. The Queen's job is to admire and adore her employees, to praise them and, in doing so, help them become more than they thought they could be. Anyone who has ever had a good King or Queen in his life (as a parent, coach, teacher, boss, or other authority) knows exactly what I am talking about—that merely being in her presence leaves you feeling more capable and motivated than you felt before. It literally strengthens your Self.

Praise serves to fan most when it comes from a leader in whom we see some of the good King or Queen. A leader with an appreciative mind-set has some of that going for her already. When praise comes sincerely from a leader who embodies the Appreciative Self, it is amplified. The same is true of *blessing*. While praise is about the past, blessing is about the future. When we bless something or someone we are giving them license to continue being what they are. Again, getting a "blessing" from a manager who just attended a course and is following his three-blessings-a-day program doesn't have much kick. But a blessing from a leader who sincerely appreciates what you are doing has an impact. And when blessing comes wrapped in tangibles, like money or resources to increase what you are doing, amplification is assured.

One of the first acts of blessing I witnessed early in my career had a big impact on my understanding of the power of appreciative process.

A regional manager who had come to the plant was shown what two skilled tradesmen had devised in their spare time. Using some discarded circuit boards and electronic parts they had gotten the maintenance superintendent to buy for them, they had been able to get two different machines on the production line to "talk to each other." They had, in fact, invented the basics for a crude programmable controller, now a mainstay of any modern manufacturing plant. At the time, however, these did not exist. The general manager said, "I've just spent the last week being told by our engineering staff that what you two have done is impossible!" He then, on the spot, gave them half a million dollars to spend however they saw fit to extend their work. You want to talk about two incredibly motivated, pumped-up guys! It affected not only them. Everyone in the plant took pride in their accomplishment and the blessing they received, and that helped to amplify their efforts in numerous ways as everyone pitched in to make them more successful.

Meta Fanning

Anything that amplifies what you want more of is fanning. A lot of things fall into the categories of attention, praise, and blessing, and these seem to be the mainstay of fanning. But people can be ingenious in the ways they come up with to amplify what they are tracking. Meta fanning is what I call their strategies for getting someone else to do their fanning for them. I've seen people use the local newspapers for giving attention, and apply for company or industry reward programs for generating praise and blessing for others. Getting a respected authority to give out the attention and praise can have a powerful impact.

Meta fanning is also about finding positive ways to deal with what appear to be obstacles to getting more of what you want. One of my favorite meta-fanning stories comes from the first clear leader I ever saw in action.

Janice, a young quality supervisor who had shown an interest in Japanese quality methods, had been placed on special assignment to help implement Quality Circles. At the time, Quality Circles, where employees meet in groups on company time to identify and solve problems in their areas, were a very new idea. Being a natural clear leader, she decided to work from strength, and targeted the skilled trades area as a place to start. Employees there were used to taking initiative and solving problems. She found a couple of supervisors who supported the idea and began two Quality Circles using company-sponsored materials.

After about a month she got wind from the supervisors that their general supervisor was not at all supportive of the Quality Circles. Rob, the general supervisor, did not think it was a good idea to have employees meeting on company time doing the work of supervisors. He figured the workers would just goof off or come up with demands that management would not be able to meet. He was worried that other employees would demand the same "hour off work" and his efficiencies would go down. Janice's attempts to persuade him otherwise had no effect. He hadn't done anything yet because his supervisors were committed, but it looked like it was just a matter of time before he would pull the plug.

Janice thought that Jim, the plant superintendent, who was Rob's boss's boss, would be quite excited by the issues the Quality Circles were talking about. She put together the minutes from previous meetings of the circles and showed them to Jim. As she expected, Jim was excited by what he saw. The skilled tradesmen were discussing issues that were always causing the department problems, and any solutions they came up with would really make a difference. Janice said, "What I'd really like you to do is go see Rob and tell him how much you like what the circles are doing and ask him to keep up the good work—and it might be better if you didn't mention you heard about it from me." That's just what Jim did. And Rob became a supporter of Quality Circles.

Notice how different this is from more traditional power plays and the use of authority to deal with issues. Janice reported to the plant manager who supported Quality Circles and could have asked him to "get Rob in line." But that would only have created a more resentful adversary out of Rob and could have created problems in her work with other supervisors. As a change strategy, appreciative process doesn't create the negative repercussions that "push" methods and "burning platforms" do. Appreciative processes are more likely to create the strong social bonds, good feelings, and sense of camaraderie that sustained organizational change requires.

Meta-fanning strategies depend on the circumstances and situation and are only as limited as your imagination. One of my favorite examples comes from the Peter Mayle book *A Year in Provence*, in which he is trying to get a host of different tradesmen to finish the renovations to his house. Anyone who has suffered through a major renovation, with contractors and subcontractors who are always disappearing before anything is finished, can relate to that. Work has now dragged on for close to a year with no end in sight when Peter's wife comes up with a brilliant meta-fan. She gets the contractors to agree that the work could be finished before the end of the year (of course, I could finish my part if those other people would finish theirs) and then invites them and their wives to a Christmas party at their home. This will give the wives an opportunity to see the husbands' handiwork. What happens next is that no husband, of course, is willing to be the source of his wife's loss of face in front of any of the other wives by not having his part of the renovations complete. The pace of repairs speeds up and everything is done in time for the party.

Exercises to Develop Your Appreciative Self

Appreciative Mind-Set

Sometimes it's hard to have an appreciative mind-set, just because life ain't that good. With all the stress and problems we face we can lose any sense of appreciation. Depression, too, can make it very difficult to pay much attention to the best in ourselves and others. I have found one thing that has worked for me and others that makes a big difference in my ability to have an appreciative mind-set (and get over non–chemically based depression). I call it "the gratitudes." It is simply spending a few minutes, twice a day, thinking about what I am grateful for. I invented this at a time when nothing in life seemed good to me. At first I would exhaust my list of gratitudes in about 15 seconds! But I would try to sit out the five minutes I allotted to the exercise trying to think of other things, and feeling almost guilty that I had so little I was grateful for. One effect of this was that I started to notice people who had it worse than me. I could at least be grateful that my life was better than theirs. Slowly I began to notice that I really did have a lot to be grateful for, and this spiraled into more and more gratitude until one day, a few months after I had started doing the gratitudes, I noticed that I was walking down the street with a smile on my face for no apparent reason at all. I was easily able to fill up five minutes with things I was grateful for, and realized that I didn't need to be doing the gratitudes anymore. Every now and then, however, when something is making it hard for me to be appreciative at work or at home, I do the gratitudes for a few weeks and it always makes it easier to track what I want more of in others.

You can do the gratitudes out loud with your partner or just silently to yourself.

Tracking and Fanning

1. Tracking and fanning go together, so although they are two separate skills, you really practice them together. To practice tracking and fanning, think of some behavior you'd like more of from someone at home or at work. Remember, it can't be something you want less of disguised as something you want more of. With your partner identify what, exactly, you'll see if and when you see more of it. Pick someone that is low-risk; if this blows up in your face it'll pass with minimal damage.

   Then simply be on the lookout for it. When you see it, notice it, praise it, bless it, and ask for more. If it is a behavior you don't think you'll ever see without some prompting, tell the person what you want more of and then fan like heck as soon as you see it. For example, one of my students wanted his mother to get along better with her sons-in-law and daughters-in-law and decided that she needed to talk less and listen more at family dinners. He began by talking with her about her relationships with her in-laws, using the appreciative mind-set that she wanted good relationships, and discovered that indeed she did, but she didn't know how to get them. So he asked for what he wanted. He asked her, at the next family dinner, to talk less and listen more, to be curious about others and to ask questions. At the next dinner she did, and he fanned, and the rest is history.

Review with your partner, at regular intervals, how you are doing. Together, think up some meta-fanning strategies.

2. If it's an attribute or attitude you want more of, tracking is trickier. Then you have to see it yourself, behind the person's behavior. Remember the stories of the "father of his nation" and Eric, the leader who wanted to be wise and compassionate. Here is where tracking is the hardest. You need to assume that the attribute you want more of is indeed behind the actions you see.

If you find tracking an attribute difficult, start by choosing one attribute you want to see more of in people in general, something like generosity or thoughtfulness. Then, at work, in every interaction you have, assume that attribute exists in everyone you deal with, even if just in little ways. Work at noticing when it might be present in their behavior. Don't worry about fanning it, just pay attention to it. You'll notice that you forget to track, sometimes rather quickly. Just start tracking again. See how long you can keep tracking for that attribute before forgetting. Each day, try to increase the amount of time you spend tracking it until you can go for hours without losing track. When you start being able to see the attribute you are looking for in most people, review with your partner any differences you are noticing in your interactions with people.

Summary

Clear leaders are not averse to problem-solving, it's just that they recognize that their effort and impact are greater if they leave the problem-solving to the people doing the work and use their attention differently.

By focusing on what is working well, on solutions that already exist, on the qualities of teams and people they want more of, they improve organizations through amplification. Instead of using their time and energy to shore up weakness, they build on strength. Clear leaders get clear about what they want more of and search for more of that.

Being an Appreciative Self requires developing an appreciative mind-set and the skills of tracking and fanning. An appreciative mind-set requires a map that says that your beliefs have an impact on the world you inhabit and that you get more of whatever you pay attention to. The Appreciative Self is about attending to and noticing those things that call out the best in us as people—the kinds of things most of us value, hope for, and want in our work lives. An appreciative mind-set is focused not on identifying and fixing what we want less of, but on tracking and fanning what we want more of.

One of the really neat things about appreciative process as a method of leadership is that it can be used by anyone regardless of his level of authority. You may have noticed that in a number of the examples in this chapter the person using appreciative process didn't have authority over the person he was tracking and fanning. Anyone can use appreciative process to influence others but, like anything else, power amplifies the effect. Using appreciative process, a supervisor can influence a few people (including people with more authority). A CEO, however, can influence a whole organization.

Tracking involves seeing what you want more of as already there. You can't fan something you can't see. Sometimes it requires a leap of faith to believe that the positive qualities or attributes you want more of are already there. Sometimes tracking requires seeing the subtle clues and tiny instances that give you a place to start fanning. Tracking is about seeing the good intentions people have in even their weirdest behavior. Most of all, tracking requires not taking all the positive effort, skills, imagination, and motivation people bring to the job every day for granted.

Fanning is about turning the little flame of positive potential into a roaring fire. By simply paying attention to something you tend to get more of it, but praise, blessing, and asking for more can go a long way in amplifying your efforts. Praise and blessing have to be sincere, and the more they come from someone (or some organization) that people have respect for, the more impact they have. When they come from someone we see as a "good King or Queen," praise and blessing are a potent kind of psychological food that strengthens our Self. That, in turn, helps to strengthen and increase our ability and motivation to do more of whatever we are being praised for. The consummate Appreciative Self uses meta fanning, leveraging her fanning efforts and removing obstacles through appreciative processes.

PART THREE

Clear Leadership at Work

Improving Organizational Learning

I am convinced that in business the only sustainable competitive advantage is the capacity to learn faster than your competitors.[1] The new, destructured, empowered organizations exist because they can learn and innovate more quickly than bureaucratic organizations. But simply getting rid of the rule book and encouraging self-management does not mean that people will be able to learn from their experience together. First people have to get out of interpersonal mush and into interpersonal clarity. It appears to me that getting clarity—that place where people really understand each other—is one of the things that separates high-performance organizations from the rest. I am still surprised how common it is for people in organizations to have different perceptions about what the goals are, what the strategy is, what the priorities are, and who is responsible for what. You'd think these would be basic areas of clarity and agreement, but often they are actually areas of considerable confusion.

People I describe as clear leaders work at developing clarity in their teams and organizations. They do that through using the four skills I have described: the Aware Self, the Descriptive Self, the Curious Self, and the Appreciative Self. When leaders who are self-aware balance description and curiosity they create organizations where clarity is the rule. When problem patterns appear, these leaders are able to use *organizational learning conversations* to get clear about what the patterns really are and what sustains them. Simply being willing to inquire into them changes them. The process of a learning conversation is useful in many avenues of life, but it is a critical act of leadership in empowered organizations.

The Organizational Learning Conversation[2]

I introduced my approach to organizational learning in Chapter 1. Organizational learning takes place when two or more people inquire into their experience and generate new knowledge that leads to a change in their patterns of organizing. Patterns of organizing are the typical interactions you have at work, the way you and others go about identifying and solving problems, dealing with conflicts, making decisions, assessing performance, serving customers, managing stakeholders, communicating up and down the hierarchy, budgeting, and so on. The purpose of organizational learning is to change ineffective patterns of interaction that are hampering performance and/or motivation.

There are a number of reasons that normal conversations at work rarely result in a change in problem patterns. Part of the problem, as I described in an earlier chapter, is a lack of awareness of one's experience and one's maps in use. Part of the problem is interpersonal mush: people are sense-making and don't realize they need to describe their experience to each other. Part of the problem is that people don't know what they want more of—only what they want less of. Part of it is that we are often so clear on how the other person is the problem that it never occurs to us to inquire into how we ourselves are contributing to the problem pattern.

Much of the tendency to avoid discussion of problem patterns comes from the desire to avoid anxiety. When people at work have a discussion about problems of organizing and what is needed to fix them, two things tend to happen out of a desire to avoid anxiety, and they make these discussions unproductive. First, the discussions often take place without key people who are part of the problem pattern being present. Usually these are the ones considered the problem people, and the discussion focuses on how to change them. Second, if the problem person is present, the separation and/or intimacy anxiety (feelings of embarrassment or shame) created by the discussion leads people to look for quick resolutions. Only the surface manifestations of the problems get discussed, the most visible behaviors and most visible effects on performance. Without a deeper exploration of the underlying experiences, lasting changes to these patterns are rarely found.

To have a productive discussion of problem patterns at work, a discussion that will lead to clarity and the possibility of change and improvement in the pattern, something different needs to happen.

People need to have an *organizational learning conversation*. The people who are part of the problem pattern must be part of the conversation. Very little change can happen if people who are part of the problem pattern are not involved in learning conversations together. These conversations need to take place with an attitude of inquiry. They begin with people describing and listening to each other's experience about the problem pattern without trying to intellectually define the problem or fix it. People describe their experience to each other until interpersonal clarity is reached.

The purpose of a learning conversation is not to explain or justify myself or try to change you. It is not an exercise in each listening to what the other wants and then trying to find a compromise. It is an inquiry in which I focus on making my internal experience transparent to you and on understanding as fully as I can your internal experience. There is no right or wrong, just your experience and my experience. That we each will be having a different experience is guaranteed, and that's not wrong, that's natural. That we will have made up stories about each other is not wrong, it's only natural. The only thing that is wrong is the interpersonal mush between us.

Let me give you an example of a learning conversation.

I was running a week-long training program for 35 managers to teach them the skills described in this book while working on real organizational issues. There was a staff of six trainers. Because of the flexibility of this course, we met frequently to discuss what was happening and what to do next. On the evening of the third night one of the staff, Bruce, voiced his desire to spend most of next day working with the small group he was leading. The rest of the staff thought that other, large-group activities were more appropriate. At this point I noticed Bruce did not participate much as we developed a plan for the next day. On the morning of the fourth day I announced the day's schedule to the assembled participants. From the back of the room Bruce called out, "What? What's the plan?" I reiterated it. He said, "That's the plan?! When did that plan get decided?" I was starting to feel a little annoyed but tried not to show it as I said, "Last night at dinner." At this point he turned away, walked toward the back of the room, and muttered loudly, "Hmmm—I wonder where I was when that plan was decided."

Later that day the entire group of 35 managers was involved in a very tense and emotional discussion as people were finally telling the truth of their experience about some recent changes that had taken place in the organization. I was leading this segment of the workshop and had some clear goals about where interpersonal clarity needed to be increased. At one point a manager, Heather, voiced some issues that were important to her but that I considered tangential to the larger purpose of the session. She had finished talking and another person was about to speak when Bruce stepped in and said, "I want to hear more from Heather." At that point I said, "I think what Heather has to say is important but I'm concerned that we only have so much time and it is not focused on the issue we are dealing with here." Bruce said, "Yeah, well I still want to hear more from Heather." I looked at him pointedly, raised my voice, and said "NO." Bruce looked startled, turned on his heel, and walked back to his seat.

It was obvious to everyone in the room that Bruce and I had a problem pattern. A few hours later we met to have a learning conversation about it. By this point I had gotten myself worked up at Bruce's "acting out" because he hadn't gotten his way. I thought his behavior that morning had been completely uncalled for and was feeling pretty self-righteous, especially because, in my mind, Bruce is more rigid about not letting others interfere in a session he is leading than I am. Here is how that went.

Bruce: *I need to talk about what happened this afternoon. I have to tell you that I did not like how you talked to me and I'm still angry about it.*

Gervase: *Yeah, well, I didn't like how I acted either, but obviously I was angry and that came out.*

Bruce: *Yeah, I've been wondering if something started going on before that incident.*

Gervase: *Of course! After what you did this morning I was pretty upset.*

Bruce: *This morning? What did I do this morning?*

At that point I started to describe to him the story I had made up about his behavior first thing in the morning. In my mind, he was still wanting to spend time in his small group and resisting the design the rest of us had agreed on. When he turned and muttered the way he did, I thought that he was complaining that his views had not been considered. I did not like him acting this way in front of the participants after the decisions had been made.

Bruce listened calmly to all of this and asked some questions to get clear about my experience. As I talked more about it I realized that I had started getting upset with him the night before. My story, which I hadn't been fully aware of, was that he stopped participating in the design conversation because he didn't get his way. By the morning I was already seeing him as petulant, and that affected how I experienced his behavior. Then I thought that he was attacking my leadership, so by the time the incident occurred in the afternoon I was primed to experience Bruce's actions as attacks on my authority. My outburst was as much in response to thinking that he was being very inappropriate in managing his petulance as from feeling attacked.

Bruce asked me questions until he and I both thought that he was clear about my experience, and then he told me his. He had not been aware that he was not participating the night before but now realized that he had been preoccupied by some bad news he had received when he'd called home before dinner. He did not care that we did not meet in the small groups—it had been his preference but not a strong preference. That morning he really had not remembered the design conversation from the night before, and his loud mutter as he turned his back was mocking himself, not me. At that moment he had felt guilty about not having been tuned in to the design for the day and was mentally attacking himself, not me, for having zoned out. So, completely unaware of the experience I was having, he was pretty shocked when I yelled at him that afternoon.

After we got completely clear about each other's experience, Bruce said that he sometimes has this effect on people—they feel he is challenging their leadership. He isn't conscious of wanting to challenge their leadership and wants to learn more about how he creates that impression in others. Bruce owned that he had a part in this pattern that is still outside his awareness and he is learning more about it. I owned that the problem started for me during the planning meeting at dinner but that I wasn't paying attention to it and it got out of hand. I realized that I should have checked the story I was making up about Bruce withdrawing because he didn't get his way instead of letting it fester just on the edge of my awareness (something I do too much of). I also owned that when I don't get my way I sometimes withdraw and act petulant, and that I had projected this onto Bruce.

I asked Bruce how he felt about my leadership and he assured me that he was perfectly satisfied with the way I was running the workshop. He asked me how I felt about his participation and I assured him that except for that meeting I was very pleased with his contributions.

We did not have any more problems for the rest of the time we worked with that organization. In fact, Bruce is one of my favorite consultants to work with.

That learning conversation lasted about 20 minutes. As you can see, once I began describing my experience I got clearer about my experience of Bruce. When he understood my experience he was able to describe his own experience and show me where my sense-making was way off. Once we got clear about each other's experience, the problem went away. Like so many organizational problems, the real issue was that he and I were operating from completely different maps and I had an inaccurate map about him. Notice that we spent no time discussing whether Heather should have been given more air time. That would have been irrelevant to understanding the underlying issues I was developing around Bruce. If we had simply focused on that and gotten into a debate about who was right, probably nothing useful would have resulted. Yet how many arguments at work revolve around who's right and lead to little or no change?

Imagine if we worked together every day but had not had a learning conversation about this incident. Can you imagine the stories Bruce and I would continue to make up about each other, the amount of conflict we'd experience, the reduction in our ability to work effectively together, and, ultimately, how we'd like going to work less and less because we'd each have to deal with "that jerk"? Does that go on between people who have to work together in organizations everywhere, every day? You bet it does. And organizations have been able to continue to pump out products and services and make money in spite of it.

As I described in Chapter 1, bureaucratic organizations can function adequately in this state of affairs. But empowered organizations can't do that. They rely on people working together to get things done. They can limp along, surviving in interpersonal mush as long as their competitors are not using the skills of clear leadership in their teams and organization, but they never achieve anything close to their potential without people having learning conversations, when needed, on a day-to-day basis.

Let me be clear about something I haven't said explicitly yet. I am not advocating that you go through life being a Descriptive Self all the time. Not at all. Not even most of the time. I am not advocating that most discussions at work be learning conversations either. If people in an organization full of interpersonal mush had just one learning conversation a week, that would make all the difference in the world. A learning conversation is something that needs to happen when there is a problem pattern that is worth putting energy into changing. Clear leaders pick and choose whom to have learning conversations with and when to have them. These conversations take time, effort, sincerity, and the right attitude. There are people I do not trust to level with me whom I have no authority over, who might stab me in the back if I weren't looking, and I would be crazy to be a Descriptive Self with them. They are not people I expect to have learning conversations with.

The Learning Conversation Process

In a learning conversation one person describes his experience, using the experience cube to remember to describe all his observations, thoughts, feelings, and wants, and any stories he is making up. The other person is curious until she is clear about the other's experience. She asks questions to fully understand the other person's experience. Then they switch roles. They go back and forth until they are completely clear as shown in the diagram. If you go back to the example of Pierre and Stan in the first chapter, or the example of Bruce and me in this chapter, you will see that this is what is happening. After you have gained clarity you then go on to issues of agreement, discussed in the next chapter.

Another way to say this is that a learning conversation is a process of both people using their Aware Self, Descriptive Self, and Curious Self. They switch these roles, back and forth, until they've developed clarity about the issue. Sometimes just that level of inquiry will lead to a change in the pattern itself. Sometimes clarity by itself is not enough because there is some other reason why you can't agree on what to do next. In the next chapter I will show you how to use clear leadership to develop and maintain agreements.

Let me remind you that I am not advocating that every interaction be a learning conversation. Far from it. But if you want to be a manager who creates outstanding teams and organizations, I am advocating that you be more descriptive of your experience of those things your subordinates are most likely to be sense-making about, things that most affect them, so that the stories they make up about you will be

STEPS IN AN ORGANIZATIONAL LEARNING CONVERSATION

Step	The Initiator	The Other
1	Check that you are willing to learn about yourself in this conversation. Check that the other is willing to explore this issue with you at this time in this place. Ask them to have a learning conversation with you.	Tell the truth about your readiness to learn about yourself, the initiator, and your relationship. Set another time and place if you need to.
2	Use the experience cube to describe your experience of the problem pattern. Check to ensure the other understands you. Once you feel finished, say so.	Actively listen and seek clarity about the other's experience and maps. Use the experience cube to guide your listening. Check to see if they are finished once you think you fully understand them.
3	Actively listen and seek clarity about the other's experience and maps. Use the experience cube to guide your listening. Check to see if they are finished once you think you fully understand them.	Describe your here and now experience—the impact of what you have just heard. Use the experience cube to describe your experience of the problem pattern. Own what was true about the other's experience of you. Check to ensure the other understands you. Once you feel finished, say so.
4	Describe your here and now experience—the impact of what you have just heard. Use the experience cube to describe your current experience of the problem pattern. Own what was true about the other's experience of you. Check to ensure the other understands you. Once you feel finished, say so.	Actively listen and seek clarity about the other's experience and maps. Use the experience cube to guide your listening. Check to see if they are finished once you think you fully understand them.

Step	The Initiator	The Other
5	Continue this conversation until you are both clear about each other's thoughts, feelings, and wants and any relevant maps.	
6	State what you have learned about your part in the problem pattern.	
7	Describe what you are willing to do differently in the future. If you don't know, manage issues of agreement.	

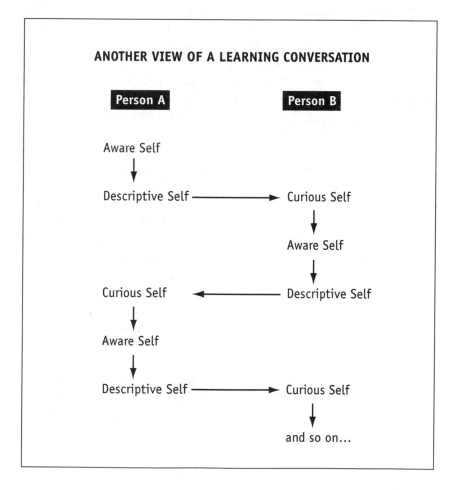

ANOTHER VIEW OF A LEARNING CONVERSATION

more accurate. And I am advocating that you be more curious about their experience, about the stories they are making up, about the maps they are using, about their thoughts, wants, and feelings. Similarly, if you want to be a professional who creates outstanding teams and organizations, I am advocating that you be more descriptive of your experience to your boss and co-workers and help them realize when interpersonal mush is present and work at developing interpersonal clarity. Helping create clarity at work is an indispensable act of leadership.

I've come to believe that a balanced approach of being descriptive and curious is one common trait among those who get great results working with people. You don't have to be an authority to use these skills to give leadership to your team, office, or department. By utilizing the skills of the Aware Self, the Descriptive Self, and the Curious Self you make a dent in the interpersonal mush and show others how they can too. If you have authority from your position in an organization as a supervisor, manager, executive, or owner, when you use these skills, your power amplifies the impact you have on developing a climate of interpersonal clarity. If you go further and ensure that the people who work for you know how to have learning conversations with you and with each other, insisting that doing so is part of their job, you are building a learning organization.

A learning conversation is a process that needs to be well managed, with a clear beginning and ending. And it requires the right attitudes. These are (1) everyone has a different experience and that is just how it is, no rights or wrongs; and (2) I am part of the system that is creating this problem pattern, and therefore have a part in it. The best attitude for entering a learning conversation is "What is my part in this problem?" The worst attitude for entering a learning conversation is "You need a lesson." And there is the rub, because we are most likely to want to have a learning conversation when we are having problems with another person. Sense-making processes being what they are, we probably already have a story in which he is the problem and he needs to change. If you try to use learning conversations to manipulate people into buying your story no one will really learn anything and people will just get more guarded when you next ask for a learning conversation. The best learning conversations are those where everyone learns something about how they contribute to the problem pattern.

No matter how many times I say this people don't seem to get it at first—a learning conversation is an *inquiry*. We are learning something together. It is not about fixing a problem or telling you what I really think or finding out what you really want. Any of those things might happen, but if you go into a learning conversation with those as your agenda you'll probably find yourself having the same kinds of conversations that lead nowhere. You need to think of a learning conversation as an attempt to understand what your part in problem patterns is. If people enter conversations with that attitude, they will have a different kind of conversation that will lead somewhere.

A leader has to model this and lead by example. In each learning conversation he has to own his part in the pattern. If the other doesn't own her part, he can express his disappointment and desire for her to continue to reflect and to talk to him until she does see her part in the problem pattern, but he will lose the fragile trust that is so critical to creating a climate of interpersonal clarity if he decides for her what her part in the problem is and bullies her into accepting it.

A map I've heard expressed by Ron Short that is useful for learning conversations goes as follows:

- I can't change you; only you can decide to change you.

- I probably can't really change myself all that much either—it took me a lot of years to get this way and that probably won't change overnight.

- But I can change our relationship pretty quickly if I choose to.

Let me own that my personal map is different. I think I can sometimes change people, at least amplify parts of them, through being an Appreciative Self. I also think I can, sometimes, change myself. But the idea that what I can mostly change is the relationship is a useful map when going into a learning conversation because it puts the focus of change not on the people but on the problem pattern, where it needs to be.

Bringing Appreciation to Organizational Learning

All of the skills and processes I've described in this book can be tinged with appreciation. Bringing an appreciative mind-set to organizational learning is about seeing the best in ourselves, others, and our

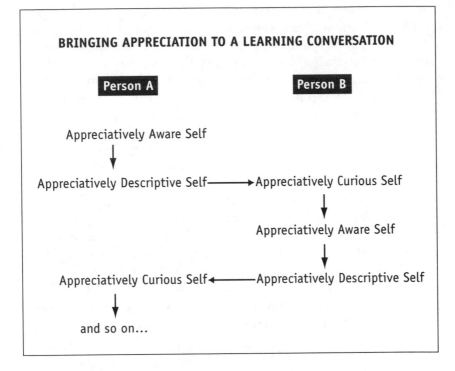

organizations even when we are trying to change problem patterns. As I describe in Chapter 10, getting past shame-based defenses in ourselves and others to uncover subjective truth is aided by compassion, a state of being most aligned with an appreciative mind-set. The Aware Self is aided by holding an appreciative mind-set even toward the negative parts of oneself. Embracing your humanity and lack of perfection as part of the greatness of the human condition helps to open you up to seeing your less-than-perfect thoughts, feelings, and wants. Seeing the positive intent in others helps the Curious Self to make it easier for others to tell their truth. Organizational Learning Conversations are less threatening when one or both people are operating from the Appreciative Self. A master at organizational learning conversations brings his Appreciative Self to the process as shown in the diagram above.

The process of a learning conversation is just as applicable to understanding high-performance patterns as it is to investigating a problem pattern. When we use awareness, curiosity, and description to understand the best in our work relationships and organizations, we are leveraging clear leadership with a powerful form of inquiry—

appreciative inquiry—that can lead to a virtuous cycle of improvement. In an appreciative inquiry we ask people to tell us their stories of work and the organization at its very best. These stories can then displace all the negative stories existing in the interpersonal mush and change the organization's inner dialogue.

One organization I worked with has a strong and deep (but changing) inner dialogue about the lack of "real leadership" in the organization. This, however, is not discussed openly. Publicly those in authority are praised and given accolades for their leadership prowess. But in the inner dialogue, just the opposite happens. Stories get passed around that depict authorities as gutless wonders who have no integrity, blow with whatever wind is strongest, and can only be relied on to act politically in their own self-interest. Little wonder, then, that almost none of the "soft" organizational strategies agreed upon during a major strategic planning exercise had been implemented three years later. The training department I was working with to develop leadership programs had no sense of partnership with senior managers, and instead tended to see them as, at best, an annoyance to be managed and, at worst, the enemy.

To redesign the leadership development process I talked the department into using an appreciative inquiry to gather stories about organizational leadership at its best. People from this department interviewed their executives about the greatest acts of leadership the executives had seen in the organization as well as what they considered their own peak leadership experiences. The interviewers were stunned by the stories their executives told—almost always stories about great personal integrity and courage where someone took the "right" stand even though it was politically unpopular or highly risky. Old stories about events from the past that involved these leaders were radically changed as new appreciations about the motives and meanings behind their actions evolved. As these stories changed, greatly different interpretations of the current actions of leaders began to emerge in this department. Leaders were now being supported by the inner dialogue where in the past they were resisted, and some really different training and development strategies were implemented with the full partnership of the executives.

I and others have written extensively on appreciative inquiry elsewhere, and I don't want to cover that territory here.[3] Suffice to say that the Appreciative Self brings to the process of organizational learning an interest in what could be by exploring the best of what is in the experiences of people.

Appreciation, Awareness, and Curiosity as Three Forms of Inquiry

The Descriptive Self is a form of expression. The other three skills I've covered in this book, the Aware Self, the Curious Self, and the Appreciative Self, are forms of inquiry or ways of knowing. In the world of work and organizations, inquiry needs to be balanced with expression to be of practical value. But we need more forms of inquiry than the ones science and technology have given us. Traditional forms of organizing tended to reinforce "objective truth" as the only kind of truth worth exploring. As we become ever more global and diverse in our social organizations, managers have to increasingly understand how to think about, explore, and validate other kinds of truth—subjective and inter-subjective truth. I believe that self-awareness, curiosity, and appreciation form a basis for exploring all these different kinds of truths in organizations and society. In the box on page 197 I list some of the important differences between awareness, curiosity, and appreciation as methods of inquiry.

The Aware Self is interested in knowing what is going on in him. He uses reflection on his here-and-now experience to arrive at subjective truth. He interprets the information he gets mostly through his body—through the sensations that tell him that he is correct or that he hasn't quite got to the truth of it yet. The Curious Self is interested in knowing what is going on outside of herself, particularly in others. She uses observation and questions to collect information that she then subjects to logic and reason to arrive at a very different kind of truth. The Curious Self operates in the realm of objective and inter-subjective truths. While the Aware and Curious Selves are interested in different forms of "what is," the Appreciative Self is more interested in "what could be." Rather than operating on the basis of hypothesis-testing and doubt that is proper for issues of objective truth, appreciation operates on the basis of faith—faith in the human capacity to create any kind of social process that can be imagined and valued. Through looking for what he wants more of and interpreting what he sees through his imagination, the Appreciative Self uncovers and creates new inter-subjective truths about the social realities he is interested in.

DIFFERENCES BETWEEN AWARE, CURIOUS, AND APPRECIATIVE WAYS OF KNOWING

	Aware Self	Curious Self	Appreciative Self
is interested in	what's inside	what's outside	what could be
form of consciousness	reflection	observation	faith
"data" collection process	awareness of here-and-now experience	asking questions and listening	tracking
interpreted through	sensation	thinking and reason	imagination
type of truth arrived at	subjective	objective and inter-subjective	inter-subjective

You can see why these three skills are required for clear leadership. They represent a balanced approach to understanding and describing the truths of our organizational lives. Through these skills we gain clarity and agreement not just where the light is brightest, but in all facets of social reality.

Summary

Getting clarity and reducing interpersonal mush in organizations requires a process I call an organizational learning conversation. In a learning conversation, two or more people describe their experience and maps, and listen to each other's experience and maps. Through sincere inquiry they work at clearing up the stories they are creating about each other to get to a place where each knows what his experience and maps are, what the other person's experience and maps are, and what the differences between them are. Through a joint inquiry into their different experiences of a problem pattern, they develop a new understanding of the pattern, which almost always causes a change in that pattern. That, I believe, is the process of organizational learning. Organizational learning comes one conversation at a time, rippling out as the climate in the organization increasingly supports people telling each other their truth and learning from their experience together.

Anyone can give leadership to organizational learning by choosing to have learning conversations with people when it is important. Learning conversations are not something to have every day. You use them when you think it is important to put the energy into changing a particular problem pattern. The skills required are the same no matter what your level of authority. Whether you are leading a major corporation or you're a techie in an R&D team, whether you're an insurance adjuster or leading a maintenance crew, high performance comes from people who are motivated and learning together; and that can't happen unless you have interpersonal clarity. With the power of their authority, managers can set the tone by their willingness to be a Descriptive Self, to listen well to others, and to seek to understand their part in problem patterns.

When you couple a willingness to find interpersonal clarity with an appreciative approach to inquiry, you have the basis for creating truly positive teams and organizations—not just ones where people put on smiley faces but ones where people really are bringing the best of themselves and others to their work.

Strengthening Decision-Making
and Creating Alignment

9

Sometimes a learning conversation is finished once you get to interpersonal clarity, sometimes it isn't. A learning conversation begins with sharing one kind of map we have with each other: the stories we are making up about each other and the situation. If doing that leads to new insight and understanding and creates a positive change in how we interact in the future, then the conversation is probably finished. But sometimes it doesn't. Sometimes we get to interpersonal clarity but still don't know how to act differently.

This is almost always related to some task process. Maybe we are clear that we have different ideas about what we should do or how to go about doing it. Maybe we are clear that we have different opinions about people's roles. Maybe we want the same thing but have different ideas about how to get it. Maybe we want different things. What needs to happen? In this case, we are almost always dealing with a situation where our maps of another area are not in alignment.

Creating Common Maps

In the world of tasks, problems, and decisions that have to be managed by groups of people, map-making is essential. "Map-making" is what I call the process of developing shared maps, that is, agreement about what something is and/or how to do something. Anyone who is able to help people come to real agreement on anything is implicitly or explicitly using some form of map-making. I have found that many of the conflicts people have at work over what to do (once the interpersonal mush is cleared out) come from having different theory of action maps. Rarely, however, are these talked about explicitly. If you pay attention to arguments you'll notice they almost always consist of proponents asserting the superiority of their proposals without first agreeing on the problem they are trying to solve, the outcome they seek, or the theory behind the solution they are proposing. For example, people will debate how to increase sales before first agreeing on why sales are flat. Sure, bits and pieces come out haphazardly as people try to persuade each other, but rarely can anyone walk away and describe the theory of action behind the counter-proposals.

Traditional organizations rely on hierarchy or expertise to decide which map will prevail. Part of the underlying theory of action in most bureaucratic organizations is that "there is an expert for everything and only he knows." The experts decide and the rest implement. If the issue is outside of recognized expertise, then it's run up the hierarchy until someone makes a decision. As a result, people in traditional organizations aren't used to shared map-making processes. But once you try to empower people, reduce the hierarchy, and rely more on everyone's expertise to solve problems, explicit map-making is essential. That does not mean that authority and hierarchy are eliminated, but the nature of authority needs to be continuously reexamined, redefined, and clarified.

One of the really important identity maps in any kind of organization has to do with who has authority and who is responsible for what. Ultimately, those with hierarchical authority must decide how things are decided. This is the basic organizing map and everything else flows from it. If team members or people in an organization have different maps or are confused about who gets to make what decisions, lots of ineffective things happen. That seems self-evident yet it is a common problem in organizations that are undergoing major change or trying to become empowered. In an attempt to empower employees who have been left out of the decision-making loop in the past, managers will unintentionally create a situation where no one is sure who can make a decision about what. This does not empower anyone. Instead it creates confusion and wasted effort. If people are given total freedom but have to put in twice as much effort to get anything done (e.g., how do I get a purchasing requisition?), they feel *disempowered*.[1]

I have worked with many managers who were adamant that they wanted their subordinates to participate in decision-making. From their point of view subordinates had valuable information, ideas, and insights to contribute to decisions, and their commitment to implementing those decisions would be increased if they participated in making them. Yet the subordinates had a very different experience. They saw the manager making decisions all the time without their participation, or making different decisions from those the subordinates favored. In these situations subordinates often became suspicious about their manager's stated desire for their participation, and distrustful of her real motives. In all these cases the managers were sincere in their desire for participation but were not clear about (1) who, exactly, they wanted to participate in what kinds of decisions, or (2) what they would do with the participation once they got it. Does the manager want everyone to participate in every decision? Usually not. What will the manager do—listen to their input and then make a decision, search for consensus in making the decision, give people a vote and decide by majority? All this needs to be clear for people to understand what is going on and be able to work together effectively

It is the job of those leaders who, by virtue of their role, have the authority and responsibility for decisions, to create clear decision-making maps for everyone to follow. Specifically, who decides what? It still surprises me how common it is for people to have different maps about that, for managers not to be clear about what their decision-making maps are, and, even if they are, for them not to have communicated them clearly. In organizations where things are changing rapidly, decision-making maps sometimes have to change just as quickly too. One of the attributes of clear leaders is that they are constantly checking in with their subordinates, clarifying and updating everyone's maps about who participates in what decisions and how.

Decision-making is just one of the many important kinds of identity maps that exist in organizations. Other maps address questions like "What are the goals around here?" People have maps about the stated goals and the real goals. For years in the auto industry supervisors were given many different quality goals, but they always knew that the most important goal was their labor efficiency, which took precedence over any "flavor of the month" goal. Any important definition of what is (e.g., what is customer satisfaction, what is acceptable profit, what is the role of a manager?) is encoded in people's identity maps, and when people who work together have very different identity maps, it's no wonder that trust, cooperation, and coordination are lower and conflict, politics, and interpersonal mush reign.

Coming to agreement requires first of all that the maps people are using to guide their decisions and actions be described and discussed. Here's an example.

Members of the plant management team were trying to decide whether to eliminate the special supervisors' parking lot and have everyone park on a first come, first served basis, or to maintain the privilege supervisors were used to of being able to park close to the plant's main entrance. Those for the proposal saw it as a further step in developing better cooperation between management and labor, part of an evolving change process to develop an empowered, delayered organization. Those opposed believed the proposal would just further upset the supervisors who were already upset by the change process. The plant manager, who was trying to create a management team, refused to make the decision. He wanted the group to come to consensus.

Arguments went back and forth about the possible positive and negative impacts of changing the parking, but no one stopped to lay out, in any systematic way, their theory of cause and effect and how changing the parking would impact that. Listening to the argument, one could have believed that these managers had very different agendas. Some of those in favor of the change in parking thought some of those against it were just resisting out of fear that their perks would be on the table next.

Only after much fruitless debate, where no one had convinced anyone else to change their opinion, did the consultant enter the picture. She listened and asked them what larger outcome they sought. It turned out they all wanted the same thing: a greater sense of "we-ness" between management and labor, and increased personal motivation from everyone to make the business a success. Then individuals were asked to write out their personal theories of how to accomplish that on large pieces of paper so that everyone could see everyone else's. It soon became clear that the real basis of the argument was some very different assumptions about how to maintain and increase personal motivation. Some people thought that a decrease in perks that separate management from hourly workers would increase people's sense of camaraderie and belonging, and this would make them more motivated. Yes, it might make some supervisors upset, but they would quickly get over it and value the increased cooperation from the workforce. Others thought that getting rid of perks would give people less to strive for and therefore reduce their motivation. Supervisors were some of the most motivated employees they had and nothing should be done to wreck that. In fact, they should be looking for more ways to single out and reward good behavior. One group thought that motivation came from rewards while the other group thought that motivation came through a sense of belonging.

Decisions as Experiments

Who was right? Often, it isn't so easy to know. When we get people to clarify their theories of action what also becomes clear are the *assumptions* their theories rest on. Often these are untested or unproved assumptions, which is why we have different theories to begin with. When it comes to managing people, we are all operating on assumptions that are, in the scientific sense, unproven. The only way to make a consensual decision when there are disagreements over assumptions is to find ways to test the assumptions. But who has time for that? We can't hold off making decisions and taking action while we test each assumption to find out which is valid. The way out of this problem, and the one that ultimately creates high-performing teams and organizations, is to pick which assumptions you will go with and then treat your decision as an experiment. Clear leaders get to the bottom of the assumptions behind different theories of action and then make *decisions as experiments* and stay open to changing the decisions as they learn. This extends organizational learning from issues of interpersonal mush to issues of tasks, problems, and strategies. Acknowledging that we are just working from maps and theories allows us to try out an action to see if it works. And we are more willing to revisit the decision if it doesn't work. This approach is crucial for organizational learning. The clear leader works at building a culture that views decisions as experiments.

Remember the case of the hospital administrators in Chapter 4 who were trying to get people to be more cost-conscious? Rose and Chuck's solution to their lack of a shared map was to keep learning. They didn't so much disagree on their basic assumptions, but they didn't know how to create an overall policy that would cover them. So they decided to stay open to learning on a case-by-case basis. When the next cost overrun came up, however, they would be faced with the dilemma of which assumption to go on. This is when they would need to make a decision as an experiment. When you make a decision as an experiment you need to be clear about three things:

1. What your theory of action is and what unproven assumption you are testing through this decision

2. When you will be able to assess whether the decision is having the desired outcome

3. How you will know if the assumption is valid or not

Getting clear about the contours of your experimental assumptions takes time and effort, just as any learning does. Managers faced
with more tasks and issues than they can deal with often prefer to just
make a decision and get on with it. Some might think it does no good
to second-guess themselves. Others have a theory of action that says
there are no perfect decisions, and execution is more important than
the quality of the decision, so it's best to just make a decision and then
put all your effort into making it work. It's more important to get
decisions made and action taken than to waste time hand-wringing
and going through "paralysis by analysis." These managers like to
quote Tom Peters's saying about one of the attributes of excellent
organizations: "ready, fire, aim." What they don't realize is that
"ready, fire, aim" is about making decisions as experiments. They forget the "aim" that comes after "fire." Decision as experiment is not
about paralysis by analysis; exactly the opposite. Decision by experiment is about making a decision and committing to a course of action
quickly (fire) and then turning around and changing that decision just
as quickly if it's not working (aim). If you are clear about the theory of
action you are using when you make the initial decision, you can aim
more effectively when you make the next decision: you are learning
which assumptions work and which don't.

People have to stay loose and flexible as they learn from mistakes
and build on successes. This can create anxiety for people who like
"strong leadership." People who are used to the certainty of bureaucracy don't like managers to "keep changing their minds"—they want
clear marching orders. They don't like to head in one direction and
then all of a sudden have to head in a different one. It feels like wasted
effort. And if there's no learning going on, then it is wasted effort. A
manager creates a climate of organizational learning when the theory
of action behind a decision is communicated and when the learnings
that have been taken from "failed experiments" are also communicated,
along with the new decision (and the map it is based on).

The problem of too many contradictory decisions, however, pales
in comparison to the opposite and much more prevalent problem,
escalation of commitment to prior decisions. In a series of studies
Barry Staw and his students have demonstrated a clear tendency for
managers to keep putting resources and effort behind bad decisions to
try to salvage them.[2] This is also known as the "trapped administra-
tor" problem, and it happens in organizations that don't allow for
"learningful failure." When any decision that turns out to have been

wrong becomes a blotch against a person's record, managers are going to work long and hard to ensure that all their decisions look like successes, to hide any failures that do occur, and to make few risky decisions. A climate like that reduces innovation and creativity and ensures that little organizational learning is taking place.

One of the most successful new leaders I've interviewed, who was able to radically change the culture of an old, entrenched, bureaucratic company to a delayered, empowered one in two years (gasp!), described his approach to decision-making in these terms:

We make plans and then we leave them behind. When we started we had a plan and had to turf it the second day. I tell people that's where we are going, but how we get there will depend on what works. The vision doesn't have to be terribly detailed. A big picture is important, though, because it must be big enough to encompass what's going to happen inside and outside the company. But everyone must understand that the plan is just that—and it may not work, so everyone has to stay flexible. I say, "We're going to reach this goal. Let's start by going down this road and if that route doesn't work we'll change directions. No decision is carved in stone. But we have to move fast to reach the goal in time so we have to plunge in, take action, and learn from it." The people have to know that the decisions en route are their own to make. I don't want them scared to act, I just want them to figure out fast if they're heading down a rat hole. As long as we reach the goal on time, that's what counts.

An organizational culture that supports the attitude of experiment toward decision-making has many beneficial effects.

1. Managers don't get trapped into having to justify bad decisions, escalating their commitment to a course of action that is not effective. Instead of bad decisions, we have failed experiments, which is OK because we often learn more from the failed experiment than the one that ultimately succeeds. The clear leader is just as likely to ask "What did you learn?" as "What did you accomplish?"

2. People are more likely to develop valid maps from experiments than from anecdotal evidence and attempts to make sense of the past. A lot of decision-making in organizations is justified by

anecdotes (well, they did X there and it worked), but research has shown that anecdotal learning leads to incorrect conclusions just as often as it leads to correct ones.

3. Risk-taking is less risky. If people have to be right every time they make a decision they are going to be very cautious in every decision they make. In addition they will avoid making decisions in areas where they don't have a theory of action they trust. By acknowledging that a course of action is an experiment to learn what the right thing to do is, people are much more willing to venture into unmapped territory.

4. Everyone's competence is continually increasing as they get clear about what their maps really are, find out what alternative maps exist, and get to check out how valid their theories of action are. New leaders drive organizational competence by continuously surfacing the tacit maps that are being used to guide decisions and challenging people to match them against external reality so that they can learn and improve those maps.

So in the supervisory parking example above, you wonder, what experiment did they do? They began by considering whether there was some validity to both theories of action, and devised a joint theory of action that used both sets of assumptions. Working off that map they came up with a totally different strategy. Instead of just getting rid of the privileged supervisory parking area, they expanded it and awarded it each month to the workers and supervisors in the department that best achieved or surpassed their total quality targets. They decided that if their assumptions were correct, supervisors would find that workers were taking more initiative to meet quality targets, there would be more of a competitive buzz between work groups, and supervisors and workers would be found strategizing together how to win. They gave themselves three months to see if the changes occurred and and then revisit the decision. It turned out that the effect was visible within weeks, and was exactly what they were hoping for: increased worker-management camaraderie and increased motivation. Notice that a belonging-individuality paradox was at the core of their debate. Are people best motivated by belonging or by individual rewards? Intuitively, they understood that a better solution was probably not either/or, but a blend of both.

In this case and so many others in organizations every day, the interpersonal mush is exacerbated by fuzzy maps. Not only do we lack clarity about each other's experience, we lack clarity about the theories of action each of us is operating out of. When you get clear about both, you have real interpersonal clarity and the basis for sustained, superior performance in teams and organizations.

Using the Skills of Clear Leadership in Meetings

Meetings are the lifeblood of empowered organizations because things there are not standardized and a lot of things are constantly changing, so coordination depends on face-to-face interaction. Yet many people find meetings dreary, awful rituals that they would avoid if they could. In this section I want to give you a real "rubber hits the road" process for how to reap the benefits of interpersonal clarity and have high-performance meetings.

The meetings I am interested in are ones where decisions need to be made. I don't think that informational meetings are all that useful, and they can be used far too much in organizations. Email can carry most of that bandwidth. Meetings where people share ideas and innovations are different and are usually well accepted by attendees. The most important reason to meet, however, is to develop a common theory of action and get agreement on who is going to do what by when, and that usually takes place in the context of making decisions.

All work systems are based on an allocation of responsibility and, if properly designed, commensurate authority. Authority is the allocation of decision-making power. For a meeting to be a useful decision-making process, the person with the authority to make the decision must be in the room. In the meeting process I will describe, the authority and her employees use the skills of clear leadership to ensure and maintain interpersonal clarity while making agreements.

The chart on page 208 shows the sequence of events that need to occur around each decision. It starts out with the manager being clear about what the decision that needs to be made is and how that decision will be made. Will the manager decide alone, get input and then decide, look for consensus or unanimity, or what? When will the decision be made? Whose input will be sought? It is part of the manager's job to be clear how decisions will be made, up front, with his employees. It is the employees' job to make sure they are clear and to point out to the manager when he is not being clear.

This process works whether you are a formal leader, like a boss, or an informal leader, like part of a leaderless software team whose

MEETINGS USING CLEAR LEADERSHIP

The Manager	The Employees
Describes the issue, problem, or opportunity that needs a decision.	Ask questions to get clear about the issue, problem, or opportunity and add any further information.
Describes how the decision will be made.	Ask questions to get clear about how the decision will be made.
Describes her observations, thoughts, feelings, and wants and the maps she is using to think about the decision.	Ask questions to be clear about the manager's maps, observations, thoughts, feelings, and wants.
Inquires into the maps, observations, thoughts, feelings, and wants of employees.	Describe their maps, observations, thoughts, feelings, and wants.
Describes what the decision is or how and when it will be made. If appropriate, lays out the experimental parameters of the decision.	Ask questions to get clear about the decision and the theory of action being used. Contribute ideas to the experimental parameters of the decision.
Asks employees what they need in order to be able to commit to the decision.	Describe what is getting in the way of committing to the decision and what they want.
Affirms the decision, what action she expects from the employees, and the consequences of noncompliance.	Ask questions to get clear about the decision, what they are expected to do, and the consequences of noncompliance.

members look to you for direction. Once the decision-making process is clear, the leader needs to go first in describing her maps and thoughts about the thing that needs deciding, what data she has, how she feels about the different options she can see and what she wants, both from the decision and from her followers. It is the followers' job to use their Curious Self skills to check out their stories with the leader and get an accurate picture of her experience. Then it is time to switch roles; now the followers talk about their thoughts, observations, feelings, and wants while the leader is a Curious Self. They discuss their maps and how they differ. Once everyone is clear about everyone else, the leader describes what the decision is or when the decision will be made and how. If there is a lot of uncertainty or many different points of view, it's appropriate to make a decision as an experiment. The leader, after getting appropriate input, needs to be clear about the theory of action the decision is based on and how that will be tested through the decision. The followers again need to make sure that they are checking out any stories that they are making up and are clear on the decision and the maps behind it. Once a decision is made, the followers need to tell the truth of their experience—what they think, feel, and want about the decision. The leader needs to listen to that, check out her stories, and find out what the followers need in order to be able to commit to the decision. Committing to a decision does not necessarily mean that one agrees with the decision, but it does mean that one is willing to make it work. The leader needs to be clear what she expects from each person in regard to the decision and what consequences, if any, will come from noncompliance. The followers need to ensure that clarity.

When managers and employees use the skills of clear leadership to ensure clarity and alignment in their decisions and actions, each of them is giving leadership to the group. That's one of the reasons why these leadership skills can be used by anyone, regardless of position, at any time, to increase interpersonal clarity in organizations.

Managing Clarity and Agreement over Time: The Organizational Learning Meeting

To maintain interpersonal clarity and keep updating agreements as things change requires some time and effort, but research has shown that the time and effort I am going to suggest managers put into this more than pays itself back in increased coordination and reduced conflict and need to fight fires. Organizational learning meetings should not be large events with lots of people. If a team or department needs clean-up, that is a different thing. They need trained consultants and time away from work together. The organizational learning (OL) meeting I'm going to describe involves only two people: a manager and one of his employees.[3] After going through a clean-up process,

---

THE ORGANIZATIONAL LEARNING MEETING

1. Review commitments from the previous meeting.

2. Share information on what is happening in the organization and get more facts about anything you are making up stories about, especially who has authority for what and who is accountable for what.

3. Discuss any problem patterns you are having. If necessary, have a learning conversation.

4. Ask for what you want more of.

5. Celebrate any recent successes and achievements at work and in personal lives.

---

managers can use OL meetings to maintain the benefits and keep practicing the skills. Or managers can simply institute OL meetings and start building a learning culture.

During an OL meeting, the manager and subordinate take 30 to 60 minutes to get clear about what is happening in their relationship and in the work setting, and to find out what they can do to help each other succeed. These meetings always have an agenda and a written list of commitments that are reviewed at the following meeting. Meetings occur about once every two to three weeks. The biggest resistance to this technique comes from managers who believe they are too busy to meet individually with each subordinate, for less than an hour, 17 to 24 times in a year. Most managers who implement this system, however, say that it saves them time from all the hassles they no longer have.

OL meetings are scheduled in advance. Each person emails their agenda items to the other a day or so before the meeting. The manager consolidates the agenda. A good template for an agenda is shown in the box above.

OL meetings are a simple, inexpensive change to implement, and the impact far exceeds the effort. When managers meet for half an hour twice a month with each of their direct reports and use clear leadership, huge clouds of interpersonal mush can be held at bay.

A time and place is created where everyone knows it is appropriate to use these skills. This is a necessary ingredient in planned cultural change: a time and place, sanctioned by the old culture, where relationships are governed by the new culture you want to establish.[4] For people used to the "normal" atmosphere of interpersonal mush it can be difficult to know when to use clear leadership skills when they're first introduced. The OL meetings help to establish their use. Within a short time, subordinates will start arranging their own OL meetings when they need them with their colleagues, and the need for formal structures may lessen.

Regular OL meetings ensure increased interpersonal clarity between managers and followers through consistent opportunities to check out their stories. There's much less chance for unconscious negative spins to be put on events or inaccurate rumors to gain momentum. Information flows up and down more consistently, and as a result large group information meetings are no longer needed regularly. Agreements are written down and reviewed regularly.

If a manager does it right, he can do everything he needs to manage the unit in these meetings—relying on his staff to manage the unit's day-to-day operations—and leave the rest of his week free to deal with people outside his authority (where he needs to spend most of his time). One of the surprising results from the long-term research on OL meetings is the positive impact they have on teams. Even though the OL meeting is not a team meeting, it helps groups be more effective. Every team has an authority, either inside or outside the team, and when members have clarity and agreement with that authority, there is less opportunity for work-related misperceptions, confusions, and conflicts.

Summary

The clear leader knows that managing people is about managing their maps. The consistency in what people say and do comes from those maps. You cannot influence someone to change what she thinks or what she does if you cannot get inside her map and show her how your map will work better for her (except maybe by brute force). The new leader in the delayered, empowered organization does not have brute force as an option. Therefore the only way he can be effective is by surfacing and altering maps, a key outcome of a learning conversation.

But simply surfacing and acknowledging the differences in our maps may not be enough to get to agreement. What if the basic assumptions underlying our maps are different? What do we do then? The boss who is fused with his maps will simply force others to use his theory of action. In traditional organizations, conflicts in theories of action are usually settled by those with authority or expertise. Decisions get made, but they aren't necessarily the right ones and, more importantly, chances are high that learning doesn't occur. This is especially true if the experts are far removed from the problems they make decisions about. I remember one plant where every time the product was changed two guys would send the same suggestion for how to fix the same process design problem back to head-office engineering and get the same large monetary pay-out from the suggestion system. This went on for four years and everyone in the plant knew about it, but the headquarters engineering group was too distant and the issue too small for them to ever learn from it.

Clear leaders know that to get the most from empowered organizations they can't simply rely on authority or expertise to force agreement on maps. Alternative maps that employees bring to the table need to be seriously considered. At the same time, the pace of business requires that decisions get made promptly. To deal with this situation, clear leaders make decisions as experiments. What that means is that they get clear about the different basic assumptions people hold in their theories of action, make their best guess about which will work, make a decision, and take action based on everyone's being clear about which theory of action they are going to try. Everyone monitors the results and stays flexible and ready to change course as soon as they see whether it is working or not. This way leaders not only ensure that they maintain a healthy differentiation from their maps, they ensure that everyone is constantly learning and updating important theories of action.

Bringing clear leadership to work is about taking the risk of getting clear—clear what your boss expects, clear why you don't support a decision, clear what theory of action the group will use to operate by, clear what the impact of your actions is. When meetings are run to ensure clarity, the hoped-for attributes of empowered organizations such as innovation, flexibility, and cooperation have a greater chance of being realized. Using organizational learning meetings between managers and employees every few weeks ensures that clarity and agreement exist between them. This has important spin-offs for relationships between co-workers and it really helps teams to work well.

Overcoming Obstacles to Clear Leadership Throughout the Organization

When I first teach people how to have organizational learning conversations their thoughts quickly turn to all the reasons that they cannot do it or that it won't work in their organization. This chapter is for them. In this chapter I describe the main obstacles that I and others have encountered to having learning conversations, and I show you what you can do about them.

Of course, the number one obstacle to having learning conversations is your hesitancy to just do it. At first it will seem awkward and difficult, like learning any new skill, but after a while it becomes a lot easier because, really, it isn't all that hard. It is our emotional investment in our maps and our fear that leveling will make things worse that keep us in the interpersonal mush. Given your willingness to try having a learning conversation with others, what other obstacles can you run into? In this section I'll discuss the most common obstacles I see and what you can do about them. These are (1) your own fusion and disconnection, (2) working with people who don't know the skills of clear leadership, (3) shame, (4) cynicism, (5) their lack of differentiation, (6) the current level of interpersonal mush, (7) authority, and (8) interpersonal triangulation. I'll discuss them in that order.

Your Fusion and Disconnection

One obstacle you face is the extent to which your experience is determined by other people's reactions to you. To lead a learning conversation you need to be a nonanxious presence, and work at not expressing your emotional reactions to what people are saying. Remember the difference between describing your emotions and expressing them. If someone says something that lands hard on me and I visibly

213

stiffen or look angry or hurt, they may back off. If I have power over them and look upset at what they are saying, they are likely to stop telling me their truth. I need to maintain the calm, dispassionate exterior that I would have if I truly were differentiated and my internal experience were not determined by you. There's a saying, "Fake it until you can make it," and I do think that we learn to be differentiated by holding back from expressing our reactions and calming ourselves when our fusion is hooked. Each time you do that, you become a little more differentiated. It's appropriate and maybe essential, depending on the content of the conversation, to describe the feelings you are having, but you have to do that in a way that doesn't seem to blame the other (e.g., you make me feel . . .) and you need to time it so it doesn't shut them down.

The image of playing catch that I described in the chapter on the Descriptive Self is a great image for learning conversations. When I am operating from a differentiated place I don't hold other people responsible for my experience—I create my own experience. You can't make me feel or think or want anything. I do that for myself. I might do it in reaction to you but I'm the one creating my experience, not you. So why throw snowballs at you? If I want you to "get it," I need to play catch.

That doesn't mean I don't need to learn about how I impact people. If four out of five people have the same experience around me, then there is probably something I am doing that creates that reaction. That is different, however, from taking responsibility for how each individual experiences me. If, as a manager, I am pursuing a strategy that requires you to do things you don't want to do, and you perceive me as mean and uncaring, well, that's too bad. I want to hear about your experience, I'm willing to show you why I think we must change, I wish you would see the nice and caring side of me, but I am not going to take responsibility for your experience and I am not going to change my strategy so that you will have a different one.

In a case like that, a manager probably has to deal with his own desire to disconnect so that he doesn't just shut the unhappy subordinate out. The only way I can possibly manage your productivity and motivation is to stay in touch with your experience. The anxiety I feel when I have to listen to the misery I am causing you makes me not want to listen, and that will be an obstacle to having learning conversations with you. If I am truly differentiated, I can listen to your misery both compassionately and dispassionately, and look for ways to lessen it without giving up my agenda. Even if I'm not really differentiated I can still listen, park my reaction, and work at being a Curious Self.

Working with People Who Don't Know These Skills

An obstacle many people focus on when they first learn these skills is that other people who haven't learned the skills won't be willing to have learning conversations. I think this is less of an obstacle than it seems at first. Sure, if the other person has not got a clue what you are doing and you launch into a learning conversation he might get uptight and defensive. The best way to deal with that is to tell him, up front, what you are trying to do and why. Explain the ideas in this book. Give him the Steps in Having an Organizational Learning Conversation guide. Show him the Experience Cube. Tell him why it is important to you to have a relationship of interpersonal clarity with him. Be open about the experience you are having with him right now, as you discuss this. If you are his boss tell him you consider it part of the job and expect him to learn how to have learning conversations not only with you but with everyone else in the department.

Be willing to coach people through the first few learning conversations. Expect that they won't be good at being descriptive or curious at first, that there will be big gaps in their awareness of their experience, that they will react before giving impact and describe their judgments instead of their experience. At first you need to just let that be. You need to keep a lid on your defensiveness and, instead, refocus them from their judgments to the story they are making up that is leading them to those judgments. Even if they are lousy at describing their experience, you can keep asking questions until you get clear. Even if they are lousy at listening you can keep asking them what they are hearing until they have heard what you have to say. After you do this a few times they'll start to understand the difference. People need to have a few success experiences before you give them critical feedback. Being an Appreciative Self is more likely to lead to their acceptance of this different way of working together, and improvement in their skills, than being critical and doing too much teaching. Once they get comfortable with the idea of having a learning conversation with you, then you can give them more coaching on the ground rules of clear language, being a Descriptive Self, and being a Curious Self.

Another thing some managers have done is use their understanding of clear leadership to create a set of simple ground rules for having conversations at work. If you are trying to build interpersonal clarity in a team, begin with the most differentiated people, those who create the least interpersonal mush. You may have an urge to try working with the people you most need to clear up the mush with, but that may be a losing strategy. If you want to start building an atmosphere of interpersonal clarity at work, start with the people who will feel least threatened and most able to tell the truth of their experience. Have them read the book or some of the chapters. Together, agree on a list of ground rules for conversations you want to have when there are problems or disagreements. This will help others better understand what you are trying to do and observe that it isn't as risky as it might at first appear.

Shame

From my studies of people learning and using clear leadership skills I have concluded that shame is the number one impediment to well-intentioned, normal people having learning conversations. To lead organizational learning you have to be able to circumvent the shame that fuels so much of the negative fantasies and reactivity in organizational life.

Shame is that part in each of us that feels unworthy, small, inadequate, bad. Guilt is the feeling that you have done something wrong, but shame is when you are what is wrong. In most of us there is a deep-down, mostly unconscious, core of rot—a place where we are convinced that we really don't fit here, that there is something terribly wrong with us, that we don't belong, that if others knew who we really were they would not accept us. That is our shame. I can imagine that there are people that don't have that core of rot, but I have never met any. No matter how successful or powerful or beautiful a person is, they probably carry shame. In fact, shame is often what compels a person to work so hard at being successful or powerful.

Each of us has some "shame buttons." These are images we carry of ourselves as in some way "less than," deficient, inadequate. Common ones are not being smart enough, not being caring enough, not being likeable enough, and not being attractive enough, but the range is as wide as human experience. People vary, of course, in how much shame they carry and how close to the surface these buttons are, but we all have them. When a shame button gets pushed we react in a defensive way, and that can stop a learning conversation dead. More often, however, shame is what stops a person from even starting a learning conversation. When I'm not sure that I'm worthy or good enough, then the last thing I feel like doing is being a Descriptive Self. Instead, I will want to fade into the background and figure out what the "right" thing to say or do is before I say or do anything.

When you think about it, infancy is a setup for shame. We come onto the planet full of energy and vitality and curiosity, but our parents wanted a "good" boy or girl. They were not as thrilled as we were by our discoveries of all the neat stuff our bodies create. They didn't think it was so great when we wanted to share the wonder of our loud screaming voices. In fact, we got severely reprimanded when we followed our exuberance onto a busy road, didn't we? As we grow from infancy to childhood we are told in myriad ways that our experience is not right—think different thoughts, feel different feelings, want different wants. Much of that is necessary survival training, but it has other consequences. Gershen Kauffman has argued that the number one way a child learns shame is when she asks a question and doesn't get a response.[1] Now how common is that—children tugging at a parent's leg while the parent is trying to have a conversation with someone else, being shushed and ignored? Who can blame the harried parent? But what happens to the child is she thinks to herself, "If I were worthy, I would have gotten a response." That sense of shame gets dumped into a "shame tank" that she carries with her at home and at school, storing all the times when she gets the message that she just isn't "right" or "good enough." Over time her shame tank becomes just something in the background, so much a part of her that she doesn't even notice it anymore. The question is not whether you have a shame tank, but how full it is and what you currently do with your shame.

Shaming Versus Confronting

You shame a person when you bring to his awareness an image he has of himself that is deficient, unworthy, bad, or inadequate in some way. This is a very important definition. It points out that shaming always serves to reinforce a belief or map the person being shamed already has of himself. The act of shaming causes that image of inadequacy to flash in his awareness for a millisecond and be followed by physical and/or emotional pain (unless the person has learned to numb himself to it). Feeling our shame hurts and we defend ourselves against it.

A lot of what passes for sarcasm and joking is really shaming, but not all shaming is verbal. We can shame others with gestures or actions. For example, if some part of me, conscious or unconscious, thinks I'm bad at planning and I tell you my new plan and you roll your eyes—wham!—I feel my shame. If I don't buy into what you are saying about me, no matter how negative, it doesn't push my shame buttons. So there has to be a kernel of truth, subjective or objective, for shaming to occur, and that is what makes it so difficult to deal with.

It used to drive me nuts in my personal relationships; I thought there was no way to win. I'd want to bring up something that really bothered me, but when I did, there would be hurt and maybe crying or anger. The other person would be angry at me for pointing out something that was wrong, but it was true, wasn't it? What else was I supposed to do? Then I'd be left feeling stuck in a lose-lose situation; either I say nothing about things that bother me or, if I bring them up, I create even more of a mess. Better to just not say anything—leave the interpersonal mush alone.

What I have since learned is that it is possible to talk about problems and issues without shaming people—I call that confronting, and I will describe the differences below. First of all, however, it takes a decision to not shame people. What right do I have to go around bringing truths about people that are painful for them into their awareness? Whether or not you go about shaming people is a value decision you have to make for yourself. I would point out, however, that shaming makes it difficult to have learning conversations. First, if you shame someone, she will have a defensive reaction and it'll be difficult to get her to be descriptive or curious. Second, if she associates a learning conversation with being shamed, she won't want to come back for more.

I have spent some time trying to figure out why people shame others. It is rarely a desire to attack or hurt another, but that does happen. We can shame someone to defend against being shamed, or to counterattack when we feel shamed. We can shame someone when we feel scared, or to push them away for whatever reason. Sometimes shame is used to get power over someone. It can also be used to try to get attention or affection, or as a response to a feeling of jealousy.

Sometimes shaming is used to protect a third party. Sometimes it's a sideways method of expressing anger. But the number one reason people shame others (and themselves) is to try to motivate change.

It goes like this. I notice that Sam is frequently late. It starts to bother me. One day when Sam's tardiness is really causing me problems I say something sarcastic about it. My hope is that he will stop being late. Instead, one of three things almost always happens: (1) Sam goes away feeling wounded and makes up nasty stories about me, (2) we get into an argument in which I try to show Sam how late he always is while Sam defends himself, or (3) Sam zings me back and we escalate our attacks until we pull back and go off separately to lick our wounds. It is ironic that even though shaming is such a common strategy for trying to change others it almost never works. Sure, with enough negative reinforcement you can get someone to change their behavior, as long as you are watching. But shame generally serves to reinforce a part of the person that contributes to the behavior you are trying to change. For example, Sam wouldn't have felt his shame if there weren't a part of him that believed he was late too often. When I shame him by noticing and validating its existence, I am reinforcing the part of him that has trouble being on time.

Can a person talk to Sam about her experience of his tardiness without shaming him? Yes she can, and it is essential if she wants to have a learning conversation about it. Confronting is when I bring to awareness (in myself and/or in others) an incongruence or discrepancy.[2] That could be a discrepancy between actions and words, the ideal and the actual, goals and results, and so on. A confrontation does not result in psychic pain, it results in a sense of clarity. Confrontations do not diminish the person. Rather, they are invitations to learn more about what is really going on. A successful confrontation results in increased awareness while maintaining or enhancing the quality of the relationship.

When I confront someone, I put my observations on the table for both of us to look at. When I shame, I am operating from the judgments and inferences I have made about those observations. I have already decided that you are the problem. When I confront, the discrepancy is the problem, not necessarily you. I might discover, in a learning conversation with Sam, how my unrealistic deadlines and my unwillingness to listen when he says he can't meet them contribute to my experience of Sam being late. I have learned that by focusing on the discrepancy I want to deal with, being open to seeing my part in it *and* being extra sensitive to where the other person's shame buttons might be, that I can often discuss difficult things without others getting defensive.

Sense-making processes being what they are, however, there is one further difficulty. Someone can take some perfectly innocent remark and use it to shame himself. When shame buttons are close to the surface, statements can be interpreted as putdowns even if there is no intention to shame. It's also true that sometimes I can shame someone unconsciously—I can block that kind of intention from my awareness pretty well. So if someone feels shamed by me and I don't think I purposely shamed him, how can I know if it's him or me? If there are witnesses, ask them. One of the really interesting things about shame is that when a person shames another, everyone present feels it. Have you ever been to dinner with a couple who are hurling sarcastic comments back and forth all night? When one of their zingers lands on their partner, you actually feel the pain, don't you? The witnesses can tell you if your remark was innocent or loaded.

Like many other problems of developing interpersonal clarity, this problem is amplified by authority. Most people are most sensitive to their shame around authority and can feel put down by casual observations from someone who has authority over them. This puts an extra burden on leaders who want to confront subordinates and have learning conversations without pushing their shame buttons.

If you want to have a learning conversation with someone but you are afraid that all you will get is his defensiveness, it's useful to plan out your confrontation ahead of time. Here are some useful steps.

1. *Identify your purpose.*

   Why are you confronting this person? Is your intention to teach? motivate? discipline? release stress? Are you there to confront or have a fight? Are you willing to learn about your part? Be honest with yourself: if what you really want is some emotional release, then go yell at her and don't pretend you want a learning conversation.

2. *Locate yourself.*

   Where are you "coming from" as you enter this confrontation? Are you coming from a place of hurt, resentment, betrayal, or other painful emotion? If so, no amount of smoothness will mask it. To be effective you will need to differentiate yourself from your reactions and get into that calm, dispassionate place where you can be descriptive and curious.

3. *Locate the other person.*

What is your history of confronting and shaming this person around this issue? How does this person respond to confrontation? What are his shame buttons? What is likely to propel him into shaming himself and how can you disarm him before he does that?

4. *Make sure you have the facts right.*

The first step as you enter into the actual confrontation is to check your understanding of the facts with the person you are confronting. Lay out your observations without your judgments and inferences and check them out first. This is especially important when confronting someone over an issue you've had problems about in the past, as such issues are most ripe for misunderstandings and defensiveness.

5. *Give specific, descriptive observation.*

A confrontation is where we point out a discrepancy between things, like promises and actual delivery. Describe the discrepancy in a clear, objective, and nonjudgmental manner. Simply *describe.* Ask the other person what her observations are. Try to come to an agreement either that there is a discrepancy or how you'll be able to both know if there is one in the future.

6. *Now have a learning conversation.*

You have overcome the obstacle of shame and are now ready to use the skills from the previous chapters.

Those who are excellent at confronting seem to be guided by a belief that every individual is his own harshest critic. When people become defensive at criticism, what they are doing is attempting to disarm their own internal critic by getting angry at you. If this happens, the confrontation has been less than effective. In the most effective confrontations the person does not experience himself being confronted *by you;* rather, he experiences you as an ally in confronting himself.

To overcome shame as an obstacle to learning conversations the place to start is with your own shame. Learn to recognize how you manage your shame and, like your other reactivity, learn to park it. Even better, get rid of the shame. That takes a process of developing compassion for yourself and probably requires the help of a therapist, but it's a great thing to do for yourself and is the basis for developing real compassion for others.

You also need to work at stepping lightly around other people's shame buttons while still telling your truth. Recognize their shame-based behaviors and notice when their buttons are getting pushed. It's helpful to know how shame manifests itself in yourself and others so that you can recognize it when you see it. Let's finish this section by looking at that.

Shame-Based Defenses

It's not just the shame, but the ways we learned as children to defend ourselves against shame, that make learning conversations difficult. Shaming someone can close down a learning conversation, but the ways most of us have learned to defend ourselves against being shamed make it likely that we won't even begin a learning conversation. Shame-based behaviors create disconnection. Here are just a few of the common shame-based responses that make learning conversations difficult:

- Wanting not to appear foolish, stupid, or inept
- Wanting to get it just right before I say or do something
- Wanting others to agree with me so I'll feel accepted
- Always looking for what is "wrong" in others
- Wanting to know what others think before saying anything
- Wanting to be fully in control of the impression I give others
- Berating myself whenever I am less than perfect
- Feeling intimidated by people
- Creating really high standards for myself

Underneath each of these is one of the basic six ways I have seen people defend themselves against feeling their shame. These are withdrawal, perfection, contempt, anger, power, and shaming others.[3] These become lifelong habits unless a person works at getting rid of the underlying shame. I'll briefly describe each and how they make learning conversations difficult.

Withdrawal

The strategy here is that if I am not visible I won't be shamed. So I fade into the background. Being a Descriptive Self is the last thing I would consider doing—way too scary—people will make fun of me! If someone asks me my subjective truth I'm most likely to say something safe until I can figure out what I'm supposed to say.

Perfection

The strategy here is that if I am perfect you can't shame me. I make sure I wear just the right clothes and do just the right things and hang out with just the right people, and so on. It's a very precarious thing, being perfect, so I only engage in activities where I know I can be perfect (or close enough). I have to control myself and the situation and a learning conversation is too uncertain an activity—too much chance for my lack of perfection to be noticed. If you start to bring up things about me that I know aren't perfect I will quickly say "I know" and try to close down the conversation before any real learning happens.

Contempt

The strategy here is that if I don't have any respect for you then you can't shame me; you are too far beneath me to have an impact. Why would I consider having a learning conversation with someone I have contempt for? Why would I care what your subjective truth is or bother trying to get you to understand mine?

Anger

The strategy here is that if I get enraged when you try to shame me, I'll scare you into stopping. A person who has learned this strategy will feel himself get enraged whenever his shame buttons are pushed. Then he either scares others off with his anger or has to put his effort into "keeping his cool," making it difficult to stay tuned in to a learning conversation.

Power

The strategy here is that if I have power then you won't dare to shame me. I may try to use your descriptiveness to get power over you. I use my power to make it very clear that you had better not shame me or else— which makes bringing up issues and wanting a learning conversation with me a very risky thing.

Shaming Others

The strategy here is to use a kind of mental jujitsu to avoid shame. Whenever some shame comes at me I just pass it along before it can land. You push my shame buttons and, wham, I shame you back. If you are too scary a target, wham, I shame the person next to me. If we are having a learning conversation and I start to feel shamed all of a sudden, you'll find yourself being attacked by me—bringing the learning conversation to a bad end.

I find recognizing the shame that underlies another person's arrogance (contempt) or fear (perfection) or tantrum (anger) or accommodation (withdrawal) or power play helps me to be less reactive to his behavior. When I focus on the wound instead of the annoying behavior, I can feel my compassion increase and my reactivity decrease. I can be more of a nonanxious presence. I can pay more attention to where his shame buttons are and avoid them when I want to have a learning conversation with him. By recognizing my own shame-based defenses, I can catch myself when I am starting to react to him and realize that it's my own stuff, not his, I am reacting to.

Cynicism

When the managers I work with first begin to contemplate trying to clear up the interpersonal mush in their organizations, one of their initial reactions is to point out people who "will never get on board with this." Almost always they are talking about people they experience as cynical. Managers can find cynical people the hardest to deal with, often because the cynic knows just how to push their shame buttons. They worry that the cynics will immediately turn off to clear leadership and try to turn off others as well.

I actually don't find cynical people that hard to work with. I think it comes from knowing what cynicism is. Cynicism is a state people use to avoid the pursuit of a worthy purpose that will inevitably fail. You see, cynical people have high ideals and are smart enough to realize that they, their organizations, family, community, whatever, will never live up to those ideals. But they are not simply satisfied knowing their ideal will never happen. Something in them pushes them continuously to do something about it. But what can they do? Any attempt to achieve the ideal will inevitably fail. Maybe the ideal is eliminating world hunger, or the racism in their community, or the dumb things the organization does to people. They can't see how to make any significant change, so they turn cynical. It is a place where we defend ourselves against having hope, because we just can't stand the pain of disappointment one more time. The ideals are still there, but the hope is gone. So now all we do is focus on all the ways in which things are inadequate.

Underneath the prickly, shaming armor of cynicism rests a starry-eyed idealist who will bring boatloads of productive energy to any change process if she can just believe that her hope won't be trashed one more time. I've never met a cynic who, once convinced of my sincere curiosity, wasn't willing to tell me a whole lot about the truth of her experience. Cynics do not find clear leadership too "touchy-feely," too "PC," or "just a load of BS," as their managers fear. Cynics are afraid of being tricked again—and they won't buy into any new system until they are convinced that the rug is not going to be pulled out from underneath them. If, however, your cynics believe that using clear leadership will make the organization more like their ideal, watch in amazement as they change from passively destructive opponents to actively constructive champions for interpersonal clarity.

Other People's Lack of Differentiation

Fusion

One of the tougher obstacles to deal with are people who are highly fused with you. Remember, fusion is a condition in which another person's experience depends on your experience. If his feeling OK about himself depends on what you think or feel toward him, he may not want to hear your truth, especially if your truth doesn't fit with what he believes he needs in order to feel OK. Most people are going to have a little fusion in important relationships, and this is just one more thing to bring into our awareness of our experience. Having learning conversations is a great way to reduce unconscious fusion in a relationship. But there are cases where people will act in extremely fused ways, requiring great patience and understanding. By extremely fused I mean they have an active fantasy life about you in which they are constantly imagining interactions with you. In such relationships people can hear any attempt at gaining interpersonal clarity as, in some way, shaming; this increases their anxiety, sometimes to such a degree that they can't even hear what is being said. They will take your attempts at being a Descriptive Self personally, as if you are criticizing them.

Generally, your best strategy is to work at helping them understand that when you are describing your experience it is *not about them*, it is about you. Try to make them see that you are trying to help them understand what goes on in your head and that you are not criticizing them. It will take patience and a willingness to not shame them for their fusion (which would only tend to reinforce it). Keep coming back to describing your here-and-now experience, what you are thinking, feeling, and wanting right now. If they get too anxious let it go and return to it later. Probably the best strategy is to be an Appreciative Self. Look for times when they are doing it right and ignore times when they are doing it wrong.

Disconnection

People who are highly disconnected in relationships can be disconnected from their own experience as well. If you ask them what their experience was in the past they may not know. If you ask them what they think, feel, or want in the moment, they may not know. It's important to recognize that this problem is not about being defensive or unwilling to tell you their truth. If you make up a story that they are choosing not to tell you the truth of their experience, you will be way off. Such people are also doing less sense-making about others. They may just not have made up any stories about something you have been obsessing about for weeks. Demanding that they level with you when they have nothing to say will just create more tension.

As likely as not, such people will not have spent a lot of time thinking about their awareness and can be somewhat embarrassed when their inability to know their experience becomes painfully obvious. Learning to be aware takes some time and practice, and you will need to be patient with that. One learning conversation may need to take place over several sessions, as these people often need time by themselves to think about their experience and then get back to you.

For quick, highly verbal people the idea that someone needs to go away and think about what they think can be hard to fathom. Don't they know what they think? Well, no. Everyone accesses their thoughts, feelings, wants, and observations at different rates of speed. Disconnected people can be really slow at becoming aware, and a leader needs to avoid shaming them if he wants to cultivate an environment of interpersonal openness.

The Current Level of Interpersonal Mush

There is no question that it is emotionally a lot easier to start and maintain a relationship of interpersonal clarity with a new person, team, or organization than it is to take one that has existed for some time in interpersonal mush and create interpersonal clarity. If I begin a personal or work relationship with you in which I am always telling you the truth of my experience and expecting the same from you, we really don't experience it as all that tough. We soon develop the expectation of interpersonal clarity. We will find that disagreements and misperceptions get worked out easily and quickly before they become conflicts. The relationship or team is able to grow stronger and develop more quickly because issues that might have been hidden in normal organizations are getting talked about and dealt with.

For a number of reasons, it's much tougher to change a relationship or team that has already existed for some time in interpersonal mush. First, there are unfavorable stories people have been carrying around about each other that they haven't told the truth about. Negative beliefs about each other can reduce any desire to develop interpersonal clarity. If people do level with each other and the negative stories are finally told, some can feel betrayed or think they haven't been dealt with honestly. Hard feelings can get generated not so much by hearing the stories but by the fact that they weren't checked out in the first place. This is especially true if someone has lied about her experience in the past out of fear or anxiety. She didn't want to cause a scene, hurt the other person's feelings, risk losing the relationship, or whatever, so she told a white lie. Now, if she tells the truth, a certain amount of trust will be lost. This can usually be regained and added to if both people keep on developing their interpersonal clarity. It is also true, however, that relationships based on deep interpersonal mush can blow apart when the truth comes out. However, such relationships have a better chance of getting healthy if the truth is volunteered—and people use the skills of the learning conversation to deal with the experience this creates—than if the truth comes out in some other way.

This is the problem of "clean-up," which can take real mastery of clear leadership skills to do well. I don't encourage you to begin learning clear leadership in a clean-up situation unless you have professionals to coach you through the process. Clean-up brings to the surface strong feelings and reactions that can cause either party to break off the interaction and close down before real interpersonal clarity has been reached. Sometimes that can seem worse than not having brought up the issues in the first place. When people hang in and keep working until they get to interpersonal clarity, I have not seen one case where they did not feel it was a good thing. But if one person disconnects and runs away (and I have seen that happen), more interpersonal mush rushes in to fill the vacuum and can leave everyone feeling worse. Relationships are strengthened when they go through a period of adversity and emerge intact. Relationships are weakened when people react to adversity by heading for the hills. If you head into a clean-up situation you have to be prepared to go all the way, get all the stories on the table, and get to a place where each of you is clear about the others' experience. All the tangled-up feelings and reactivity make this very difficult to do without skilled coaching.

A different problem occurs when one of the people in the relationship wants the relationship, and the interpersonal mush, to stay just the way it is. He is in this relationship because the interpersonal mush is comforting, and is not interested in interpersonal clarity. This problem occurs mostly in personal relationships, but it can also occur at work. A leader, for example, wants to change the work environment to one of interpersonal clarity, but an employee is not interested at all. At work or in your personal life, if you become a Descriptive Self, telling the truth of your experience and asking others to do the same, the situation will probably become unbearable for a person who does not want interpersonal clarity, and he will simply leave (if he can). As a manager, that is probably what you want to encourage with subordinates who have no willingness to try.

Authority

I have described the problem of authority for interpersonal clarity throughout this book. In simple terms, unequal power tends to increase anxiety, leading people to distort communication and reduce interpersonal clarity. As the boss you have the advantage that you can require people to seek interpersonal clarity with each other, but you have the disadvantage that the person they are likely to be most afraid of telling their whole truth to is you. As a result you have to work harder than others at understanding the patterns of interaction that swirl around you and ameliorating those patterns that tend to close people down.

Russell, the regional VP, was pretty dedicated to interpersonal clarity and, as far as I ever saw, treated people more than fairly and did not punish them for telling their truth. Eighteen months previously he had taken over a large geographically dispersed region of a large organization and had implemented a major reengineering of their work processes, dramatically flattening and democratizing the organization. Prior to our work together there was a common story in the organization that he was ambitious, ruthless, and not to be trusted. I, who was not in an authority relationship with him, found him incredibly open and sincere, and saw that he held a vision of this organization's greatness that was much dearer to him than any vision of his own greatness. I was at first confused by the amount of fear and anger that was directed at him in the organization.

I came to realize that when Russ talked with subordinates about issues that mattered to him he would get very energized, his brow would furrow, and his voice would get louder. People interpreted his demeanor as expressing anger, and they would shut down, thinking that he was not interested in hearing their truth. Actually, he was just getting excited. It took him quite a while to be able to recognize when he was doing this, stop himself, and describe his experience; and it took even longer for people in the organization to learn to trust that he really was not getting angry with them and really was interested in hearing their truth.

In this organization some people were never willing to try telling their truth to him to see what would happen. They were convinced that he was untrustworthy and they would be punished if they expressed views different from his. They wanted me, the consultant, to convey their views for them instead. This I refused to do because, as I describe in the next section, I have come to believe that would only maintain the interpersonal mush and not change anything. Instead I worked at creating opportunities for them to have a learning conversation with him, but some never took the opportunity. So these highly educated, intelligent, dedicated men and women continued to be stuck in a situation they felt was awful based on a set of stories they would not test and not let go of because they were convinced that to do anything different was too dangerous.

As an authority trying to be a clear leader, one of the things you can do is find people who are perceptive and not afraid to tell you the truth, and who will be willing to let you know when you are unconsciously shutting people down. These can be subordinates, peers, or internal or external consultants. They are worth their weight in gold. They can act as "process consultants" helping you and people you have authority over create effective learning conversations in which you really hear each other, don't close down prematurely, and get to interpersonal clarity. Their job should not be to speak for others or gather information for you. Rather, they help others speak for themselves, help you understand when the message you intend to send is not the one being heard, and function like the court jester, deflating you when you are being pompous and making you seem more human and less scary to everyone else.

Interpersonal Triangulation

Triangulation is a term coined by Salvador Minuchin to describe how most of us manage our anxiety by talking about our issues with one person to someone else.[4] Here's how it goes. I work for you and I am making up a story about you that leaves me feeling tense and upset. The more time I spend around you the more tense and upset I get. If something didn't happen, my tension and discomfort would get to the point where I couldn't help expressing it. That would probably be a good thing because then there would be a lot less interpersonal mush. But instead, I find someone else I can complain about you to, preferably someone whom I can get to agree with me that you are the problem. I go and talk to this person until the tension and discomfort are reduced to a level I can manage, so the next time I am around you, you don't have a clue how upset "you make me."

This is called the process of triangulation because a third person is brought in to manage the feelings going on in a relationship between two people. It goes on all the time inside and outside of organizations. It is how we manage to maintain a calm exterior and get by without ever doing anything to change work situations that would otherwise be unbearable. It is a great system for absorbing anxiety. It is what causes stability in dysfunctional work systems and ensures that nothing ever changes.

Notice what happens in the typical triangulation. First I check out my sense-making with someone other than the person I am sense-making about, so I am guaranteed to have an inaccurate story. Second, I never learn anything about my part in the problem pattern because I have someone who agrees with my story that the other person is the problem. Third, the triangulation acts as a tension escape valve. I never have to deal with problem patterns because whenever they get unbearable I go let off steam. So what happens in an organization full of people triangulating about each other? The interpersonal mush is extra thick because not only do I make up stories about things I'm sense-making about, but I also hear the stories you make up about things you are trying to make sense of. Fantasy is layered upon fantasy.

Triangulation blocks learning conversations by removing all the urgency for having them from the system. As long as I am getting my needs met talking about you to someone else, I don't feel much need to talk to you. It also creates an atmosphere where people know things they don't feel at liberty to disclose. If an important part of my experience of you comes from something Frank told me, but I don't feel I can say so, how can I level with you? We end up with half-baked learning conversations filled with "Someone told me . . ." that leave people feeling more upset than clear.

Some organizational consulting projects that deal with "people issues" seem to me to be more like professional triangulation. The consultants come in and people tell the consultants the truth of their experience with the guarantee that this will get passed on, anonymously, to those in authority. The people telling their stories get to feel a little better from having the escape-valve session. Maybe hope stirs that something will change for the better. Those in authority get to feel a little worse hearing all the stories that they are now supposedly responsible for doing something about. Maybe the authorities try to change a few things. But for the most part no one feels, afterwards, that these efforts really accomplished much. They are right.

Hearing anonymous stories does very little good for anyone. What does an authority do when confronted by anonymous feedback when her story is completely different from the stories her employees have? How does she go about developing interpersonal clarity with the people who have such a different story? Even if she tries to tell her story to the masses, who is going to ask the hard questions, counter with their different perspectives, ask the "yes but" questions that are required to find common territory out of contrasting experiences? How does she learn what is creating these very different stories? How do the people who have passed their stories through the consultant learn why their stories are so different from the authority's story? How do they learn to get clear with each other now and in the future? The short answer is that they don't.

If there is a recurrent theme or pattern to the issues, then yes, there is probably something there that needs looking at and that might warrant changing. But what really needs to change is the interpersonal mush and the process by which it is maintained. Anonymous feedback, done either through surveys or through consultants, does nothing to change the interpersonal mush. In fact, it helps to maintain it by giving the illusion that something is being done about it when nothing really is. People may feel good for a while and then it's back to the same old same old. Anonymous feedback is, I believe, an elaborate form of triangulation.

When people first hear about triangulation there is an instant recognition, a kind of, "oh yeah, I do that and I know other people at work do that." And there is an immediate recognition of the problems it creates. Right off, people want to agree that they won't do that anymore, but it is not so simple. Some triangulation we like. I can feel warm, close, and included when you choose me to share your tale of woe with. If you are my boss and you are telling me about your problems with your boss or peers in the organization I get to feel like I am being let into the inner sanctum. Some managers feel it is their job to "get in the middle," so to speak. Some want their subordinates to come to them with issues they have about co-workers. Some want other managers to come to them with issues they have about their subordinates rather than dealing directly with their people.

Whole departments can exist that maintain their power and status by making people dependent on them to communicate information up, down, and sideways. Human Resource departments are often well intentioned but inadvertently part of the problem of interpersonal mush when they see their job as being go-betweens for others.

One HR vice-president I worked with realized that the whole organization used her to triangulate around their problems with senior managers. Once she decided to stop doing this, problems that had been ongoing since she took on the job started to clear themselves up! For example, there was one plant manager who refused to go to work much before 10 a.m. First shift started at 6 a.m. and the rest of the management organization were in by 8. The plant manager reasoned that since he stayed at work until at least 9 p.m., it was OK for him to come in later. He was just a night-owl type and liked it. Since taking on the VP job the HR manager had been fielding almost weekly phone calls from people who were upset by this plant manager's behavior. Mostly she tried to calm them down, ask them to look at it from his point of view, and remind them that his plant was one of the most productive in the company. Now and then she would have a heart-to-heart talk with the plant manager and tell him about the impact his behavior was having on anonymous others, but he didn't change. On the day following her decision to stop triangulating she got another of these phone calls, but this time she said, "Look, it's not my problem, you need to talk to him directly and deal with it. I don't want to talk about it anymore," and hung up. Then she called the plant manager and told him that she was not going to field calls about his hours and apologize for him anymore, that she was sending all complaints to him and he would have to deal with them. Three months later she met the plant manager at a company strategy session. Over drinks he told her that at the time he had been quite angry at her taking that position, but now he was glad she had, because he had not been aware of just how much animosity his late hours had created. He was now getting to the plant by 8 a.m.

So how do you overcome this major obstacle to organizational learning? By naming it. Really it is as simple as that. You begin by describing what it is and encouraging the people who work for you to have a conversation about what they think and feel about triangulation. I've never seen such a conversation where people didn't unanimously decide triangulation was a bad thing that they didn't want to do anymore. After that you just point it out when it is happening. It won't go completely away, but much of the wind can be taken out of its sails. Talking to person A about person B can be useful when you use it to get your thoughts together and figure out what your experience really is before approaching person B to have a learning conversation. If you don't let me get away with pretending that "she" is the whole problem and I have no part in it, you can be helpful by listening to me, as long as I eventually get around to talking to her about our problem pattern. As your boss I can coach you on how to talk to the co-worker you are having the problem pattern with and I can act as a process consultant while the two of you have a learning conversation. But you two have to talk to resolve the issue. I cannot change your relationship for you. Interpersonal mush is the problem and interpersonal clarity is the solution. You cannot arrive at interpersonal clarity with someone who is not a part of the conversation. It is as simple as that.

Summary

Many of the obstacles to having learning conversations in the workplace can be understood as obstacles to speaking and hearing subjective and inter-subjective truths. People need to learn how to express their subjective truths in ways that didn't imply they have "the truth." People need to learn how to listen to someone else's subjective truths without getting reactive or feeling shamed. These are real problems for people, even those who have had training in clear leadership. Perhaps the most widespread problem is shame, that mostly unconscious part in each person that feels unworthy. Our fear of feeling our shame, and the defenses we develop for avoiding that, run counter to the skills of awareness, description, curiosity, and appreciation. There is a vulnerability in everyone that gets surfaced when people are telling their truth, and people have to believe that they and their truth will be treated with respect or they will close down very quickly.

Probably the single best way to overcome obstacles to learning conversations, especially when you are first developing relationships of interpersonal clarity, is to do them with coaches—third parties who have no emotional investment in the conversations. The coach's job is to keep reminding people whose turn it is to be curious and when it is time to be descriptive, and to remind them to use the experience cube and use language that doesn't mystify. I have found that a good coach can help me and someone I have a sticky problem pattern with, one that we haven't been able to resolve in months, get to a new level of clarity in just a few minutes.

Conclusion

Choosing Our Paths
in Tomorrow's Organization

As we enter the 21st century the structures and processes of organizations are going through as big a revolution as they did a century ago. The industrial revolution brought along with it the bureaucratic form of organizing. It was a much better way to organize than had previously existed, and it was the basis for successful businesses that grew to span the globe. We are now deeply into the next technological revolution, and this is spawning just as radical a change. I can't be sure what word will come to characterize this form of organizing, but "empowered" seems to have picked up a lot of steam. It is a fundamentally different way of structuring organizations than bureaucracy because the underlying logic of the division and coordination of labor is completely different. Bureaucracy rests on standardization as the key way to coordinate the actions of people doing different things: by standardizing the work itself (e.g., assembly lines), standardizing the skills of workers (e.g., universities, hospitals), or standardizing the outputs of people (piecework) or larger units (component manufacturing) and creating a standard procedure for anything else that can be imagined. Coordination is a big cost of organizing, and standardization proved to be the most efficient, most cost-effective way to coordinate the actions of many people. Standardizing procedures meant that the best methods of accomplishing objectives could be applied over and over, and everyone would be treated, in a sense, equally. In essence, this form of organizing rests on command and control, where a small group of people try to control what a large group of people do. As long as the world was simple enough for a small group of people to be able to react quickly enough and get their ideas implemented, bureaucracy was the most successful form of organizing for business.

But bureaucracy has a big drawback. As a system it is slow to learn, innovate, and adapt. It trades off flexibility for efficiency. And it wastes huge amounts of human resources. Many employees' problem-solving abilities and creativity are stifled and their motivation and energy squandered. That worked fine as long as companies didn't need a lot of innovation or a high level of commitment. As the pace of change and competition has increased, however, bureaucracy has not been able to keep up. The last 30 years have seen numerous experiments with new forms of organizing that attempt to optimize both efficiency and innovation, to learn and adapt while still keeping costs down. It's become evident that any organizational design that can do this must simultaneously engender people's striving, learning, and sense of belonging.[1] And that, in turn, requires a method of coordination not based on control but on people's willing participation. The new organizations depend on everyone bringing their creativity and problem-solving talents to the table, which means much more negotiation, cooperation, and sense of partnership.

The microprocessor revolution will push this to the extreme as organizations increasingly become made up less of employees and more of organized collections of subcontractors. I don't think big organizations or bureaucracy will disappear completely. There are business environments where they will continue to prosper. But we can all see what is happening because of the communications revolution, the decreasing importance of unskilled work, and the increasing importance of "knowledge work" in the northern hemisphere. The most employable people, those with the skills and expertise that businesses need, can telecommute to work via the Internet, faxes, and cellular phones. Increasingly, these people choose to be self-employed, doing various projects with various clients. And there are many reasons that businesses would rather subcontract work than hire full-time employees. The quality of organizing required for success is no longer command and control but partnership and mutual alignment. For social, demographic, economic, and technological reasons, I think we can only expect this trend to expand.

Even though our organizational designs are now rapidly turning away from bureaucracy, our styles of leading and managing are not. We have not seen as much of a radical change in leadership styles, but I think that will come. It will come because to be really successful in these new organizations requires a different leadership style from bureaucracy. The processes of perception generation and sense-making create a number of problems in organizations, such as fragmentation, subcultures, and an environment of distrust and cynicism. People, especially leaders, can't see the consequences of their own actions. An active organizational unconscious is created that leads to poor implementation and follow-through on decisions. Bureaucratic organizations, designed to work in spite of such problems, can still be successful in slow-changing environments. Organizations in rapidly changing environments, which must quickly adapt and innovate, cannot. So they require leaders and followers who can manage perception generation and sense-making processes differently, and, instead of living in what I have called interpersonal mush, create a state I have called interpersonal clarity.

In this book I have described the new skills and attributes needed from people for a form of organizing that is empowered. These are not *all* the skills needed from leaders. There are many other skills, such as running meetings, setting goals, managing conflict, and coaching, that make a leader great. But these are techniques that rest on a more fundamental platform. I've been interested in that basic, underlying platform, the absolutely essential and different ingredients that make a person able to use the usual assortment of management techniques and get outstanding results. That is what this book is about.

Descriptive Self in the Virtual Team

One of these key skills is the ability to be a Descriptive Self. The Descriptive Self not only knows what his experience is and is able to describe it to others, but also knows what part of his experience it is necessary to be descriptive about. What thoughts, feelings, and wants are other people most likely to make up stories about, and what information about his experience would most help them work effectively with him? The Descriptive Self doesn't just wait to be asked to be descriptive, he makes a point of being descriptive whenever he wants others to understand where he is coming from. I think this is a necessary skill to lead people in a way that encourages their striving, learning, and sense of belonging. I think the increasing numbers of teams whose members are geographically separated, where communications take place via email or other computer-based means, only increase the need for this skill. Email is a much leaner form of communication than face-to-face. We get less information for sense-making, so our sense-making is even more prone to projection, fantasy, and error. Leading virtual teams effectively requires, therefore, an even greater ability to manage the sense-making process by getting people to describe their experience to each other to increase interpersonal clarity. The upside is that the relative coolness of electronic media creates less anxiety than face-to-face communication and probably will make it easier for people to tell each other their truth (if asked appropriately).

Taking the Skills to Work

With these four skills in hand, through a balance of inquiry and expression, you can facilitate conversations that create new insights into people's experiences and lead to lasting improvements in patterns of organizing. These can be inquiries into problem patterns or into the best of what we know. That's what I think organizational learning is all about, and it happens one conversation at a time as people learn the skills and accept the legitimacy of having that kind of conversation. An organizational culture can then be built that values interpersonal clarity and no longer tolerates interpersonal mush.

The ability to lead these kinds of conversations depends on the degree of differentiation in the work relationship. The more people's internal experience depends on what others are saying or doing, the harder it is to manage the anxiety of saying and hearing people's truth. Fear and anxiety, particularly the avoidance of fear and anxiety, underlie a lot of the mediocrity in organizations. People who can create learning conversations are able to contain their own anxiety and act as a damper on others' anxiety. They don't do this by repressing or being unconscious about their anxiety, but by (1) being less anxious because they are not in a fused or disconnected state and (2) being aware of their feelings without being controlled by those feelings.

Clearing out the interpersonal mush makes it much easier for people to learn and for us to have a sense of belonging. Interpersonal mush comes from people having different maps about each other and about situations, and acting on the basis of those maps without ever checking them out. Maps are extremely important in work environments, particularly identity maps and theories of action. Map-making and making decisions as experiments extends the organizational learning process from patterns of interaction to the goals, roles, tasks, and procedural decision-making of organizational life. If everyone has to operate off the boss's map, then map-making is not so important. But when organizations are partnerships, then findings ways to describe, discuss, choose, learn about, change, and discard maps among everyone is critical to effective striving and learning. Having common maps is part of what belonging is all about, and the success that comes to groups and organizations that learn and strive well also increases belonging.

After years of teaching this material in various permutations, it is clear to me that most people can learn the skills and can increase their differentiation and appreciative mind-set, but these two ways of being require a commitment to living a certain way that a person can only choose for herself. In a sense, each is a path. By choosing them, other things get excluded. If you choose to lead a differentiated life you can't also choose a life where you are responsible for other people's happiness, or one where you are an island and nothing touches you. You can't lead a life of indifference to your inner world, ignoring the forces of your unconscious mind. Choosing differentiation entails a desire to fully explore and understand yourself and the other people you choose to be connected to.

If you choose the path of appreciation you can't also choose the path of "scientific doubt." If you begin from a place of doubt (I'll believe it when I see it), where other people's goodness, trustworthiness, and so on have to be proven before you acknowledge them, you won't be able to track well. Choosing appreciation requires a willingness to work from a basis of faith, not only believing that something is true even if you haven't already seen it, but believing that your choices affect the social world you live in, that your way of looking affects what you find. If you try it I think you will be amazed at the power of the appreciative mind-set and the uses of appreciative processes for managing people and change. Without command and control the old push-and-pummel methods of getting people to do what you want them to do (veiled threats, asserting authority, use of punishments) are not viable. But leadership is still the art of creating followership—getting people to do what you think is best to do. Tracking and fanning are, as far as I've been able to discover, the most powerful means of influencing attitudes and behavior in relationships that aren't based on authority. One reason they work is that they increase, not decrease as so many other change strategies do, people's sense of belonging.

I am an idealist and I am hopeful. I am hopeful that we can create business organizations that are wealth creating, serve their customers well, and are good for the planet and good for the people that work in them. I think the business environment increasingly selects out those kinds of organizations for survival. I am sure that the new organizations we are creating will be less oppressive to the human spirit, places where our collective efforts bring out the best in each other. I am also sure that the new organizations will have their shadow sides as well. It is one of the paradoxical realities of human relations that every new form of organizing contains within it the seeds of its own destruction, which is another way of saying that every solution, including this one, will eventually create new problems. Isn't that wonderful!

Are you interested in applying the principles of clear leadership to your work or organization? If you

- are interested in developing your clear leadership skills

- want to help others develop their clear leadership skills

- want to create a group of friends or colleagues to practice the skills

- are looking for training products for your company or consulting practice that build on the techniques of clear leadership in such areas as supervision, teamwork, and customer relations

- are interested in changing the culture of an organization to get rid of interpersonal mush and increase interpersonal clarity

- are looking for a consultant who can do some serious clean-up work with a management group and transfer the clear leadership skills to them

then explore the possibilities at www.clearleadership.com or contact Gervase Bushe directly at Gervase@cheerful.com or in Vancouver, B.C., at (604) 253-7117.

Endnotes

Introduction

[1] I learned this way of defining experience from John Runyon and Ron Short. See Ron's (1991) *A special kind of leadership: The key to learning organization.* Seattle: The Leadership Group; and (1998) *Learning in relationship: Foundation for personal and professional success.* Seattle: Learning in Action Technologies.

[2] Mintzberg, H. (1979). *The structuring of organizations.* Englewood Cliffs, NJ: Prentice-Hall.

Chapter 1: Where Interpersonal Mush Comes From and What It Does to Organizations

[1] Welck, K. (1995). *Sense making in organizations.* Thousand Oaks, CA: Sage.

[2] Jaques, E. (1989). *Requisite organization.* Arlington, VA: Cason Hall & Co.

[3] Taylor, S., & Brown, J. (1988). Illusion and well-being: A social psychological perspective on mental health. *Psychological Bulletin*, 103, 193–210.

[4] Mills, D.Q. (1991). *Rebirth of the corporation.* New York: Wiley.

Chapter 2: Understanding the Foundations of Clear Leadership

[1] Here I am building on the work of Murray Bowen and Family Systems Theory [Bowen, M. (1978). *Family therapy in clinical practice.* New York: Aronson]. My way of thinking about fusion and differentiation is a little different from Bowen's. For example, Bowen described fusion as a characteristic of a person. I am more inclined to see it as a characteristic of an interaction, but I'm going to use his labels to acknowledge my intellectual debt to him.

Chapter 3: Leadership and the Four Elements of Experience

[1] People familiar with this field will notice the similarity between this conception and the work of Chris Argyris and his students on what they call "the ladder of inference."

[2] Harvey, J. (1988). *The Abilene paradox*. Lexington, MA: Lexington.

Chapter 4: The Aware Self: Gaining Self-Knowledge

[1] Weick, K. (1969). *The social psychology of organizing*. Reading, MA: Addison-Wesley.

[2] Argyris, C., & Schön, D. (1974). *Theory in practice*. San Francisco: Jossey-Bass.

Chapter 5: The Descriptive Self: Communicating Honestly

[1] This "left column–right column" approach to displaying interactions was developed by Chris Argyris and Donald Schön to help people learn about their defensive reasoning.

Chapter 6: The Curious Self: Helping Others Communicate

[1] Culbert, S. (1996). *Mind-set management*. New York: Oxford.

Chapter 7: The Appreciative Self: Inspiring the Best in People

[1] Srivastva, S., & Cooperrider, D. L. (eds.). (1990). *Appreciative management and leadership*. San Francisco, CA: Jossey-Bass.

[2] I want to acknowledge Tom Pitman's early influence on these ideas, contained in the following essay: Bushe, G. R., & Pitman, T. (1991). Appreciative process: A method for transformational change. *Organization Development Practitioner*, 23(3), 1–4.

[3] Cooperrider, D. L., & Whitney, D. (1998). A positive revolution in change: Appreciative inquiry. Unpublished working paper, Case Western Reserve University.

[4] White, T. W. (1996). Working in interesting times. *Vital Speeches Of The Day*, 62(15), 472–474.

[5] Homans, G. (1961). *Social behavior*. New York: Harcourt, Brace and World.

[6] Eden D. (1990). *Pygmalion in management*. Lexington, MA: Lexington Books.

[7] I think Kohut and his students' work has been overlooked in managerial psychology for too long. They have some important things to teach us about leadership, especially their ideas on self–object transference.

[8] From a Jungian point of view, religious stories are viewed as tales of the psyche, as personifications of the deep forces that drive human behavior. Instead of reading a religious text literally, Jungians read it metaphorically. They do the same with dreams. Contrary to what some fundamentalists say, however, Jungian analysis does not negate the possibility that God(s) exists. What Jung and his followers may have discovered is how God(s) influences human nature.

[9] Moore, R., & Gillette, D. (1992). *The king within.* New York: William Morrow.

Chapter 8: Improving Organizational Learning

[1] An idea first pointed out to me by Bob Guns. See Guns, B. (1996). *The faster learning organization.* San Diego: Pfeiffer.

[2] My ideas about organizational learning conversations build on the work of Ron Short and his notion of "feedback as mutual inquiry." See Short, R. (1991). *Learning from experience with people.* Seattle: Learning in Action Technologies.

[3] The theory of appreciative inquiry was developed by David Cooperrider and Suresh Srivastva. See Cooperrider, D. L., & Srivastva, S. (1987). Appreciative inquiry in organizational life, in W. Pasmore & R. Woodman (Eds.), *Research in organization change and development* (Vol. 1, pp. 129–169). Greenwich, CT: JAI Press. For practical applications see Bushe, G. R. (1995). Advances in appreciative inquiry as an organization development intervention. *Organization Development Journal,* 13(3), 14–22, and Bushe, G. R. (1998). Appreciative inquiry in teams. *Organization Development Journal,* 16(3), 41–50.

Chapter 9: Strengthening Decision-Making and Creating Alignment

[1] If you are interested you can find my map of what makes people feel empowered and disempowered in Bushe, G. R., Havlovic, S. J., & Coetzer, G. (1996). Exploring empowerment from the inside-out, Part 2. *Journal for Quality and Participation,* 19(3), 78–84.

[2] Staw, B. M., & Ross, J. (1986). Understanding behavior in escalation situations. *Science,* 246, 216–220.

[3] I have been strongly influenced by the research of Wayne Boss, which has demonstrated a very strong positive impact on measures of team performance from using what I'm calling OL meetings.

[4] A point I emphasized in Bushe, G. R., & Shani, A. B. (1991). *Parallel learning structures.* Reading, MA: Addison-Wesley.

Chapter 10: Overcoming Obstacles to Clear Leadership Throughout the Organization

[1] Kaufmann, G. (1996). *The psychology of shame.* New York: Springer.

[2] I picked up this way of defining confrontation from Torbert, W. (1976). *Creating a community of inquiry*. London: Wiley.

[3] This is a slightly modified list based on the work of G. Kaufmann (1996). *The psychology of shame*. New York: Springer.

[4] Minuchin, S. (1974). *Families and family therapy*. Cambridge, MA: Harvard.

Conclusion: Choosing Our Paths
in Tomorrow's Organization

[1] Lawrence, P.R., & Dyer, D. (1983). *Renewing American industry*. New York: Free Press.

Index

active listening, 145–147

anecdotes, 205–206

anger, 223

anxiety: authority effects, 55–57; avoidance of, 93–94, 184; awareness of, 82, 94–95; behavior effects, 94–95; embarrassment, 94; experiences caused by, 90–91; intimacy, 47, 49; prevention of, 238; separation. *See* separation anxiety

appreciative inquiry, 195

Appreciative Self: assumptions of, 168; attention benefits, 164–166; behaviors associated with, 156–157; characteristics of, 12, 155–157, 196–197, 239; development of, 176–178; fanning. *See* fanning; gratitudes, 177; inquiry nature of, 196–197; learning conversation participation of, 193–196; mind-set of, 157–161, 176–177, 179, 194; skills of, 12; summary overview of, 178–180; thoughts and feelings that affect others, 162–164; tracking, 166–170, 177–179

archetypes, 172–174

Argyris, Chris, 106, 109

assumptions: Appreciative Self, 168; experimental, 204; truth, 10; unproved, 204

attention: Appreciative Self's focus,

164–166; benefits of, 164–166; to experiences, 90–91; fanning of, 170–176; mental map effects, 103; paraphrasing for maintaining, 145; positive reinforcement nature of, 170–171; tracking of, 166–170

attribution errors, 31–34

authority: anxiety effects, 55–57; bad vs. good, 173; bias against, 55; in empowered organizations, 13; fusion effects, 55–57; hierarchy vs., 13, 200; identity map of, 200; in meetings, 207; obstacle effects of, 228–230; power and, 28–29; reactions to, 27, 122; shame and, 220; workplace influences of, 55–56

Aware Self: anxiety, 93–95; characteristics of, 12, 91, 196–197; components of, 89–90; definition of, 89; development of, 112–117; feelings, 93, 95–96; fusion effects, 97–98, 225; inquiry nature of, 196–197; language effects, 98–102; mental maps. *See* mental maps; skills of, 12; summary overview of, 116–117; thinking, 91–93; wants, 96–98

behavior: anxiety effects, 94–95; effects of thoughts and feelings, 162–164; shame-based, 222–224

belonging, 47

245